The Long-legged View

To: Susie + Sarah

The Long-legged View

From Life in the Big Apple to Life in Apple Country in the 1940s, 50s, and 60s

Created by Patricia Carr
Edited by Nicki Carr Tiffany

To order additional copies of this book, contact:
Xlibris Corporation
1-888-795-4274
www.Xlibris.com
Orders@Xlibris.com
62512

Contents

PREFACE

This book is the creation of the second wife (Pat) of William Mortimer Carr, Jr., my paternal grandfather. My sister, Ruth, wrote a brief family history:

> Myrtie Powell (our grandfather's first wife) was born September 17, 1884 in Ransomville, New York, and died December 21, 1943. She married our grandfather, William Mortimer Carr, Jr., on March 20, 1909 in the Eagle Harbor NY Methodist Church. William was born September 28, 1886 and died June 26, 1960. About a year after our grandmother's death, he married Pat (also known as Helen or Helena) Carty on November 22, 1944 in New York City at the Actors' Church. That day is also Pat's 40th birthday—she was born in 1904.
>
> Pat had one sister, Mary, who was a kindergarten teacher and competed in ballroom dancing all over the country. They had a brother who died in infancy. Pat lived to enjoy her 99th birthday and died three days later on November 25, 2003.

Our grandparents' home is located on West County House Road in the village of Albion, New York. It was built in the early 1800s (see photo on cover) and was a working dairy farm for many years, until the barns burned in the late 1950s. Our grandparents raised four children in that home: Mariam Ida Carr, born January 21, 1910, died November 18, 1976, no children; William Franklin Carr, born February 17, 1912, died March 24, 1970, one adopted daughter, Laura Ann ("Janie"); Ruth Alice Carr, born July 12, 1913, died October 10, 1992, nine children James, William,

Linda, Alice, Madeline, Joseph, Ruth, John, and Mark; and Charles Arthur Carr (our father), born May 14, 1926, died October 18, 2002, two children, Ruth and Nicki. After Pat's death, the home lay empty for a couple of years and was eventually bought by Scott Root and Tony McMurtrie, who are working to refurbish "The Pillars" to its once beautiful grandeur.

When Grandpa Carr married Pat and brought her to the farm, Pat began her new life as a farmer's wife. While her stories are entertaining, often amusing, and sometimes sad, they are somewhat embellished. In any case, the names of non-family members have been changed. Things were not always rosy for her, my grandfather, or my father, aunts, and uncle after the marriage. After grandpa's death, Pat estranged herself almost totally from our family; however my sister Ruth and her daughter, Julie, did visit her in her later years and they became good friends.

Pat gave this manuscript to my niece, Julie Carr Miller Trembley, a couple of years before she died, and we decided to share her stories because, at the very least, we thought they were good representations of farm life in rural Western New York. I hope you enjoy them as much as we do.

Nicki Ann Carr Tiffany, Editor

"Patricia Helena Carty circa 1922"

PROLOGUE

by Patricia Carr

What happens when a "nice" teenage girl with no money, no backing, and no experience tries to crash into show business? I was struggling along trying to get my start, taking any job I could find to keep going. I was an usherette, a hat-check girl, an "Amateur Night" contestant, a dime-a-dance girl in a dance hall, a terrible singer, but a pretty good "hoofer"! One night, Bill Carr, who was in New York City for a convention, came into the tiny club where I was appearing as a dancer. He turned out to be a farmer *and* a justice of the peace *and* a widower *and* a rural Upstate New Yorker. I had lived in hotels and eaten in restaurants for most of my adult life. Crazy as it sounds, we got married. All of a sudden, I was transplanted to my husband's cozy little Victorian pad with twenty-some rooms, and I learned to cook on a wood-burning stove! The grown-up stepchildren didn't approve of me. Along with Bill, I married the house, some sheep, some cows, some cucumbers, some tomatoes, and a couple hundred acres of land. Now we're in the process of "living happily ever after".

At the height of the war restrictions, we converted the house into six apartments. We were about thirty miles between Rochester and Buffalo, but we found the magic words that lured fathers of families into driving out to Albion: "Ideal for Baby" our ads read; whatever that meant. I learned to run a snack bar for sheep, oversee a clipping service for cows, and to boss field crews. Oh, yes, and how to be managed by a husband. Our tenants had fourteen children and five dogs and the wells went dry every summer. I kept learning new roles and, through every step of my present life, seeped something from my former life.

11

As I write this, the snow is floating lazily through the branches, blurring the edge of the roof: white on white, with leaf-striped bark for accent. It looks like a Currier & Ives print. My mind is floating lazily, too. That is, half of it is. The other half knows that the milk truck hasn't come yet; it's probably stuck somewhere or the driver stopped off to chat with someone and twelve cans of milk are waiting for him.

The storm windows aren't up yet. I called the handyman three weeks ago! There's snow on the porch that needs to be swept off. Ah, yes: the sweet repose and peacefulness of a snowy day in the country. It sure beats a hectic day in the city!

When I was working in the city, the country beckoned like Shangri-La: a place for suntans and dreaming. This summer, the hired hand's wife and I fertilized the orchard by hand. And in New York City, they talk about "curbing your dog"!

Bill was twenty years older than I. After we had been married for ten years, he had a stroke. The day he came home from the hospital, the bank informed me that they would start foreclosure proceedings in three months because no woman could run a farm!

While I wrote most of this book, I would read to Bill what I had written and expect him to say: "My, aren't you wonderful?" Bah! I knew he wasn't going to feel very secure with it or the "home-is-my-castle" attitude, which I was going around with blithely. "Do you like it?" I would ask anxiously. "Do you think it's funny?"

Bill would consider, and then, as he edged toward the door, would say over his shoulder: "I think it would be funny if you actually *sold* it!" That's my Bill!

The situations in *The Long-Legged View* are commonplace, but my show-business background taught me to search for a punch line with a "twist", and often Bill topped me! This is a glimpse of an era when people were more than Social Security numbers, when money was easy, and the young could afford to be light hearted. Relax and enjoy!

"William F. Carty circa 1912"

"Patricia, Mary, and Annie Carty circa 1913"

CHAPTER 1

So, You Want To Be An Actress!

Mom tucked a St. Cecilia medal in my purse. "There!" she said. "Now I feel better about you. You're awfully young to go to New York City alone, but if you want to be an actress . . ." The bus driver slammed the door, and I was on my way. New York! Broadway! A star overnight? Well, not exactly. I was sixteen. Anything could happen. And it did!

I stayed at the Y.W.C.A. (transients pay in advance). Each morning I packed my bag and checked it at the desk. All day I trudged from one theatrical agency to another; at night, I grabbed any job I could find: a hat-check girl, an usherette, a theatrical contest with a cash prize, anything that would let me pay for another night. I got so tired that I dozed off in the subway and woke up in Mott St. in Chinatown at 2 a.m.! I stumbled over a corpse tossed in a doorway before I found the Uptown subway. (I didn't dare tell Mom!)

I ate in one-arm joints and almost lived on coffee, "extra cream and sugar, please." One afternoon, when I stopped in at the Actors' Drug Store, our unofficial message center, the waitress at the soda fountain whispered, "Auditions today, Honey". "Where?" I demanded. Auditions were very hush-hush; the fewer who knew about them, the less the competition. Actors didn't tell their best friends, and of course, *no one* told me any thing! "Back stage in the Shubert Alley, and hurry!"

I gulped my coffee and ran. The alleyway was dark and sort of spooky, but I was too excited to be scared. My first audition! I found the stage door, clutched my St. Cecilia medal, and walked in. The theater was deserted;

The Long-Legged View   Chapter 1

the house was dark. On stage, a single bulb burned so fiercely that I felt naked. "Sorry" called a voice from the wings. "Auditions are over. You're too late." Too late! "St. Cecilia," I muttered reproachfully, "Mom trusted you." I turned away with such a beat up look that the man relented. He walked to the piano and sat down.

"Let's hear you sing" he said. Sing? I was an Actress! But my room rent . . . so I sang. The first scales were easy. Maybe I was a singer after all! But the notes soared higher and my breath got hoarser, and on the final note, I let out a squawk and burst into tears. The director walked over to me (he was a chubby little man with a slight paunch that made him look fatherly to my teenaged eyes) and put his arm around me. "What's the trouble, little girl?" he asked gently.

At this touch of sympathy, the dam broke and I really bawled. "My father's dead," I blurted, "and I'm all alone and I'm broke." And I started to bawl all over again.

"There, there little one," he said soothingly and put his other arm around me. His eyes changed from blue to liquid black, his paunch quivered, and he began to breathe kinda funny. I felt sort of queer myself.

"Hey, you guys!" yelled a coarse voice. "Break it up, will ya? I wanna go home!" It was the doorman waiting to lock up.

The man stepped back abruptly. "Report tomorrow in practice clothes. Rehearsal at 9 a.m." I had a job!

I rushed out to call Mom (collect, and could I borrow some money?), promised St. Cecilia a candle (I got the job, didn't I?), pawned Mom's watch, and bought the skimpiest pair of dancing pants I could find. They were so short that they barely covered my "vee" of hair, but Mom always said "Make the most of your good points, Dear." And I had nifty long legs. I slept with the pants under my pillow, and I dreamed that I was a star overnight, and then I had a nightmare that I had only dreamed that I had a job.

The next morning, I was the first to report and Pop, the doorman, smirked when I came in. Never mind; someday I'd show him! The stage was lighted and four sets of chairs were grouped around the piano. Soprano, alto, tenor, and bass—we were all ready. The music director (the man who had auditioned me) assigned our seats. "You," he said to me, "sit with the altos." (He wasn't taking any chances with my high C!) Then the stage manager passed out sheets of music. I couldn't read a note! I tried desperately to follow the alto sitting next to me, but it was no use. I kept sliding off into the soprano and stepping on everyone's toes as I slid. Finally the director stopped short. "YOU!" he said, pointing straight at me.

16

"Switch over to the sopranos. That seems to be where you're heading." Then he smiled at the rest of the company, muttered "one trouble spot taken care of," rapped on the piano, and said brusquely, "OK boys and girls, let's take it from the top!" I slunk over to my new seat and sat down, crossing my legs, but I could hear the snickers around me.

When we "took ten", everybody stood around talking to everybody else, except me. I drank three cups of water at the cooler before one of the girls came over. "First job, huh Kid?" she asked. I nodded. "You're just a baby! How did ja get in this racket?"

So I told her about my being the lead in the school play and all, and how Mom worried about me in New York City.

"Yeah, but how did ja get into this company?" So I told her about the audition and how awful I felt when I cracked on the high note. She laughed until she cried. "You stage-struck kids!" she sputtered. "Honey, you've bought the farm . . . well, maybe not. He shacks up with our leading lady and she's quite a bitch. Holler if you get in a jam." She sat next tome when we went back, and I knew I had made a friend.

After rehearsal the director drew me to one side. "Now listen, little girl," he said sternly. "Papa [the Big Boss] will be here tomorrow, and if he stops behind your chair to listen to you sing, shut up at once and start coughing. Papa signs the contracts." The next day, when he walked in, I wondered why they called him Papa—he didn't look the least bit fatherly—more like Scrooge (after he had reformed). He was as tall and gaunt as Abraham Lincoln and he wore a silk top hat and carried a gold-handled cane. Even the chorus boys called him "Sir", although I heard someone mutter "Old Bastard" when he went by. He stopped behind each chair to listen, and when he got to me, I didn't have to fake a cough—I choked! Papa patted me on the back, handed me a cough drop, and walked away chuckling. Papa knew a stage-struck kid when he saw one! The next day we all got our contracts and Papa winked when he handed me mine.

So, now I was in Show Business, and it wasn't glamour and it wasn't spotlights and applause. It was work, work, work. It was music rehearsal and line rehearsal, and costume fittings. It was learning not to bawl when my feelings got stepped on. "You there, ya got two left feet? Get the hell on and off on cue! Exit clean! Keep your line straight! Take 'ten' before I murder the lot of you!" On a good day, we were Papa's children; on a bad day, he would snarl, "What do you think this is? A strawberry festival? Hundreds of kids out there in the alleyway are begging for your jobs!" (There were, too.) But, when the music director lost his cool and threatened to toss a chair at the tenors, Papa would sit there snickering. Jeepers! Mom would never have put up with such tantrums!

One time, the leading man called to me: "Come out into the sun [the spotlight], Baby. You have such beautiful long legs." The stage manager yanked me to one side. "He wants you to do a specialty step with him. Now, I know and you know that you can't do it. And when *he* finds out you can't do it and tosses you out, if you bawl, I'll fire you." I didn't bawl, but I sure didn't do the number, either!

Once, when we had a long break (the principals needed the stage), one of the chorus boys took me for a hansom cab ride in Central Park. "My God," he exclaimed, leaning over the side of the cab while I sniffed the fresh air. "There's a tree! An honest-to-goodness tree! Not one painted on a backdrop!"

Finally, the countdown started for launching time—Opening Night. There was the last music rehearsal, the last "on and off" brush-up, and the final dress parade. It was out to dinner (I was so nervous I couldn't even drink a malted milkshake), then back to the theater in time to hear the call boy knock on the dressing room doors and yell, "Half hour. Everybody in? Half hour!" The VIPs, of course, had private dressing rooms with a gold star on the door; us peasants in the chorus shared one big room. There was a rail for clothing in one corner, and a shelf for make-up ran along the other walls. We sat on benches like picnic table seats, and I watched the other girls and did just like they did (I thought); but when my friend saw me, she let out a shriek. "Good God!" she said. "You look like a circus clown! Here, wipe all that goop off of your face, and hurry!"

"Fifteen minutes!" yelled the call boy.

My friend rubbed the "foundation stick" (grease paint) on my cheeks and patted it in. Then came the cream rouge skillfully blended, and the powder was dusted over it. She drew on my eyebrows and painted my lips. Then she picked up a pan the size of a half-dollar, held it over a candle, dropped a chunk of solid mascara in it, and when it was melted, dipped a toothpick in it, ran it along each of my eyelashes, and twirled it so that a tiny ball formed at the end of each eyelash. "There," she said when she had finished. "At least you look human!" I put a tissue over my face and the wardrobe mistress zipped me into my costume. Then came the magic call: "Places, places everybody! Curtain going up!"

From the wings, we could hear the rustle of the audience being seated, then the house lights dimmed, the musicians swung into the overture, and the curtain went up. We were ON!

It was glamour, it was spotlights, it was applause, it was ecstasy, it was Heaven. The curtain went down to a standing ovation. When we came out, the alleyway was crowded with people waiting to congratulate us. The VIPs went to Sardi's Restaurant to wait for the early bird reviews. Most of the girls had dates, and the "stage door Johnnies" were gunning for pickups. "Don't let me catch you going out with some John you don't know!" my friend warned me. She needn't have worried. I could just hear Mom telling the neighbors about "my daughter in show business in New York City."

The critics were enthused. *Variety* (the show business Bible) termed us a "boffo" and "a must-see for those who enjoy good music and good dancing", and, "the chorus was well-trained." We sure had worked hard enough. By noon the next day, the ticket line for advanced sales stretched around the corner onto Eighth Avenue. "And there ain't a decent leg in the lot of you!" growled our stage manager, who had worked in Burlesque. Papa called us "his children", and the music director sent me to a voice teacher. Run up the flags!

I was smart enough to keep my mouth shut and my ears open (thanks to Mom), and the things I learned! "Mom," I said one day when I got to visit home, "do you know there are men who like MEN?" That should jolt her! "Of course," Mom said matter-of-factly. "Royer [the local voice teacher] has his favorite tenors." Now how in the world did my Mom know that?

As the run of the show stretched into months, we began to get careless and, one night, eight of us almost got fired (as we should have been). At one point in the plot, the tenor stood stage center and serenaded the moon suspended from the "flies" stage right. The eight of us, dressed in fairy-like gauze, entered from the woods stage left, swooned gracefully to the floor on our sides, and gazing soulfully at the whole schmeer and accompanied the tenor on our lyres, which were made of paper. The nymphs down-stage left, the tenor stage center, the moon stage right: a charming picture. But wait! We had previously come off stage right, and we were supposed to dash behind the scenery in order to be in position to enter from the left. On this particular night, however, we were all involved in a "So he said . . ." "No, she said . . ." Until someone else bawled, "Girls! You're ON!" And we were on the wrong side! There was only one thing we could do, so we did it. We dashed on from the right, flopped on the floor, gave the tenor a view of our rear-ends, and then nearly twisted our heads off trying to gaze soulfully in his direction. The tenor gulped, the orchestra seats snickered, and we got the giggles. We giggled so hard that our asses waved up and down and the tenor (never a stalwart soul at the best of times) broke up!

The orchestra leader waved his baton in a frenzy and the stage manager hopped up and down in the wings hissing frantically, "Shut up, damn it! Shut up or I'll murder every one of you when you come off stage! And I'll work the b'jeezes out of your tomorrow!" He did, too. Fortunately, Papa wasn't there that night.

During a break in rehearsals, I noticed an older woman hanging around the stage door. "No openings," the stage manager said curtly. She looked so drab and dragged out that I felt sorry for her. I remembered how I had felt when I couldn't get a job. "Don't waste any pity on that one," my friend advised me. "She's been coming to auditions for years, but no one has ever heard her sing." I walked over to her, but just then the stage manager yelled, "On stage everybody! Everyone on stage!" So she gave me her address and I promised to hunt her up.

"What a crummy neighborhood," I thought, when I finally got the time to go see her. It was in a rundown section of Eighth Avenue sandwiched in between a Chinese eatery (dinner 25¢) and a pawnshop. Her house number was an old-fashioned walkup, and the front door was unlocked. I trudged up the stairs (Mom would have had a fit over the dirt on the stairs), and, as I paused on the landing, I saw that small rooms opened into the hall on both sides. Most of the doors were open and the girls inside smiled and waved to me. It was in the afternoon, but none of the girls seemed to be dressed for the street. Jeepers! Didn't anybody in this house go to work? The woman I was visiting lived on the top floor, and I was a little out of breath when I knocked on her door. She was home, but she had on a bathrobe! "I came to see you," I said, "because I know what it is like to be out of work and broke."

"But you have a job now," she reminded me.

"I know," I said sighing, "but I sure would like to be able to send more money home to Mom."

"Sit down," she said, "and we can talk about it. Would you like some coffee?"

"Sure thing!" I said, giggling. "When I was short of cash, I lived on coffee. It was all I could afford."

She ran hot water from the faucet and stirred in the instant coffee. She dawdled over the coffee and fiddled with the cups. She seemed uneasy, and I began to feel the same way. Something was queer. Finally I looked at my watch. "Jeepers!" I exclaimed. "I didn't realize it was so late. It took me quite a while to find you. I've got a dinner date and the show to do."

She looked at me without saying anything, and I started back down the steps. I noticed that this time, all of the rooms were closed and there were

20

no friendly, smiling faces. And, when I got to the front door, it was locked! I twisted the knob every which way and pulled at the jamb, but I couldn't budge it. I was locked in! I ran back up to my friend's room so fast that I tripped. Over the thudding of my heart, I seemed to hear Mom saying "Keep cool. Use your head." My friend opened her door. "S-so sorry to bother you," I stammered, "but I can't seem to open the front door. I left word at the hotel that if I were late, my dinner date should pick me up here."

The woman stared at me and at last said, "OK, Baby, you win. Either you're not as dumb as I thought you were, or you're a lot dumber. I'll go down with you." She pressed a button and there was a click. The door opened and I walked out into the street.

"I was sorta scared," I admitted to my friend in the show.

"You were right to be!" she retorted. "God in Heaven, can't I let you out of my sight? Honey, that house is a 'white slave' whorehouse! You were lucky to get out!"

I decided not to tell Mom about this one. Mom didn't have to know everything.

After an extended engagement, we were scheduled to go on tour. We are *not* a road company (a second-rate company playing in the sticks); we were the entire original cast, straight from Broadway. We were booked into a chain of theaters—the Shubert Chain. This meant three months in Philadelphia, two or three months in Boston, and "split weeks" in the smaller towns. On a split-week deal, we would arrive late Sunday night or at 6 a.m. Monday morning (if it had been a "sleeper jump"), hunt up a hotel, unpack, report to the theater for a brush-up rehearsal, do dress parade so that the wardrobe mistress could mend a torn skirt or repair a fouled zipper, find a decent restaurant, and get to the theater for the "Half-hour" call. On matinee days (Wednesday and Saturday), we rushed to our rooms after the last show, packed, checked out, and dashed to the train depot. Trains don't wait! The VIPs always got special theatrical rates from the best hotels (good publicity), but the rest of us holed up wherever we could. The South had excellent theatrical boarding houses with brunches and supper after the show. In Boston there was the luxurious Cushman Club supported by wealthy women to house young girls in show business who didn't have much money. On the first few trips, I dutifully hunted up points of interest and museums to write about to Mom. But it wasn't long before I joined the clamor of "Hey! Anybody know a cheap hotel with clean sheets?"

The VIPs always had a private car, and then there was a baggage car, and then the company car. The VIPs usually wandered into our car because it was more fun. On sleeper jumps, I always got the upper berth. "You're so skinny, if you roll off and fall on the girl below you, you won't hurt her," they explained. Jeepers! One Sunday, I was standing in the middle aisle of the train watching the leading lady play poker with the stage hands and added some new words to my vocabulary (Mitzi sure hated to lose!), when the train gave a sudden lurch and I grabbed at an overhead cord to keep from falling. At once, the train ground to a halt and a tough-looking man came into the car. "Who pulled that cord?" he demanded. (He was a security guard.) The others glared at me, and I stood there like an idiot. What had I done now? "Don't you ever do that again!" he said sternly. "That's the emergency cord. If there had been a train in back of us, there would have been a wreck!" I collapsed.

And then, in Boston, then the musical center of America, St. Cecilia took a hand. The girl who was the second lead got laryngitis forty-five minutes before curtain time. I knew the part; I knew all of the parts, including the bass viol. "That kid can't sing," the stage manager argued (he had a pet of his own). "She's been studying," the music director retorted. "Costume won't fit," the stage manager fumed. "Fix it in a second," the wardrobe mistress promised. Papa glanced at me. "Smile at 'em, Baby," he said, "and they won't care how you sound."

I was so overjoyed at getting my "chance" that my happiness reached right out over the footlights and the critics were kind. "Interesting new face," and "Might bear watching." I bought every newspaper that I could find and sent them home to Mom. Now she would really have something to show the neighbors! After that, I was made the official understudy.

We closed in Montreal. Shows are always opening and closing. The meaningful relationships split, and we all promised to keep in touch, knowing damn well that we wouldn't.

Back in New York City, I headed straight for Madam's studio. She was the voice teacher that the music director had sent me to. Madam was a gracious English gentlewoman, the kind with a hyphenated name. At the moment, she had the "in" studio. Voice studies in New York City run in cycles, like fashions. This year, it would be Mr. X ("My dear, he knows *everybody*! All of his pupils work!"). Next year, it might be Mr. Y, who held such elegant soirees. Madam had been coaching several of the Metropolitan Opera divas, and she was highly regarded.

"The critics said," I told her, loftily pulling out my notices, "that I would bear watching." Madam had been sipping tea. She paused with her cup midair. "So," she said icily, "now you're a Prima Donna. Well, I know how to deal with that, too!" And she set her cup down in the exact center of her saucer. She offered me a scholarship if I would stay in New York City and do nothing but study. Well, nothing ventured, nothing gained. I trudged up to her studio every day, opened my mouth, and sang. For a while, I progressed rapidly, and Madam was delighted. I even conquered the high C. However, I soon struck a plateau, and, after weeks of hard work, Madam said casually that "The Voice," (it was always "The Voice"), "had been ruined. Such a pity. You would have been such a charming Mimi, such a piquant Butterfly. You have the temperament, but you were sent to me too late."

Back to square one. I certainly couldn't go home to Mom. Not after all the bragging I had done. Once more I tramped from one office to another, and my savings dwindled. Once I thought I had it made. I was waiting in an office where they were casting for a dramatic play. It was a typical New York City scorcher of a day, and I was pouring a drink from the water cooler when a tired-looking man came out of the office and I offered him a drink. He smiled and asked, "What are you doing here?"

"What everybody else is doing here," I answered, "keeping both fingers and toes crossed, hoping for a job."

"Report backstage tomorrow," he said, "and tell the casting director you are to read for the part of 'Maureen'. Tell him I sent you."

"And who are you?" I asked, thinking that he was joking. He smiled at my ignorance.

"Jed Harris," he said, and walked away. Jed Harris! The producer! But, when I reported, the casting director said curtly, "Mr. Harris doesn't seem to know that that part had been promised to someone else."

On another occasion, I had an appointment to see David Belasco. David Belasco! I got goose bumps at the very thought. It was another scorcher of a day when I went to his office. There were five of us waiting and I watched the girls file in and out of the inner sanctum while I kept daubing my makeup. Finally, the list was down to two when the secretary came out and announced, "Mr. Belasco is not feeling well. Please come back tomorrow." Unfortunately, overnight "they changed their minds" and decided that the cigarette girl should be a willowy blonde instead of a pert little brunette like me. Where was St. Cecilia this time?

Once more all of my money was gone. Riding on the subway, which I hated, from 72nd Street to Times Square, I noticed a placard that stated: "GIRLS! BIG MONEY! Apply at the Roseland Dance Hall." Well, I had to do something, didn't I? It was a job, wasn't it? I was hired at once.

"It's your corn-fed heifers from the sticks that gets 'em every time," the manager said. So now I was a "dime-a-dance" girl. The rules of the house were strict. The girls sat in one corner of the hall, and the customers bought tickets at the door. Each ticket cost a dime. A customer then picked the girl of his choice and was entitled to one dance for each ticket. If he preferred, he could "sit it out" (sit down and chat instead of dance). At the end of the night, the girls turned in their tickets and collected a percentage of the profits. Some of the men, who were trying to make time, gave the girls rolls of tickets, but no one was allowed to leave the floor during working hours. When someone suggested a date later, I learned to smile sweetly and say, "Sorry, but my cousin, Tom (or Dick, or Harry) is picking me up tonight." My time was always filled, and I began to save money.

"William Mortimer Carr, Jr.
circa 1955"3

"The Carr Homestead aka 'The Pillars' or 'The White Pillars'

CHAPTER 2

I Meet My Husband And The House

"**I**'m shrieking!" I yelled into the receiver.

"That's better," said the voice on the other end. "At least I can tell you're on the other end. When are you coming?"

"That depends," said I, "on a number of things. Like, for instance, on how much you can afford . . . ."

"I'll write to you," said the voice hastily. He had heard that all right! There was a series of little clicks, and somebody shushed somebody else. "Is there someone else on the line?"

"Probably. This is a party line. Please hang up Mrs. Jones. I'll tell you all about it at prayer meeting tomorrow night." There was an indignant "Click!" and the connection got better.

"I'll write," said the fellow. "There are eight parties on this line, and I've counted six clicks. I'll write."

"Bang!" went the seventh receiver, and that was my introduction to the community where I now live, and it hasn't changed much since that hectic night. I was interrupted.

"Come on, Pat, let's get started on time tonight," said Dutch, "two shows!"

"OK, OK," I said and went back to my dressing room to get into my work clothes. I was dancing in a small (nope, not "select") nightclub.

"Hurry up," said Nikki, wriggling efficiently into her sleek, tight-fitting evening gown. "Two shows tonight."

"My God," I said. "For why? There's not a customer in the joint. We'll have to round 'em up out on the street."

"Oh, Dutch is in a lather. He's griping about business again."

"Nikki," I said, "what do you suppose we'd look like in the daylight, with nothing but our faces? Have you ever wondered?"

"Don't know and don't care," said Nikki. "There's Dutch! Come ON!"

I forgot about the letter I had been reading and the reason for the phone call. It was time to dance for my supper.

Nikki woke me up the next morning yelling up the stairs, "Letter for you. Airmail special. Looks important!"

I propped it up on the sugar bowl and read while I gulped my orange juice. I had an appointment with Bev to plan costumes, a run-through with Dewey at the piano, a dinner date, and the grind of the club. Another typically uneventful day. By 3 a.m. I was so tired I pulled the mascara beads off of my makeup and just slapped powder over the rouge. "Stell," I yelled into the next dressing room, "where can we go to eat? I've got something weird to tell you . . . someplace where we can talk."

"We'd better go to the Main Drag, then. Everybody yells so loud there, they can't overhear anybody else," she replied.

"Not that they would be interested in what I have to say! It'll be crowded," I said.

"So what?" said Stell. "It's always warm and the coffee's good."

The Main Drag was jammed. Dinner jackets blended with the dull uniforms of bus drivers. Just about every performer in town was there, too.

"Stell," I said, "Wait till I tell you!"

"Let's order first," said Stell. "I'm starved. Hey! Jeannie!"

"Hi, girls," said Jeannie, our favorite waitress. "What'll it be?"

"Just soup," I said. "And coffee—black."

"Better eat," said Stell. "You gotta keep up your strength in this racket, otherwise you might collapse on top of me while we're on stage, and I don't know if I could take that. Here, Jeannie, give her a menu."

"I gotta fit into my costumes," I said. "Bev won't make me a new set. Make it soup, Jeannie, that'll be just fine, really."

"Well, I always say your health comes first," said Stell. "Scrambled with, Jeannie. And some cheesecake, if it's fresh. None of that left-over-from-last-week stuff, or the week before's, for that matter."

"Stell," I said, "You remember that character I told you about, the one I went out to breakfast with last week, you know, the farmer?"

Stell looked blank. "Oh, you know," I said. "one of the boys on that convention hassle."

"Oh, yeah, yeah," said Stell. "I'm still beat from that tea-fight. Funny ain't it? I bet at home they go to bed early and support the March of Dimes. Wives, too, most of 'em. And kids they take to Sunday school, I bet. Never did dig the regular life much, though I can't say this is a whole lot better. Breakfast at 7:00 a.m., hot cakes and sausages on the maid's night out, and Saturday Night Bridge Club. Funny how half the world lives, ain't it?"

"You should talk, Stell," I said. "With your two kids married. Well, this character bought me a steak at the club and danced with me all night. We went to the drug store for breakfast, and he bought me perfume and a marvelous box of candy."

"Thought you were watching your costumes," said Stell.

"I am," I said, "I didn't tell him, though! I sent the candy to Mom for her birthday. He'd have bought me more, too, but the drug store was the only place open. Well, anyway . . . ."

"Here's the soup," said Stell. "Sure you don't want some eggs? Bring her some eggs," she said to Jeannie. Just then, Beverly came over. Stell greeted her: "Bev, what'd you think of the band tonight, huh? Lousy, huh? Way too fast on that first number and the racket they made, you had to yell your lungs out. I've got a good notion to complain to Dutch. Not that it would do any good."

"Now, Stell," said Bev. "Nobody can beat you when you get right in there with both lungs. Sounded good. You did alright tonight, Baby," she went on, turning to me. "Dutch was knocked off his ear with that new routine; everyone really liked it."

"Well, you deserve the credit. You're the one who planned it," I said. "All I did was wear the costumes. Look gals, stop talking shop. I've got some REAL news!" I hauled out my letter, which was signed "Bill".

"He's a farmer," I said, "and a widower. And he needs a housekeeper for him and his draft-age son. And he thinks maybe somebody like me . . . like, well, me and my mother . . . to come for a month and see if I like it. And he added 'it's coming to spring in the country' and that sounds mighty tempting."

"Smart man," commented Stella. "He knows 'Momma' will rustle up some square meals. As far as you're concerned, Honey, there isn't an apron in the act."

"Stell," I said, wounded. What did she take me for, anyway?

"Don't mind her, Baby," said Bev. "She's just jealous."

"Huh?" asked Stell.

"Listen to this," I went on. "He gives a bank president and two ministers for reference."

"Hmm," said Stell, "I'd rather have two bank accounts and a check book. Then I'd be out of this lousy rat race but fast."

"Hold out for the minister and a marriage license," said Bev.

"Shut up, you two dearest friends," I said. "Listen to the postscript: P.S. Please come right away as my oldest daughter, the one who never married and has always taught school and comes home every weekend, is also looking for the right woman for the job. I think you'd be nicer than anyone that she could find. Besides, I want to beat her to the punch."

"Oh, stop!" said Stell, blowing on her coffee.

"Goons," I said dreamily, "it's getting close to Easter, and jobs will be slack. I thought maybe, I was wondering, well, why shouldn't I anyway?"

"For heaven's sake, have you gone nuts?" screamed Stell. "Don't you have any sense? Going way up there? That's just the way young girls get murdered! References or no references. Hand me the sugar, Bev. Go way up there where nobody knows you, and they'll find your body in the truck, that is if you're lucky."

"Hear, hear!" said Bev, pounding the table, "Ellery Queen, Page 1."

"Police all over the joint," said Stell. "It don't mean a thing."

"But, Stell, he wants her mother, too," said Bev.

"*That's* a pitch," said Stell scornfully. "TWO bodies! More blood. I can just see the gory headlines now!"

"Stell," said Bev mildly, "could we stanch the flow of blood till I'm done eating?"

"But he knows two ministers, and a bank president . . . ."

"I know, Baby," said Bev. "He's probably a nice enough guy, but what about those new dances that we planned, and the costumes we looked at? Dutch promised to feature you. Are you just going to turn your bank on all of that?"

"Just think of getting sunburn from the *sun* instead of a sunlamp!" I said.

"Alright, alright," said Stell. "Go right ahead and go up there. But, mark my words. You'll be glad to come back, if you can *get* back. What kind of a fight could a little shrimp like you put up? That guy could take care of you and your Ma with one hand tied behind his back!"

"Look, Stell," I said, "so I'm 'Our Little Patsy'. But I've pounded 42nd Street and walked down dark stage alleys and taken the subway home from Brooklyn at 3 a.m. I even got hung up in those phony New Jersey club raids, remember? And what has it all got me? I'm still here drinking coffee. Don't you think maybe I could handle a man who is on speaking terms with a bank president and two ministers?"

"But you're such a nice kid," said Stella.

"We like you, Baby," said Bev.

"Alright, alright," I said, "if things get too tough, I'll trade him in for a bank president, and my mother can make a deal with one of the good reverends."

"That's my girl," said Stell. "Hey, Jeannie, another piece of cheesecake!"

I finally bypassed the whole thing by calling up Mom, who was keeping house for my schoolteacher sister, and asked if she would like to go. I figured that I was safe. I was sure she would react just as the girls had, but no! Mom was bored and she said she'd love to go. Fine thing when a child can't rely on her own parent! Mom came in from New Jersey the next day. When Mom makes up her mind to do a thing, she does it. When Dutch heard she was in town, he invited her to the club. It was the first time that she had watched me dance since I had left regular shows. It was really a well-bred striptease, but Bev had choreographed it so artistically that Mom never caught on. "It's swell for your inhibitions," Bev had said when she taught it to me.

A young sailor walked over to Mom's table. "Will you have a drink, Mother?" he asked politely, much to Mom's astonishment. "Can I order you a drink?"

Mom beamed when she told me. I think she felt that life begins at fifty, and in a club like that, she may be right.

We got our tickets the day after. Upstate Western New York: eight hours, as the New York Central goeth, two hours as the Capital line flieth, and several light years as the mind runneth. I wondered why Mom had come. Perhaps she wanted to keep an eye on me. Of course, we had always gone to Aunt Mary's in the summer and listened to the birds and the bees, and Mom had always kept a geranium on the windowsill. But I felt, somehow, that this was going to be a bit more drastic. She wasn't that used to country life. When we got to the station, a tall broad-shouldered man with the walk of a Dutch boy doll came over. "Oh, my," whispered mother to me. "He's handsome."

"Well, sure," I said. "Look who snared him."

"Quite a ride to my place," Bill said apologetically. "Trains don't stop in small towns."

We drove through the spring rain until, with no fanfare, we reached The Pillars. I've never been quite sure whether I fell in love with Bill first or the house.

The Pillars was over a hundred years old, and its columned porch, lovely high pillars (which gave the house its name), and broad hospitable steps spelled "home". There was warmth and spaciousness, solidness and tolerance. The whole place just made a person feel good again. Whoever designed that house had a song in his heart and good stout workmanship at his fingertips. The driveway curved up to the stone steps, and the trees were old and majestic, the lawn a piece of green velvet. All in all, it was quite lovely.

Five generations had lived and loved and begat in that house and the essence of their comings and goings still lingered. It was solid, like a firm handclasp.

Off to one side stretched a meadow bright with buttercups and clover. "Night pasture for the cows," Bill explained.

Mom was delighted. She was so pleased by all the room. After Dad died, our home had been broken up. Mom's culinary talents and homemaking abilities had been cramped up in apartments. These were the rooms that she had been used to. The inside of the house was as exciting as the outside. The windows were twelve feet high and went from the floor to the ceiling. The ceilings, of course, were beamed, and the doors were massive and took a good amount of strength to open. They were hand-carved with heavy ornate hinges. The stairway curved in exquisite harmony with the sweep of the upper and lower hall ceilings, and at the very top there were slender fluted columns to partition off the hall. In addition, there were two attics, and, of course, a cupola. I stood at the foot of the balustrade, and I practically filmed a remake of "Gone with the Wind" right then and there, with myself in crinoline. The whole scene was unbelievably romantic. I felt like a little girl again. I went to sleep in an 18—by 20-foot bedroom. I was thinking of some of the terrible hotel rooms that I had slept in in the past. In the summertime, I kept the window shut and suffocated, or opened it and stayed awake wondering if a rapist would climb up the fire escape and come in through the window. But in this room, I opened the window wide to hear the crickets chirping, and a beautiful red-gold and white collie dog slept just outside my door. I dreamed that I was back in New York City rehearsing for a new show.

The next thing I heard was a terrific snorting and bucking and backfire, like a machine gun. "For heaven's sake," I said to Mom. "It reminds me of Chicago during the gang wars!"

I ran to the window and looked out frantically. Coming up the lane was a tractor as big as a moving van, and driving it was our host. With one eye on my window (show off!), he shot that tractor up to the gas tank, skidded it around a thin dime, and strode off into the barn, whistling.

"Ham!" I muttered, and started to crawl back into bed.

"Oh, no, you don't!" cried Mom, as she grabbed my leg. "Young lady, get up right now!"

"But, Mom," I protested. "This is the time I always go to bed!"

"Right now!" Mom insisted, and yanked me upright. "Bill will come in any minute, and he'll want breakfast."

She slipped on a housedress and tied an apron over it. She bullied me into a simple gown that I had bought for the occasion, and we set out to find the kitchen. The first set of stairs landed us in the parlor. The next set of stairs led to the library.

"There's got to be a kitchen somewhere!" Mom said. "That man looks well fed."

"Never find it without a road map," I giggled. But, on the third try, we made it. We found ourselves in the dining room. Brown peacocks with jeweled tails wandered all over the brown wallpaper, and the heavy silk curtains were green. The table was walnut and the chairs were intricately carved. A cozy little party of twenty comers could have eaten at that table without rubbing elbows, and a party of five could eat there without getting within shouting distance. "Oh, Mom," I said, "I'm in the wrong studio! Miscast! Not the type! The write-ups will be awful!"

"Keep going," said Mom pushing me. "Where there's a dining room, there's got to be a kitchen." The kitchen ran the whole width of the house from east to west. It watched the sun rise in the morning and set at dusk. The walls were paneled halfway up with fumed oak. There was an old-fashioned sink and a refrigerator with a round honeycomb motor on top; a cook stove that burned wood, and a plain wooden table in the middle of the floor big enough to seat the "harvest hands". My mother's eyes were bugging from her head, as were mine.

"Oh, Mom," I said. "A big yellow mixing bowl, just like the one I used to lick chocolate out of when you used to make us cookies, when we were kids!"

"And a pantry!" exclaimed Mom. "I haven't seen a pantry in years!" Just then, there was a rattling at the door and Bill came in with an armload of wood. He and Mom took to each other right off. "Oh, yes," said Mom, "I've used wood heat. Nice quick heat, isn't it? And the oven . . ."

"Good for cakes," said Bill, grinning. "Chocolate ones!"

"Well, fried oysters are my specialty," said Mom. "Can you buy oysters up here?"

"If I have to go to Rochester for them," said Bill, "I'll be only too happy to oblige. Now the hot water tank is right here in this end of the stove; I keep forgetting to fill it."

"Now, let's see," said Mom. "For breakfast . . ."

"Toast and coffee," I said. "Black."

"Hotcakes," said Mom.

"Sausage," said Bill. "There's leftover pie in the pantry."

"Tomato juice?" asked Mom.

"Naturally, Ma'am, and milk, warm right out of the cow," said Bill, putting a four-quart earthen jug on the table.

"And cream," said Mom. "I haven't seen cream like that since we used to go to Aunt Mary's."

"There's plenty more where that came from," grinned Bill. "And maple syrup, and rolled oats and cream. I always have oatmeal and cream every morning for breakfast."

"Set the table, Dear," said Mom. "How many?"

"Just us three and my youngest boy," said Bill. "Chuckie's just out of high school and he's facing the draft like most young fellows his age."

I went out on the porch. "You're the most beautiful dog in the whole wide world," I whispered into the collie, Jack's ear, and he was my dog from then on. It was so refreshing out there. The smell of the open earth and the smell of the sausage frying, and the sun-cured air did queer things to my stomach. "Make that another order of sausage," I yelled to Mom. I felt like I could have eaten four more orders!

Bill took me down the lane after breakfast. He showed me the woods, the fields, the brook, and the hog pens. Mom was doing the dishes. "We're diversified farmers," said Bill. "We go from baby lambs to baby calves to baby pigs. We do all of our own haying, we bale our own straw, and we trim our own orchards . . ."

"Orchards!" I said. "I *love* apples!"

". . . combine our own wheat and oats, pick our own tomatoes, cut our own cabbage, and fix our own machinery," he added. "In short, we decide what's best for us at a given time, then, by golly, we do it!"

I looked intelligent. (One of the secrets of my charm is to look intelligent when people are talking.) "I know," I said. "We used to go to my Aunt Mary's every summer."

Mom had lunch ready when we got back.

"I've got to plow this afternoon," said Bill, "but we could drive into town and then over to Lake Ontario tonight."

"All the butter I can use," said Mom. "This is really wonderful, for there's nothing makes good cooking taste good as melted butter poured over the top of it."

"Plain food, well cooked, and well seasoned," said Bill.

"And plenty of salt," said Mom.

"Steaks well-done," said Bill, "and gravy!"

"I'm famous for my gravy," said Mom modestly.

"We'll fatten you up," said Bill to me.

"My costumes!" I said. "I have to work in those costumes. What will my faithful audience say?"

"Now, let's see," said Mom. "Roast chicken and dressing?"

Bill drooled.

"I make good dressing," said Mom.

After dinner, Bill drove us into town. After parking on Main Street, he claimed that he had an errand to do, and we agreed to meet back at the car at eight o'clock. Mom and I walked to the corner. There were five shops, including the hardware. We looked at blankets, had some coffee, bought some thread and some picture post cards with local scenes on them, had more coffee, and went back to the car.

Bill drove us to Lake Ontario that night. The countryside was even more beautiful by moonlight. The wind ruffled little waves right up to our feet and we could look clean over to the Canadian shore. "I love the water," said Mom.

Bill looked right at me. "It's kinda nice up here, sometimes," he said.

Mom baked and roasted and lined the pantry shelves. I put on my playsuit and soaked up the sun. It was like a fantastic holiday, and it started so suddenly.

Bill wanted to show me the farm. He drove the tractor and I stood on the hitching bar, which was fastened to the back of the tractor. It was only a foot off the ground and ten inches wide, so I reached up and grabbed Bill around the waist so I wouldn't jounce off on the bumps. "Hang on!" he said and away we went!

An early morning shower had washed the air. The piglets oinked, the lambs bleated to their mammas, the hogs (dumb things) greedily chomped their way to the butcher's, the cows placidly snubbed us, the creek and the swimming hole rushed by, and we ended up at the pine woods.

"See that tree over there?" asked Bill, pointing. "The big one off by itself, with all of that soft grass around it? Well, if your Mom wasn't waiting for us . . . ."

When we got back, Mom had dinner ready. That night Mom had decided that we would dine in state because Chuckie brought home some of his friends. I spread the Irish lace tablecloth on the cherry wood dining table. From the dining room, a double doorway opens to the fireplace in the living room and a short curved passageway glimpses the fireplace in the other living room. We can sit at the table and see the two fireplaces with the flames making dancing lights. Think of the dinner parties we could have!

"We're not far from Buffalo," said Bill, "but we don't get the chance to see too many shows."

"They have shows in Buffalo and Rochester, too," I said.

"She can't cook a lick," said Mom.

"But I can make beds," I said. "The most beautiful, neat, smooth, square-ended beds you've ever seen. Grandpa taught me when I was a little girl and I've always been proud of it. I think he learned in the Army."

"We could buy cookbooks," said Bill.

"Now, you listen to me," said Mom. I knew what that tone meant.

The spring flowers were just starting. I could look out of the kitchen window and see the peony border begin to turn green. There was an oval-shaped shrubbery bed on the corner, and the snowdrops and hyacinths made a delicate still life. I could've sat there looking at them for hours. As it was, I filled the kitchen with them.

"I learned to dance, Mom," I said. "Maybe I could learn to cook, too."

"Now, you listen to me," said Mom.

I went down early the next morning to start breakfast. Bill came in with an armload of wood. He took the stove lids off. "You know," he said, laying the sticks in and not looking at me, "you know, I kinda like you!"

I perked up in spite of myself. The first spring robins took up the refrain. I ran upstairs and shook Mom awake.

"Mom! He practically proposed!" I said.

"Well, what did you expect?" she replied.

"I could dance weekends," I said. "My career need not be shelved completely. Dutch would love to have me work weekends at the club. After all, he complimented me on my last act."

"You're still young," said Mom, "and you've never lived on a farm. You've picked armfuls of flowers and you've gone riding every day. You've never really worked hard in your whole life."

"I have too!" I said.

"You're used to colors and lights and music and dancing. Bill will rarely scold you and almost never praise you, and you've been spoiled a bit in show business, Child. You think you can be a dancer *and* a farmer's wife? It won't work out that way."

"I've never met anyone like him," I said.

"That's just what I mean," said Mom.

"Approaching Nuptials," said the *Orleans Republican Democrat* (published every Tuesday). "Mrs. Florence Carty announces the engagement of her daughter, Patricia, to Mr. William Carr. Date for the ceremony to be announced later." And the deluge broke. I had never dreamed that I, a stranger, could be the subject of such interest.

"Have you heard?" said one party line to another.

"What's she like?" said the Home Bureau.

"We heard she was an actress," said the Grange.

"The most beautiful voice," said Mrs. James, the plumber's wife, "but Jigger went out there on a job and when he got back, well he was just shocked! She was barefoot! Yes, of course, I've heard that dancers . . . it'll *never* last."

"Such a waste of talent," said my friends in New York City. "Shut off, way up there in the country. Nothing to look at but the cows. Work her fingers to the bone, and for what? Such a waste! My Dear, they get up at six o'clock. In the morning! She was being featured, too. It will *never* last!"

"Think carefully, Baby," said Beverly. "I want you to be happy, but you dance well and it's a life you're used to. We want you to be happy."

"You take the next train back here," said Stell. "Are you nuts? What's gotten into you, anyway? Dutch has got you advertised for next weekend!" Yakety, yakety, yak!

"I've got to go home," said Mom. "Your sister Mary needs me." Things were becoming hectic again. Mary had honey blonde hair and an infectious giggle. Her coloratura is floating and pure and she can dance circles around me. Naturally, she is the one who teaches school, while I've been terpsichording. Naturally.

"Mom," I said, "you can't go! Mary doesn't need you."

"Oh, yes, she does," said Mom firmly. "Anyway, I'm all packed."

"I've been packed for years!" I said.

"To think of all that life and color on County House Road!" said the Home Extension. Even the Ladies Aid entered into the fray. I was invited to join the church. A general state of confusion set in.

"Honestly," I said to Bill, "I never dreamed that putting flowers in the kitchen would stir up such a hornets' nest!" Between "what Father ought to do" and "that crazy mixed-up Pat", we were a little confused ourselves.

"Now, don't fret a bit," said Betty, who lived on a nearby farm. She was a girl who'd already become a fast friend. "You just bring your cookbook up to me. I've never seen Bill look so well or so happy!"

The oldest stepdaughter bought a plane ticket to Detroit to see the oldest stepson. "It's his money," they agreed. "Poor Father; it will never last." The oldest stepson bought a ticket to Washington, D.C., and spoke to the second-youngest stepdaughter. "It will never last," they agreed. The second-youngest stepdaughter telephoned Bill.

"I'm bringing your grandchildren for a visit," she said, "on the 22nd."

"We won't be home," said Bill. "But don't let that stop you, now. You come up anyway, and we'll cut our honeymoon short and be home by the 29th."

"Oh, no," said the second-youngest stepdaughter. "You be there on the 22nd."

"That's our wedding day," said Bill. And that was that.

I went to New York City first and bought clothes. Since it was the only wedding I was ever going to have (Right, St. Cecelia?), I splurged. I kept in mind that Bill had good taste, so I chose my clothes carefully. While I was tearing around shopping, Bill was tearing around on the farm. Was his "year man" reliable enough to run the place for a week? Would the bred cows abort? Would the ewes be all right? Would the plowing get done? The result was that he got to New York City a little later than he planned. He was an expert driver, and none of the state troopers at home had ever bothered him. The car was new (for our honeymoon), and there wasn't too much traffic. What, with one thing and another, he took his eye off the speedometer, and, in the highway circle at the foot of Bear Mountain, he got scooped up in a speed trap.

"I saw the trooper coming," he told me later, "but I was so busy thinking about everything . . ."

So we marched off to the local Justice of the Peace, an elderly man who wore glasses and had a reputation for speaking his mind. "Aha!" he said to Bill as he stood before him. "And what brings you, an upstanding citizen, to my court?"

"Well, I . . . . I guess I was driving a mite fast," Bill admitted sheepishly. "It's this way, Your Honor. I'm on my way to New York City to get married and I got started a little late . . . . By the way, I'm a JP upstate!"

Needless to say, he got off scot-free!

We were married in New York City at the Actor's Church. It was an oasis of serenity tucked into a corner not far from the bedlam of Wall Street. Many famous actors had gone there for a quiet wedding. It had tradition and charm. What more could a girl want?

The day was just like an opening night, and I got stage fright! Bill pretended to be perfectly calm, but he wasn't. He had even nicked his chin when he shaved. When we walked through the lichen gate down the flower-bordered path, I looked at my new shoes and fingered the corsage of orchids that Bill had pinned on my coat. We entered the church and waited for our bridal party. Mom, my sister Mary, and her boyfriend were to see us married. They were late, but they finally arrived. The minister read the service, my sister's boyfriend gave me away, Mom sniffed, Bill kissed me, and then the minister pronounced me Mrs. Carr.

"Glad that's settled," said Bill. He had been getting flack from both the Methodist Ladies and the Presbyterian Ladies in his small town.

We went to the Russian Bear for our wedding breakfast. The balalaikas serenaded us as the customers toasted us, Mom managed another sniff, and we were off on a Great Adventure. The curtain had gone up.

When we returned from our honeymoon, we found that everything had gone well on the farm and Bill was pleased, but I felt a little sorry for him. Nothing is so deflating to one's ego as to discover that things have gone well without you. Then Bill and I got right down to what's known as "adjusting to one another". We soon discovered that each of us had one trait that the other would not tolerate. Ever since I had been a child, when I got mad, I smashed dishes. Mom gave me a spanking every time, but I figured it was worth it. There was such a satisfying "thump!" when the dish hit the floor. It was the ultimate retort. So, when Bill riled my French-Scotch temper, I grabbed a dish and let fly. Bill was shocked. "I work hard for my money," he said, "and I paid good money for that dish." (A quarter at Henry's, but it was the principle of the thing.) "Young lady," he said sternly, "don't you ever do that again!"

"No, Sir," I said meekly, and then I sneaked another dish out and went behind the barn to smash it.

Bill, on the other hand, shut up like a clam when he was mad. "Good morning," I would say. No answer. "Nice day," I would offer. No comment. I was at once a non-member of the human race. I was a nothing, a nobody, a zilch. "Young man," I said in my best imitation of Mom's voice when she was scolding us kids. "You speak when you're spoken to. Do you hear me?"

"Yup," Bill said, and then grinned. One time, after an especially earnest spat, Bill disappeared. I was terrified. Perhaps I was reliving one of those dreadful childhood memories that linger through the years. It was Christmas and Santa Claus had been as generous as usual. My sister and I (she was ten years old and I was twelve) had been so absorbed in our gifts that we didn't notice Pop was gone. "Maybe he's in the cellar fixing the furnace," Mom said. "Honey, run down and tell him dinner's ready."

I went into the cellar, which was a huge basement. Pop was sitting on a crate staring at the pipes that cross and crisscrossed overhead. A piece of rope was dangling from one of the pipes and I knew somehow that my father had meant to hang himself. Our family had always been considered "well-to-do", but in our town, the really wealthy people owned silk mills. So Pop mortgaged his stores and wiped out his bank account and bought a silk mill. Unfortunately, his partner was crooked. "I'll kill myself before I declare bankruptcy," I heard him say to Mom. So I stood there in the cellar, and Pop and I stared at each other. "Daddy," I finally quavered, "Mom said to tell you that dinner's ready. Please come and eat your dinner, Daddy. Please."

With a sigh, he got up and climbed the stairs. Pop died in a hospital a year later following surgery, but I was never able to forget that moment.

So, when Bill disappeared after that knock-down-drag-out spat, I hit the panic button. I searched the attic; I looked (shrinkingly) in the cellar, then the carriage house, the well house, the barn, the haymow . . . dear God! The haymow! I dragged the rickety old ladder from the wall and started to climb. "St. Cecelia, please let him be safe!" I begged, "and I'll never ask another thing from you again. Not ever."

St. Cecelia sighed. "That's the ninety-ninth time she's said that," she observed to the Angel Gabriel, as she put a dot next to my name. The haymow was littered with ropes the men use to haul up the bales, but Bill . . . Bill! He was sitting in one corner contentedly enjoying a fit of the sulks. "Darn you!" I yelled.

And Bill went through the same rigmarole when the car and I disappeared. He chased after me once in a neighbor's car. He vowed, "I was doing eighty and I couldn't catch her!" He knew I wasn't an expert driver, so he called the sheriff, the state troopers, and the hospital. Had I crashed into a tree? Gone over a bank into the Canal? Didn't I w he loved me? In time, we both adjusted. If we had a spat, I went to the hayloft first, and he snatched the car keys.

"Pat Carr circa 1945"

CHAPTER 3

I Tangle With Local Customs

Not long after our return from our honeymoon, I bumped up against what Bev termed "the generation gap". In New York City, we had floor maids and cleaning women, janitors and busboys. The names were simply categories for the payroll. But, in all the length and breadth and depth of Upstate, there was no such thing as a "cleaning lady". There were, of course, one or two neighbors who, for a slight stipend, were willing to help out that nice Mr. Carr and that "poor little young thing who doesn't know a thing about housework", but nobody told me about the local hang-up. So, when a stranger came to the door and asked to use the phone I, unawares, said apologetically, "The house is sort of messy; my cleaning lady hasn't come yet."

The man reared back and said frostily, "Your 'cleaning lady' happens to be my wife!" The Ladies Aiders snubbed me for a week after that!

As for whimsy, forget it! If Peter Pan had soared over the treetops of Upstate New York, he would have been shot down as an unidentified flying object! I had a pet lamb, known as a "cosset", that figured I was its mama and the hell with letting me out of its sight. It "baaa'd" so heartbrokenly when I was out that I tied a bow around its neck, slipped a pair of rubber panties over its hind legs, put a leash through its collar, and took it downtown shopping with me. We stopped traffic. Later that week, when I was helping at a quilting bee and got up to leave early saying, "My lamb will miss me," the ladies all urged me to stay. I explained, "Well, it's this way. Bill said if I could raise a lamb, he might trust me with a baby." I *waded* through the silence to the door.

When Kipling wrote "East is east and west is west", he undoubtedly had in mind the local Upstate sense of humor. The only chance I ever got to go shopping in the city (not THE city, but a small city upstate), was on a rainy day. Farmers don't work on rainy days, not because they pamper themselves, but the ground gets too soggy to work. So, when a cloud the size of my fist appeared on the horizon, I would begin to pester Bill. "Bill, will it rain so that we can go shopping? Bill? Will it?"

"Wal-l," he would drawl, scanning the horizon from east to west and back again, while I hopped impatiently on one foot. "Allus has somewhere along the line." This was supposed to be funny! Yuck! But, once in a while, I got my comeuppance. Bill sent me on an errand in the "North Country". It sounded ominous. Should I pack a gun? (I found out later that it was only twelve miles away!) I got lost once or twice and floundered around in rutted lanes, but I finally found the house. The door was off its hinges and all sorts of livestock wandered in and out. The kids were playing in the chicken roost, and the chickens were roosting in the parlor. In the front room, there was the last remnant of an ancient grandeur: a rosewood grand piano! Some hens were cackling on the top! When I told a neighbor about it, I said indignantly, "What if some of the eggs those hens were hatching had cracked open and dripped down on those priceless ivory keys?"

"Mi gol," the neighbor responded. "And eggs at two dollars a dozen!"

Bill threw back his head and roared, "Did Jim really say that? Why the old so-and-so! Honey, where's your sense of humor?"

Bill could be really cute about getting his own way. I was trying to get a closet cleaned out one morning, and he kept teasing me and teasing me. Finally I exploded. "Who told you that you could pick me up and toss me on the bed and rape me whenever you wanted to?" I demanded.

"The minister!" he said. Oh well . . .

The one local custom that really hog-tied me was the communal cemetery complex. One of my friends in New York City, on hearing where I was headed, assured me that "those people up there never die. They just sort of dry up and blow away." Well, maybe they did, but you'd never prove it by the cemeteries. They are beautifully kept. The lawns are manicured, the lily ponds have lilies in them, the massive iron gates work, and there are acres and acres of headstones. Social prestige was established by the quiet elegance, the ornate ostentatiousness or (V.I.P.s only) the impressive mausoleums. Every person in the family had a headstone, living or dead. One of our neighbors, a Catholic married to a Protestant, had a headstone in both denominational cemeteries!

"Betty," I said, giggling, "where will you end up?"

"Oh," she said, "I talked it over with Pop Sullivan," the easy-going middle-aged parish priest, "and he figures they'll let me commute."

I knew darn well what was going to happen, and sure enough it did. On my birthday, we went for a ride, and Bill swung in at Mt. Albion Cemetery. "Want to show you something," he said, and drove up to the Carr family plot. And there was my tombstone! I was relieved to note that while the birth date was chiseled in, the "died" date was still blank. When we got home, I said to Bill, somewhat diffidently, "Dearest, I feel sort of uncomfortable with your first wife there, and all." (Second wife syndrome?)

"Now, now, Little Girl," Bill responded. "You know you want me close enough so that, in the middle of eternity, you can poke me in the ribs and say 'Bill, wake up! There's a mouse nibbling at my toe!'"

He had a point, but the next day, when I was wandering along the creek, I came across a huge oak tree off by itself. "Bill!" I yelled to him. "I know where I want to be buried. Under that oak tree. The leaves will keep me warm in the autumn, and the creek will keep me company."

"And the old sow will come along and root you up!" Bill said.

That night I had the most horrible dream. The kind of dream where you know it's a dream, but you think it's for real. The old sow did come down the lane and she did root me up, and she started chewing on my leg. I screamed.

"There, there, Little Girl," Bill said, getting awake at once. "You're having a nightmare. Nothing's wrong."

"It was the old sow!" I sobbed. "She was eating me!"

"Now, now," Bill soothed me. "No old sow is going to get you while I'm here." He pulled me closer to him, and I snuggled into his arms. The warmth of his body felt so comforting.

When I was growing up, I had always tagged after my father in the store. So, while I was a whiz kid at "gross profit" and "net profit", I couldn't tell the difference between a double boiler and a frying pan. In fact, Mom had confided to my new husband, "You'll have to be patient with her, Bill. Pat can't boil water without scorching." How about that?!

So, I signed up at once for a course in cooking. "Cooking is an art," the university lecturer proclaimed to the politely spellbound ladies of the Grange. Like hell it is! Not when it's a wood-burning stove versus a new bride, it's not! It's more like a knock-me-down, no-holds-barred wrestling match! "In this corner, Ladies and Gentlemen . . ."

Before we left on our honeymoon, Mom had drawn Bill to one side and said diplomatically, "Bill, I'm a little worried. You and I both know that there's nothing like a wood-burning stove for good baking, but these young girls today . . . ."

"I'll order a new one right away," Bill assured her. "You know, I had to send clean to Kalamazoo for that wood-burning stove. They just don't make them like that anymore. Cost me a lot of money, that stove did, but these young girls today . . . ."

So he phoned in an order to the Village Hardware, and they promised him it would be delivered by the time we got back from our honeymoon trip. However, the wholesaler put it on backorder and "backorder" meant delivery within the next six weeks and/or the customer's lifespan. In our quaint little hamlet, you never, never pressured your tradesman. He was your peer, your social equal, and he sat next to you in church. Amen. In the meantime, you used the old stove.

The Stove had a rigid schedule and bucking the schedule was like bucking the establishment: 6:00 a.m.—Shake out the ashes, lay fresh kindling, and pour coal on top. Easy! (When Bill did it.) 6:30 a.m.—Breakfast over; pull out the damper so the coal burned slowly, and, from "time to time", pour on more coal so that the fire wouldn't go out. It was the "from-time-to-time" business that screwed me up. Was I supposed to babysit that damn thing all day long? I would get dinner organized, meatloaf ready in the oven, peas shucked and in the pot with cream and a pat of butter handy, salad crisping in the fridge, potatoes sliced and put around the meatloaf, half of last night's pie (thank goodness), coffee measured in the percolator, anything else? Flowers! Jeepers! Couldn't set the table without fresh flowers! So I wandered down the lane, and the prettiest flowers were always a little way farther on . . . and on . . . . Suddenly I would look at my wristwatch. Yikes! The Stove! I would race up the lane in a panic. The fire had gone out. I would blow on the coals in a frenzy, but the ashes were so dead that not even mouth-to-mouth resuscitation would revive them. At this point, the Standard Operating Procedure was to shake out the ashes, put in fresh kindling, and scatter coal on the top. But, there wasn't time! Bill would be up from the fields in half an hour, and he would be hungry! I had to move quickly. So I put kindling over the ashes, scattered coal on top, grabbed the kerosene can, and poured with a lavish hand. WHOOSH! The flames leaped. WHOOSH! I leaped. The fire blazed so red hot that it was a case of which would crack first: me or the Stove?

When Bill came in, he asked anxiously, "Pat, are you running a fever? Your cheeks are so red."

"It's been a hot day," I said, as I dished up dinner.

If you live in the country, you just don't amount to a hill of beans unless you join. Join the Women's Auxiliary. Join the Farm Bureau. Join the Library. And, yes, by all means, join the Grange. So, when I got a letter inviting me to the Annual Dinner and Business Meeting of the Grange, I was all braced to "help the ladies in the kitchen and to please bring a dish of baked beans and some escalloped potatoes."

When I told Bill about it, he said solemnly, "By gol, Honey, you're in!"

"How come?" I inquired. "What's so big about this baked beans and escalloped potatoes bit?"

"Honey," he said, "you just don't understand. It's the most important dinner of the year, and only the best cooks are asked to bring something. Look at it this way: suppose you were still in show business and you were asked to give a command performance for the Queen of England. How would you feel?"

"Damn scared!" I said, but I got the message.

"Now, you run up to Grandma Werner and get her recipe for baked beans. Granny got first prize for her beans at the County Fair last year; and I'll help you with the potatoes. Also, while I think of it, here's some money. Go down to the dry goods store and pick out their best apron. Then bring it home and wash it. The ladies will notice if it's new, and I want them to think you've been cooking all of your life."

D-day dawned. Bill left the field hands to their own devices and came up into the kitchen and hovered. There is no other word for it; he hovered. He inspected each and every potato and sliced it paper thin. He tested the temperature of the milk and poured in extra cream. "You'll make it too rich," I wailed.

"Can't make it too rich," he retorted, and poured in another cupful of cream. He personally regulated The Stove. The Stove never talked back to Bill. Granny's prize-winning recipe was done at last and everything was ready.

Now for my make-up: almost no rouge, very little lipstick, and my hair piled high on my head to make me look dignified. With my new apron (washed twice), I was the spittin' image of a proper matron. Laden with our spoils and shaking with stage fright, we drove to the hall. Since the hall was used for meetings, square dances, and doubled in brass for exhibits, the inside was completely bare. None of your intimate restaurant tables,

47

instead, the men laid long planks of wood on trestles and lugged the chairs from Bigg's Funeral Home. The tablecloths were from the Five & Dime and the cutlery was plastic (ugh!), but the kids had picked gobs of flowers, and there was a nosegay at every table. There was such an air of excitement that I felt the old familiar butterflies in my stomach on opening night.

We had sold 150 tickets, and the crowd was clamoring to get in. "Come on, you gals!" one of the men shouted. "Open up! We're hungry!" The chairwoman pulled back the doors and in they came. There were young men, teenaged girls, harassed mothers, middle-aged grandmothers, and heavy-set farmers. The young men looked over the young girls; the young girls streamed into the ladies' room to freshen up their lipstick; the mothers yelled at their kids; the kids raced up and down; and the grandmothers beamed over the din. It was a ball! The men yelled to each other across the tables. "Hey! You know what hogs sold for today?" And then they settled down to telling each other how the country should be run. It was a nice ball.

As soon as I came in, the chairwoman of the Kitchen Committee had taken my dishes of beans and potatoes (my, how good they looked!), and put them in the warming oven. I was supposed to be a waitress, and I carted platter after platter of fried chicken, baked ham, and potatoes to the tables. However, the dishes I brought stayed in the warming oven. Two or three times, one of the women had pulled them out and looked at them, but then shoved them back in. What had I done? Those women were sure being mean! I looked at Bill sitting there so hopefully, and I could have bawled.

At last, it was over. The crowd thinned out. "Now, WE eat!" said the chairwoman of the Kitchen Committee. A table was cleared, and we sat down. A platter of baked beans and escalloped potatoes was put before us. Bill took one look and almost burst with pride. "Honey," he whispered, "I'm so proud! They always save the best food for themselves, and they saved yours!" Our marriage was safe.

On the way home, I snuggled up as close as I could to Bill. "You did alright, Little Girl," he remarked.

"Well, you did most of it," I said modestly. "Oh, Bill, what would I ever do without you?"

He beamed. It's always nice when the little woman appreciates her spouse, and vice versa.

Bill was so solid. His muscles were hard, and his head was screwed on tight. He was like the Rock of Gibraltar. Sometimes he took my part and sometimes he took the opposition, but he was always there. He was supposed to be easy-going, but underneath his easy-going viewpoint, there was a hard core of intensity. He told me once that when he was in his teens, he had gotten into a brawl and realized that he had a murderous temper, so he learned to control it. "Overlook a lot of small things," he advised me, "or you'll always be in hot water. But, if you have to crack down, do it!"

During the dog days in August, when the heat and the humidity were both unbearable, brawls would break out in some of the overcrowded migrant worker camps. Often a trivial incident would ignite the spark. One of our juiciest murders was over possession of a chicken wing! The appearance of an officer in uniform would only pour fuel on the flames. The officers, understandably reluctant to have one of their own men killed in the melee of flying knives, sometimes ignored a call. "Let them fight it out among themselves," they said. So, the neighbors fell into the habit of calling Bill, the Justice of the Peace. "The Judge will settle it," they would say.

One night after dinner, the phone rang. After hanging up, Bill said he had to go out for a few minutes; that there was trouble at the South Labor Camp.

"Please don't go," I begged. "What if you should get hurt?"

"Don't intend to get hurt," Bill answered, as he started the car.

"Wait for me!" I yelled. "I'm going with you! If anybody's got to lug your dead body home, it'll be me!"

"Well, hurry up!" he said crossly.

You could hear the fracas a half-mile away from the camp—the yells, the thumps, the curses. "Stay in the car," Bill ordered when we got to the driveway. "And keep the motor running."

"Be careful!" I yelled idiotically after him. (Like a mother cautioning her youngster.)

He pushed open the door and said in a hanging judge voice: "WHAT'S GOING ON HERE?"

Within seconds you could have heard a pin drop in that camp. "Now," Bill said. "This is the last time I'll come down here tonight. I'll see you fellows in the morning."

Wow! Was it any wonder he was the man of my life?

There were times when Bill could be cutting. For a week he had been complaining to me about a girl who wasn't doing her share of the work. "Why don't you speak to her?" I asked.

"Been sort of hoping she'd shape up by herself," he replied. But, one sultry afternoon, when he went in the field and saw this girl sprawled under a tree drinking a bottle of cola while the others were pulling weeds in the hot sun, he blew.

"Do you intend to vacation on my payroll all summer?" he asked scathingly. The girl got back to work at once.

At other times, Bill could be so damn reasonable in getting his own way. When I left the club where I had been working, I promised Dutch that I would come back and work on weekends. Bill had agreed, but, oh dear, you never saw such reasonable excuses! On Friday, when it was time to drive to the airport, the car wouldn't start. "Damn carburetor," Bill exclaimed. It would be a cow that picked that particular time to abort a calf, or the hogs would get out and raise hell in a neighbor's cornfield, or . . .

It was all perfectly valid, you understand, but damned annoying. After this happened several times, Dutch got teed off and I read the scene as it was. I auditioned for the nearby radio station and got the job; in fact, they wanted me badly, but I did a long, slow double-take. Did I really want to be cooped up in a windowless room changing records and making cute comments when I could be out in the open riding on the tractor with Bill? Well, not really.

As I explained before, riding the tractor was a somewhat tricky business. It called for precision. The passenger stood on a ten-inch-wide bar fastened low down on the back of the machine. There were no loops, like on the subway, to hang on. The passenger (me) had to grab the driver around the waist and hang on. One day, when one of the field hands was driving, I miscalculated the distance and I grabbed where I shouldn't have! I hurriedly yanked my arms away and started over. The man never said a word; I never said a word; he was a very nice man.

When I told Mom that I guessed I was out of show business for good, she was pleased. "I didn't want you to get married," she said, "but since you did, you better work at it." It was traditional that in Mom's family all of the women had been good wives and helpmates. In fact, there was a great-great-aunt (a missionary) who had married a Fiji Islander chief. I had been told that she served a delicious fricassee, but she would never divulge the recipe. Well, if I was going to be a model housewife, I might as well tackle the laundry. We had been sending it out to be done.

One night we had been invited out for dinner, so why not rinse out one of Bill's dress shirts and iron it myself? I had a vague recollection of getting a toy ironing board for Christmas when I was five and ironing out my doll's dresses, so it must be easy, right? I squirted on the liquid starch with a generous hand, humming contentedly to myself. Bill would be so pleased. I got out the ironing board, plugged in the iron, and let it heat up. Now for the game plan: I pushed the iron away from me over the sleeve with a professional little wiggle. Beautiful! The wrinkles all came out! I pulled it back toward me and the wrinkles came back in! Out . . . . In . . . . With the smart money betting on the IN, I was starting to get teed off, when the phone rang. Saved by the bell!

My caller was one of the Grange ladies, and she told me how surprised they had been that I was such a good cook. I sat there with the receiver glued to my ear, lapping it all up. "What are you doing this morning?" she asked casually after we exhausted the topic of my skill at cooking.

"Ironing one of Bill's shirts," I said casually.

"Did you turn the iron off?" she asked.

"Oh, my God, no!" I shrieked and raced to the kitchen. The iron had burned through Bill's shirt, burned through the ironing board cover, burned through the ironing board, and was busily burning through the floor! Bang! The door opened and Bill strode in. "What in . . . ?" he yelled, as we collided in the smoke-filled room. He yanked the cord out of the socket, snatched the iron off of the floor, and poured water on the wood where it was smoldering.

"I wanted to surprise you," I said, whimpering.

"Well, you sure did!" Bill retorted. "Now, Honey, I know you want to help me all you can, but we can afford to have our laundry done, and Nellie is glad to get the extra money. Now, you go wash your face, and I'll hustle down to the men's apparel store and buy another shirt so we can still go out to dinner."

I stopped bawling. Clearly, Bill didn't love me in spite of my faults or because of my virtues. He just loved me.

After I learned to drive the tractor, yes, ME, on top of that huge thing (I looked like a pimple on a giant's nose), I began to pester Bill to let me get a license for the car.

"Look at all of the errands I could do for you," I pointed out.

"Eyeyuh?" Bill said, and went on reading the newspaper.

"Eyeyuh" in Upstate New York is the equivalent of "yes", and although I tried my damnedest, I could never pronounce it like a native. It's pronounced the way it's spelled: eye-yuh. Hell of a lot easier just to say "yup"!

Well, Bill hadn't said "no", so I took out a driver's permit. But, when it came to having a licensed driver go with me for the test, Bill put his foot down. "My blood pressure would get downright unreasonable if I had to teach you," he stated flatly. "Go up and talk to Old Man Andrews."

Old Man Andrews lived with his daughter, and his daughter was a teetotaler. Old Man Andrews was not. He was on Home Relief, and the community was a little uptight about Home Relief. "Nobody's going to buy beer with my tax dollars!" one of the church elders observed sanctimoniously. But, a Home Relief worker confided that in Old Man Andrew's case, she was careful not to inquire where his money was going. So, Old Man Andrew's home life was one long siege, and he was delighted to get out. At first, we went once a day, but Old Man Andrews plugged for twice a day, and I soon found out why. No matter where we planned to go, we always ended up in Henryville. Old Man Andrew's favorite bar was in Henryville. After a pause for liquid refreshment, he would slump comfortably in the seat beside me and utter no words of protest, not even when I yanked on the emergency brake for a hen that looked as if she might cross the road.

With all of this expert teaching, I soon felt ready to take the test. I failed. "Don't let it worry you," my women friends advised me. "That inspector flunks all of the women. He thinks women drivers are a menace."

Bill grumbled, and he was the chauffer on our family outings

As long as I could get out on the farm, I was contented, but, when the weather closed in, I was restless. Bill swore that I would move his chair one inch to the left and then one inch to the right and say imploringly, "Which way is better?"

"Neither," Bill would retort. "Leave it the way it is."

Among our furniture was a beautiful piano. Over a hundred years old, it was an heirloom, an antique. It was literally a harp laid flat on ornately carved legs and encased in ebony-finished rosewood. The tone had a singing quality, but it was flat. If there is ever a teeth-gnashing provocation, it's a chord that is flat. I love to play the piano, but this was gruesome.

"Bill," I said one night after dinner, "isn't there someone that can tune this piano?"

"Well," Bill said thoughtfully, "there's old Mr. Ambt." (I noted that he said "old Mr. Ambt" not old man Ambt.) "He's tuned pianos ever since I can remember. Guess he could do it, if he's still alive."

I hunted him up in the phone book. Yes, he would be pleased to come out, but someone could have to come and get him as he no longer drove.

"I'll got get him," I said to Bill. "You want to read the paper. After all, what do you have a little wife for?" Bill just grinned.

When I got to Mr. Ambt's house, I saw at once that here was a passenger to be handled with care. He wore a frock coat, gaiters, and a top hat, and he carried a small black bag. Man and boy he was close to ninety and he teetered, but he didn't totter. He looked like a gentleman accustomed to the best of everything. The effect was slightly marred when his daughter came running out with a scarf.

"Your throat, Father," she scolded, and tied two more scarves around his neck. With such a cargo, I decided at once that I would be the charming hostess. This meant (unfortunately) that I had to turn to him politely when he spoke, and it meant that I had only one eye for the road. Oops! The car ahead of me stopped without warning and I had to shoot around it, but there was another car coming toward us! I speeded up and we got by, barely.

"Well," I remarked cheerily, "we made it all right!" Then I glanced at Mr. Ambt. He sat as stiff as a ramrod clutching his bag with a manic grip. "Oh, Mr. Ambt," I said earnestly, "just relax. Really. There's nothing to worry about. Just hang loose. Relax!"

"Dear child," Mr. Ambt said solemnly, "I refuse to go through that windshield limp!"

"Oh," I said, and the conversation languished. Until we got to the traffic light. This is the only traffic light in the village, and it is at the intersection of Routes 31 and 98. We could keep straight ahead on Route 31 and turn south later, or we could go at right angles onto Route 98 and turn west later. In view of the general atmosphere, I decided to go straight ahead on Route 31, as the sharp turn to the right might be tricky. Absorbed in my calculations, I kept on going.

"RED LIGHT!" yelled Mr. Ambt.

In a panic, I slammed on the brakes, hit a sneaky piece of ice under the snow, skidded into a full turn-about, and headed up Route 98.

"Dear child," said Mr. Ambt, and I think he added I think he added under his breath, "Dear God."

I hadn't planned to go home that way, but what the heck, it was just as short. We reached home without further incident and Bill (the louse) helped Mr. Ambt out of the car. I was the one who needed helping out!

The piano was duly tuned. Mr. Ambt admired the mellow tone of the sounding board (there was nothing metallic in that piano). Polite compliments were exchanged, and Mr. Ambt partook of a small glass of port (the gentleman's drink). By that time, it was almost dusk, and I hate to drive at dusk; the sun is setting and the headlights don't show up. "Bill," I said, "do you want to drive Mr. Ambt home?"

"Oh," said Bill, who was getting a big kick out of the situation. "Time for me to do the milking. After all, what do I have a little wife for?"

But Mr. Ambt intervened. "Bill, Dear boy," he said. "Your wife is a charming woman and we had an interesting ride, but when I am called to those Pearly Gates in Heaven, I hope to enter with dignity and due decorum. I refuse to be skidded in. Bill, Dear boy, you will drive me home."

Bill got his coat.

"Aunt Alice Ann Carr Bolster"

CHAPTER 4

My Husband's Folks Arrive

During my first winter in Upstate New York, I got the flu. Ninety-nine percent of Upstate New York got the flu. Flat out. There weren't enough nurses to go around. The doctors (sneezing their heads off over the phone) prescribed rest, fluids, and aspirin. The local hospital set up army cots in the halls to take care of the overflow. Our village hospital had been waging a stiff competition with the hospital in nearby Medina, and, when the Medina Hospital was bucking for an addition (they reported that they had to put their newborn babies in bureau drawers), we made a snappy comeback with the flu and army cots in the hallways. We needed an addition, too.

Bill decided that I would be better off in my own bed than in an army cot in a hospital hallway with a desperately overworked staff, so he took care of me himself—temperature charts, intake charts, aspirin schedules, the whole schmeer. When I got a little better, he made homemade chicken soup from our best hens.

"Come on, Honey," he said one noon, when he brought up my lunch. "Slip on your robe and sit in this chair by the window. Time you got some sunshine."

He set up the card table in the bay window and put the tray on it.

"Soup? Again?" I moaned, when I saw the menu.

"Good for you," he assured me. "Now, you be a good, little girl, and eat it all up while I read the mail." He had scarcely opened the envelope when someone knocked on the kitchen door, and Bill went down to let him in. I was listlessly dabbing my spoon into the soup when I happened to glance at the last page of the letter lying spread out on the table. I read it. Twice.

"I can only pray," the writer stated, "that this marriage, which is so unsuitable for you both, will not end in disaster. For her sake as well as yours." It was signed "Aunt Allie".

Aunt Allie was Bill's dearest relative. She was his half-sister. Bill's father had married twice, and, since his second wife (Bill's mother) was thirty years younger than her husband, Aunt Allie and Bill's mother were almost the same age. They had babies at almost the same time, too. Bill swears he remembers that when he was six months old, a neighbor had leaned over his crib and said, "William, you're an uncle now!" Imagine! Six months old! But no amount of teasing would budge him from his story. He *remembered*. Since they lived close to each other, Bill spent most of his time playing with his nephew and lording it over him. Aunt Allie knew things about Bill that his parents never dreamed of. Now Aunt Allie was saying that our marriage was a disaster. The room lurched around me, and the bureau got very sharp and then blurred. I was a mass of uncertainty. I didn't know which way to turn. Well, there was only one thing I could do. Get out of here. Right now. Quick! While Bill was downstairs.

"If I could just find my stockings," I thought. I found them and put them on. "I can manage my dress and shoes, and I'll just go right back to New York City, where people like me."

I clutched at the walls and I made it to the head of the stairs, but there I was stuck. My head had been floating on and off all morning like a pendulum. On, off, on, off. But this time it floated clean off and no amount of coaxing would bring it back. I couldn't manage the stairs, even by hanging onto the banister. Just to stand at the top and look down at those twenty-two steps was like peering over the edge of a precipice. So, I sat down and slid to the bottom the way the kids do. It was raining and I had no hat or coat on. There was another problem; I seem to remember that I had no money with me. I wobbled to the car and put the key in the ignition. I had no idea where I was going. Anywhere would do, as long as it was away from here. The road weaved from side to side. A tree would come rushing towards me from one side and then a telephone pole would get in my way on the other side.

Bill had heard the car start up and he jumped into his caller's car and came after me. He told me afterwards that he was in a cold sweat for fear that I would see him coming and step on the gas. But, I was in my own world of fever and heartache. I saw a car driving along side of me. Gently, ever so gently, he shunted me onto the shoulder of the road and reached in and grabbed the brake.

"Honey," he said, "What happened? You can't drive the car; you're sick! Get in the car with me now Pat." As gently as he'd quiet down a horse, he got me into the other car, drove me home, and carried me back upstairs. "You're home now," he said, "where you belong. Where were you going?"

"The letter," I sobbed. "Aunt Allie said our marriage was a disaster. I had to get away from here."

"There, there," Bill soothed me. "You just snuggle up close. You're not going anywhere. Don't you understand, little girl? You belong here. This is your home."

When I was well again, he talked to me about it. "It's this way," he explained. "After my first wife died, just about every woman in the village picked out a second wife for me. They were all middle-aged good housekeepers who would invite them over for dinner and give them patterns for their knitting. But I did my own picking! Now, be fair, little girl. If a flying saucer landed in your backyard and a Martian stepped out, you'd be a little leery of him, even if he didn't have four eyes and a green nose, now wouldn't you?" I giggled. Trust Bill to be reasonable!

When I had everything under control again, I looked around for new worlds to conquer. The house? The house! The muted Victorian splendor had been getting me down. I longed for *color*—Splashy! Warm! Vivid! Down with the formal satin drapes. Up with the airy marquisette! The kitchen was oak paneling halfway up the walls and painted a drab tan above, which didn't show the dirt. I wanted my kitchen to be happy. The Hardware Store had to mix the burnt orange paint special. Whoever heard of burnt orange in a kitchen? I did the ceiling in lime yellow. Bill was pleased with the warm, welcoming color, but he was secretly afraid of what the neighbors would think. So, when a friend dropped in to talk business, Bill was a little on edge.

"My gol!" the friend observed. "Your kitchen looks really nice. Wonder if Minnie would like our kitchen this color? Guess I'll drop by the Hardware and pick up a can of this paint. What do you call it?"

At once, Bill became the Landed Proprietor. "Oh, you can't just walk in and get that color," he said loftily. Had to get Lem to mix it up for us special. Here, let me see if there's any left. Take this can along for a sample."

"You big ham!" I said, after the neighbor had gone. "You know darn well that I dreamed up that color and I painted it on the walls almost over your dead body!"

"Eye-yuh," Bill agreed. "But *he* doesn't know that!"

The next point at issue was the bedroom. "Just what," I demanded, "is so sacred about trotting up twenty-two steps and down twenty-two steps every time you want to change your shirt? We sure don't need a dining room, a parlor, a living room, and a library! One of these rooms would make a beautiful bedroom."

I had my eye on the parlor, where we could put the bed between the windows and have the birds chirping outside.

"And we've got a powder room downstairs, and that huge linen closet is big enough for a shower. And," I added magnanimously, "*you* can pick out the wallpaper!"

"My, my, my," Bill retorted. "And here I was thinking all along that my share would be just to foot the bill."

So at it I went. It was the busiest time of year on the farm, and I trotted back and forth on errands and fill-ins, and I hacked away at the wallpaper in between. Old wallpaper is misleading. The first yank tears away a quarter of the wall in nothing flat, and then the next yard and a half takes all day to come loose. "Oh, well," I thought, "as long as there's nobody but Bill and me to see it."

So we moved the bed downstairs and we were in business. Bill admitted he wasn't quite as tired as when he raced up and down those stairs a few times a day.

Bill and I were watching television during a rare long lunch break one afternoon when the phone rang.

"It's for you," I said to Bill. "Long distance."

He talked for a few minutes and then hung up the receiver. When he turned to me, he looked absolutely pale. Bill the unflappable!

"What's wrong?" I asked anxiously, braced for all sorts of unpleasant things. "Who was it?"

"Beautiful news!" Bill said in a hollow voice. "My nephew, Arthur, and his wife and son, along with Aunt Allie, are in Buffalo, and they're coming here for dinner! I urged them to stay all night, because it's a long drive back to their home in Binghamton."

"You didn't!" I wailed. But of course, he had. Mom had always said, "Baby, your own folks will understand, but when his folks come, they won't!"

The wallpaper was hanging in strips in our new bedroom; the laundry hadn't come back; there would be three bedrooms to air out and clean; two stairways to polish and a third one to sweep; the new curtains had come, but they weren't hung; the carpets needed vacuuming; and there were going to be four extra people for dinner!

"How soon will they be here?" I demanded (as if I didn't know how long it took to drive from Buffalo to Albion).

"Wal-l," Bill said somewhat sheepishly, "I sort of figgered you'd want a little time, so I told Arthur that the Thruway was sort of crowded and Aunt Allie would most likely want to see the countryside, so if they took the back roads, it should take them about two hours."

TWO HOURS! I couldn't cope. I just couldn't cope! I didn't *want* to cope!

All I wanted to do was to go down to the cellar, gulp rat poison, and quietly expire before they got here. I couldn't even do that because the house wasn't fit for a funeral!

"Now, now, pull yourself together," said Bill. "You can do it! All you need is a system."

"A system? Hell!" I retorted. "What I need is a miracle!"

"A miracle?" the little imp on my shoulder jabbed me. "Like a flat tire on the way here? Give you another half-hour." Now that was an idea. "St. Cecelia," I began . . . but the angel on my other shoulder flapped her wings and said, "Shame on you!"

"Aw, forget it, St. Cecelia," I muttered, and tossed in the towel.

I started to make out a list (for the System). "Bill," I said. "Three beds, and there isn't a clean sheet in the house."

"Buy some," he said.

I opened my purse. "No money," I reported.

"Charge them," he roared. "Gol-darn-it. Charge 'em! Crisis intervention!"

"Pillow slips and guest towels," I wrote down. "Quart of paint for the walls where the paper is off."

"Oh, my gol!" Bill moaned in his turn. "The lawns! Meant to mow them yesterday, but I couldn't spare a man. Honey, I'll go down and bring some of the men back with me."

We were using Jamaicans that year (offshore labor), and because our wages were so high, we had storekeepers and teachers. They were all family men, so when I explained that it was Bill's folks, they understood at once.

"Curtains to be hung," I said.

"Where's the ladder?" James asked. "Stairs swept and polished."

"Broom, dustpan, cloth, and wax?" Jerry asked.

"Four beds to be made as soon as I get those sheets," I went on.

"That's mine!" Johnson said. "I used to be in the army."

"Carpets to be cleaned."

"Best to take them right out and beat them!" John offered.

"By gol, you're right!" Bill chimed in. "Get a carpet beater from the woodshed.

"Shrubs to be trimmed and bouquets for all of the bedrooms, the dining room, and the front hall."

"That's for me!" Albert volunteered. "I used to be a gardener."

"Do you think he'll do a good job?" I whispered to Johnson.

"If he don't, he'll hear about it tonight." Johnson promised.

The bugle sounded, battle stations were manned, supplies were mobilized, and the Crisis Intervention Crew was on the march. At that point, the phone rang. Again? It was Arthur's wife, Edna. She was a second wife, too, and she knew what I was up against.

"I think it's outrageous," she said bluntly, "to dump four people on you without warning. So I'm going to stay in Buffalo and visit my folks."

"Bless you," I said, and hung up. One down, three to go.

There was a knock at the door. "Good Lord!" I thought, "More company!" It was Mary, my neighbor from across the road.

"Hey," she said, "What's all the commotion? Saw all the men milling around up here instead of down in the field. What happened?"

"Bill's folks," I said. "Three of them, dinner and they'll spend the night. And, oh Mary, everything is a mess!"

"Oh, my gosh," Mary said sympathetically. "What are you going to have to eat? Three extra people can sure put away a lot of food."

"Well, for starters, home-canned tomato juice from the cellar," I answered.

"Baked potatoes," Mary suggested. "They're so easy. Just rub butter in the skins and stick them in the oven. You'll serve white and yellow both, of course."

"Standing rib roast," Bill chimed in. "Be sure to tell the butcher it's for me." (Bill always got the seventh to the fourteenth ribs.)

"Fresh peas," I decided.

"With plenty of butter and cream," Bill warned.

"You drank all of the cream this morning at breakfast," I said crossly.

"City slicker!" Bill snorted. "Had a can of milk left over from the early milking. The cream will be up by the time they get here. I'll go down and have Willie pull the peas."

I started to bawl as soon as he left the kitchen. "Mary," I wailed. "Roast beef means gravy, and I can't make gravy! I've tried mixing the flour and water and then pouring on the grease, and I've tried the grease and cold water, and the grease and boiling water, and it always comes out lumpy!"

"Now, don't fly off into a tizzy," Mary said. "You just shut the door from the dining room to the kitchen, and I'll sneak over and make the gravy. Nobody will ever know."

"Mary," I said solemnly, "You've sure earned a trip to Heaven with no stopovers."

She grinned. "You won't have time to fuss with a salad," she went on. "I've been pulling vegetables all morning in the garden, and I've got a mess of stuff all washed and ready to cut up. Just let me have that big wooden bowl you bought at the auction last week. Let's see now, tomato juice, peas . . . how about some corn on the cob? Boil it in a little water . . ."

"Swimming in melted butter," I suggested.

"Gracious me!" Mary said. "They love to slather it on themselves. That reminds me; I churned last week, and I've got a pound of butter left over. Oh, and the relishes. Get out a half-a-dozen small dishes. Now, don't blow a fuse. There's dozens of jars in the cellar, all homemade. All you have to do is dish it out. Now for dessert . . ."

Well, at least I had that nailed down! Homemade ice cream from that little place on the corner, where they freeze it themselves."

"Honey," Mary said sternly, "Aunt Allie will expect a choice of at least three desserts."

"Oh, My God!" I moaned, and shut my eyes.

"Isn't it lucky I baked this morning?" Mary mused. "A custard pie, a lemon meringue pie, and a chocolate cake, sitting there all ready to be cut."

"But, your family!" I protested.

"Won't hurt them to eat bread and milk for once. Honey, we all know what it is to have a visit from our in-laws. That reminds me; I didn't bake bread this week, so you'll have to go to the Home Bakery Store and pick up some rolls. Stick them in the oven and serve them hot, and they'll never know the difference. Just sit tight and don't worry!"

I sped downtown and did the shopping. Rolls, pillow cases, sheets, and guest towels. On to the hardware store for a can of paint. Then, on to the butcher shop. "Rib roast, seventh to fourteenth ribs" I told the butcher. "Please give me a nice one. Bill's folks are coming for dinner."

"Oh, in that case," he remarked, shoving the roast he had been about to weigh up back into the showcase. "Wait a minute," he said as he walked into the cooler. He came back with a roast that looked delicious, even raw. "I've been saving this one for my own family," he said. "But Bill's done me a lot of favors."

On to the ice cream parlor. "Maple nut chocolate swirl?" I asked hopefully. "Bill's folks are coming."

"If you will permit me," Mrs. B. said diplomatically. "I think Bill's folks would enjoy good old-fashioned chocolate and vanilla."

Ye gad! Didn't I know *anything*? Back to the battlefield laden with my spoils.

"Sheets and pillow cases, and paint" I yelled up the stairway, and James came running.

The ice cream went into the freezer; the salad that Mary had brought over was in the refrigerator; I rubbed the roast with plenty of salt and pepper rubbed into it (Bill liked things well-seasoned); the peas were shucked; the corn . . . where was the corn? I ran down the lane and pulled it myself so it would be sure to be fresh.

"Help me set the table," I yelled up to Johnson. I spread Mom's Irish damask tablecloth (the kind you test by spitting on your finger and then touching the cloth; if it's real, it doesn't leave a spot) and laid out Mom's Rogers grape pattern settings, along with the candlesticks Mom gave me.

Five o'clock and all was well. The beds had square corners; the carpets had had the hell beaten out of them and glowed richly on the floors; the curtains were hung; the stairs were so polished, you could see your face in them; two walls in the bedroom had been stripped of paper and painted with fast-drying paint; the shrubs were trimmed; and the bouquets were beautiful (Albert really had been a gardener). The truck came to pick up the men and drive them back to camp, and Bill and I strolled to the edge of the driveway to welcome our guests. It was two hours since they had phoned. Ten after five, no guests. Twenty after five, no guests.

"Now, keep calm, keep calm," Bill said through chattering teeth. "They're sure to love you. But, if they don't come soon, they'll be god-awful hungry!" (I hadn't told him about our neighbor, Mary.) "But, don't you worry!"

"Oh, shut up!" I said snottily. "I like to worry!"

At five-thirty, their car pulled into the driveway. "Sorry," Arthur apologized, as they got out. "Know we're late, but it couldn't be helped. You know, it's a funny thing. Haven't had trouble with my tires in months, but the other side of Gasport, we had a blowout! Held us up about a half-hour."

"Oh, my Lord! A blowout!" I thought to myself. St. Cecilia giggled.

Arthur's son, Henry, got out next. He was an all-American boy, and we smiled at each other. Then they both helped Aunt Allie out. She wasn't at all what I expected. She was short, she was plump, she was beaming, and she bustled. She reminded me a little of the Irish grandmother I had loved, my father's mother.

"My, how fresh the house smells," she said as she stood in the hallway, while the men carried the bags upstairs. I blessed Jackson for opening all of the windows. "And how clean everything looks! Little girl, you must be a good housekeeper!"

"I try," I said modestly, crossing my fingers and toes.

As soon as they had washed up, we sat down to eat. The table did look scrumptious. I saw Bill raise his eyebrows at John's expertly polished silverware. I saw Aunt Allie surreptitiously wet her finger and test the tablecloth; I figured Aunt Allie would recognize good Irish linen. When we were seated, I said in my most gracious "hostess" tones: "Well, now that we're all here . . ."

But Bill chimed in with "Pat, Dear, perhaps you would like to say grace." The louse! The unmitigated louse! Just wail until I got him alone! All heads were bowed waiting for the leading lady to recite her lines. Frantically, I searched my childhood memories. "God is great," I began. And there I got stuck. What in hell was the second line? I saw Bill open one eye, and then it came back. Miraculously, it all came back.

"God is good. And we thank Him for this food. From His hand may we be fed. Give us this day our daily bread."

"Amen," Bill said loudly, and we drank our tomato juice. Then I "dished up". The roast was done to perfection (my new stove had a whole deck of pushbuttons and a timer!). Mary had kept her word and the gravy . . . ah, the gravy!

"Almost as good as your Mother's," Arthur said to Henry. Then he winked at me and confided. "Don't dare say it's better than *my* mother's!"

Bill puffed up like a pouter pigeon at all of this praise. The peas were perfect, firm but not tough, and the home-churned butter was exquisite.

"Where on Earth did you find home-churned butter?" Aunt Allie asked.

"Oh, I have my sources," Bill said airily.

"And, these rolls," Aunt Allie said, as she buttered her third roll from the Home Bakery. "Little girl, how did you ever find the time to bake them before we got here? They're delicious! Pat, dear, you must give me the recipe."

I shot one of those anguished wife-to-husband-looks to Bill, and he came to my rescue.

"Now, Aunt Allie," he said. "You'll be here such a short time, you don't want to talk about recipes! Pat will mail it to you," Dear Bill!

All of the little side dishes of applesauce, pickles, jam, and watermelon rind disappeared like magic. When I served the corn on the cob, Bill chomped on it for a moment, then said, "Pat? Where did you get this corn?"

"Why, down the lane," I said. "In the corn field. Where else would I get it?"

"Right side or left side?"

"On the right-hand side," I answered. "Why? What difference does it make?"

"Wal-l," Bill drawled, "the corn on the left-hand side is for us. The corn on the right-hand side is for the cows."

"Never you mind," Aunt Allie said to me. "If it's good enough for those pampered cows of Bill's, it sure is good enough for us."

And they all laughed, but it was an affectionate laugh. Nothing makes people so kindly as to share a bit of superior information and a laugh.

By this time everybody was so stuffed, I didn't see how they could possibly eat another bite. However, I offered dessert.

"There's custard pie, lemon meringue pie, and chocolate cake," I announced. "Bill, would you cut the pies? And I'll dish up the ice cream." I thought Bill would pop! The look he gave me was one I would always cherish.

Stuffed to the ears with food and friendliness, Bill and the men retired to the parlor to settle the State of the Nation. "Wouldn't you like to walk through the gardens?" I asked Aunt Allie. "The dishes can wait."

"Let's do them now," she said. "I'll help you." Bill had told me that if Aunt Allie offered to help with the dishes, I should be sure to let her. "Womenfolk get acquainted with each other over the kitchen sink," he explained. We worked for a while in a friendly silence and then suddenly Aunt Allie paused and turned to me.

"Little girl," she said, "the house looks beautiful, and Bill looks happy and well fed. And I've never had a better dinner! I was a meddlesome old fool when I wrote that letter. Will you forgive me?"

Soapy dishcloth and all, we hugged each other.

I got up early the next morning, but Mary had been over even earlier. There was a pan of hot cornbread on the kitchen table. We had cornbread along with freshly squeezed orange juice, oatmeal, toast, sausage, bacon, and sour milk hotcakes with syrup from our own maple trees. Bill played chef and made the hotcakes. He was famous for them and makes them as a feature at the church suppers. He could toss them in the air like a real chef, and he hammed it up to the limit.

"You're the one who should be in show business!" I reminded him for the umpteenth time.

After breakfast, the in-laws left in a flurry of kisses, hugs, promises to write, and urges to visit them soon. Then we waved to them until they were out of sight.

"Honey, I was right proud of you." Bill said. "And Aunt Allie told me I couldn't have picked a better wife."

"See that you remember that, Mr. Carr!" I said sternly. "Wow! I'm pooped!"

I pulled off my shoes and flopped on the sofa.

"Poor child," Bill said, sympathetically. "Bossing is hard work."

Weeks later, when Bill had business in Binghamton, I went with him and it was fun. Every minute of it.

"I told you that you and Aunt Allie would enjoy each other, once you got to know each other," Bill said smugly.

"Well, for once, you're right," I admitted. "For once."

But, when I unpacked our bags at home, I sensed that something was missing. I checked and rechecked and, wow! I knew what it was! When we were dressing, Aunt Allie had called upstairs to leave the bed unmade.

"Bill," I said, giggling. "When I pushed the sheets down, I must have left my pajama bottoms in them! What will Aunt Allie think?"

"Just what she's supposed to think," Bill said. "That you are Mrs. Carr!"

Two days later, we got a parcel in the mail. Inside were my pajama bottoms. No note was with it; nothing but a sheet of paper with a child's drawing of a moon face and a grin stretched from ear to ear. Three cheers for Aunt Allie!

CHAPTER 5

That Dillingham Puts In New Plumbing

"You know, Baby," Mom had said when I was freshly home from our honeymoon, "you won't be properly married until you and Bill have your first serious quarrel."

"Mom!" I protested, "Bill and I will never have a serious quarrel."

"Oh no?" Mom questioned and grinned.

And, for the first six months, we didn't have one; but, one morning when the Judge and I were on our way to market with a load of pigs, I suddenly yelped "Hey! Let me out! I'm going to puke!"

Bill obediently pulled over to the edge of a field, and I climbed out. When I got back in somewhat shaken from my efforts, I said, "Jeepers! That's the third morning in a row that I've puked. What do you suppose is wrong? I've never puked before."

"Wal-l," Bill drawled smugly, "you've never been married before, either."

"What's that got to do with . . . ?" I began, and then it dawned on me. "Oh!" I gulped. "Bill! Honest? Do you think . . . ?"

"Might be," he said.

"How wonderful!" And we hugged each other. "Yikes!" I gasped a moment later. "Get your hands back on the wheel, young man, or we won't be here to have that baby."

Bill pulled back into the road, and the pigs in the back of us snorted and oinked in protest.

Both of us were desperately anxious to have a baby. Bill because, as he told me many times, his father had been sixty-six when he was born, and

66

Bill wanted to go the old man one better. I wanted a baby because I had never had time to play with dolls when I was growing up; I was too busy helping Pop in the store. So, I had my daydreams in which I would wake up and find a real live doll curled up beside me and smiling up into my face. Such prosaic items as diapers and morning sickness had not been brought to my attention. I had never been around babies much since I had left home. Show people always had scads of snapshots in their wallets, but the little ones were "with my wife's folks" or at boarding school, or "with my sister's kids". Also, I had never actually met any of the old-time vaudevillians who had been cradled in a trunk lid, carried on stage at the age of two weeks and lisped their first lines at the age of three—the little dears! I had never been exposed to "stage brats"; not even the most ambitious stage mama could book her young into night clubs.

"Shall I call Mom and tell her the news?" I asked, eager as all hell to get the show on the road.

"Oh, let's wait a while," Bill advised. "You know your mother, she'd take the next train up here. This is our secret for now."

After we had pulled in at the market, sold the pigs, and started for home with our pockets full of money, I began to tease Bill to stop at the first drug store we came to and buy a glossary of names for the baby. "It's terribly important to give a child the right name," I informed him. "Psychologists say that a child can be marked for life if his parents give him a kooky name." (I had often blackmailed Bill because I knew that his middle initial, M, stood for "Mortimer". A Mortimer on the varsity team? No way!)

"'Spose I could stop and get you one," Bill grumbled, "as long as you don't want a pickle with it!"

"Annabelle, Arletta, Aresthusa," I began reading.

"Ugh!" Bill grunted.

"Abigail. Oh, Bill, can't you just see Abigail with prim little braids? Hmm? How about Anna Alice? Anna for my mother and Alice for Aunt Allie Carr. Proper, pleasant, and no chance for a kooky nickname. Right?"

"Now wait a minute, Sis," Bill broke in. "Back up and start over." He grabbed the book from me. "How about James, Jonathan, Jethro . . . after all, Honey, we're picking out a name for my son!"

"Is that so?" I yelped. "Bill Carr you don't love me. You're my very own husband, and you don't love me. If you loved me, you'd want a little girl and she would look just like me!"

"Now, hang on a minute, Sis," Bill retorted. "That shoe fits both feet. If you loved me, you'd want a little boy that would look just like me!"

Stalemate. We rode in silence for a few minutes, and then Bill turned to me and said, "We're going to settle this once and for all."

"How?" I demanded.

"You," he said, giving me the hairy eyeball, "are going to produce twins!"

I swatted him. "Bill," I sighed, as I nestled close to him, "how can I wait for nine whole months?"

As soon as we were sure it was not a false alarm, I took a long hard look at our local health delivery service. It was lousy. A philanthropic citizen had willed his mansion to the community and it had been converted into a hospital (Arnold Gregory Memorial) as cheaply as possible. It had a stunning sun parlor, beautiful gardens, and it was a gorgeous place to spend a luxurious convalescence surrounded by visitors and bouquets, but the maternity wing consisted of two beds with a nurse's aide in complete charge at night. As for obstetricians, forget it! The stork just dropped a memo through the mail slot of the family doctor.

Bill's family doctor was Old Doc Johnson and Old Doc was a delightful soul with a philosophic bent and a gut-level perception. I was in his waiting room, which was the parlor of his home—no chrome-plated streamlined gadgets or plush-lined secretaries for Old Doc!

I heard a patient say, "I gotta get a note from you, Doc, or I won't get paid for my time while I was sick."

"'Tis a crass and materialistic world we live in," Old Doc observed gloomily. "My boy, you shall have your note."

I liked Old Doc, but when it came to delivering a baby . . . . I broached the subject with Bill as delicately as possible. "If anything went wrong, they have so much more to work with in the city!" But I was attacking Bill on two fronts at once: his loyalty to the village in which he had served on the town council for twenty-five years, and his respect for Old Doc and the local customs.

"Nonsense!" he snorted. "Nothing's going to go wrong! My father and I were born at home. Perfectly natural process. Cows have calves, sows have piglets, hens have . . . er . . . Well, anyway, I've heard of women in some Slavic countries who work in the fields, go home and have their babies, do the laundry, then come back to work the next day."

"Well, I'm not Slavic," I said, "I'm Irish!"

"And a thick-headed one, too" he said as he headed for the door. "Aw, nuts!" He exploded. "You don't fool me. You're just looking for an excuse to spend a week in the city!" And he slammed out. Two seconds later, he came back in. "I didn't mean it, Honey," he said. "You know I didn't mean it." He picked me up and rocked me, tears and all.

Of course, our little secret wasn't a secret for very long. Trust a country woman to spot another woman who is pregnant. How the party lines buzzed! A friend of mine told me afterward that when I came to the Quilting Bee and sat and rocked with my hands folded complacently over my tummy, it was a dead give-away. Then they were sure, so they taught me how to knit booties: pink for me and blue for Bill.

"Poor child," Bill muttered sympathetically. "Gonna wear a different color on each foot."

Then, for the first time since we had met each other, I began to be conscious of Bill's age. He was sixty now and, by the time the baby was fifteen, sixteen, or even seventeen . . . I did a little mental arithmetic.

"Bill!" I exclaimed in a panic. "For Heaven's sake, take care of yourself! What if you should up and die and leave me to take care of the baby all by myself?"

"Now, don't you go worrying about that," Bill drawled. "Reckon the Lord has got sense enough not to yank me away and leave that poor child up to you."

Well! Just how was I supposed to interpret that?

"You're always telling me how old your father was," I said. "How did you really feel about him?"

"Don't remember too much," Bill said, "except that the Old Gent (he always called him that) used to come stumping after me with his cane, but he couldn't catch up with me. No way. He used to say, 'Now, Bill, I won't be here much longer, so you've got to learn to look out for yourself.' So he gave me a piece of land when I was still in school and I had two men working for me by the time I was seventeen. But, it wasn't all work! My gol, no!"

"So, what did you do for fun?" I asked, playing the straight man.

"Well, the Old Gent gave me a blooded mare; beautiful animal, but skittish as all get out, and a neat lightweight buggy to go with her. One Fourth of July, I figgered on tucking a small case of dynamite in the back of the buggy and driving to the community picnic. Come the right time and I'd set it off. Shake up some of my old maid aunts a bit. But, some dang fool set off the firecrackers and that mare went pure crazy. Reared and skittered and that box of dynamite was in the back."

"What did you do?" I demanded.

"Wasn't much I could do," Bill answered. "Couldn't let go of the reins to steady the dynamite, and I couldn't jump out and let 'er go. That mare would have tore through the crowd like a hot knife through churned butter."

"What happened?" I asked.

"Nothing much," Bill admitted. "Uncle of mine knew I had the dynamite in the buggy, and he grabbed the mare's head and gentled her down. The Old Gent figgered something was going on and he came stumping up, but it was all over by the time he got there."

"So, that's what happens when you have an older father?" I sniffed. "Bill Carr! Are you going to raise your son that way?"

"Oh, my gol, no," Bill said. "I'll run him on a tight rein."

All this time we had avoided discussing an obstetrician. Bill and I were so uptight about it that I hated to have a showdown. Old Doc stopped in once in a while when he was in the neighborhood, but he never said anything. One afternoon, when he stopped in to pass the time of day, Bill waylaid him at the door.

"I'd appreciate it if you'd take a look in the barn," Bill said. "Got a sick cow."

When we were alone, I asked Bill curiously, "Why did you ask Old Doc to look at a cow? Shouldn't you have called the veterinary?"

"Well," Bill said, hesitantly, "not too many people know it, but when Old Doc first started out, he was a veterinary."

That tore it. My little girl wasn't going to be brought into this world by a reformed veterinary! I didn't care what Bill said!

I brooded over my wrongs all night while Bill snored. In the morning, I made up my mind. I would go back to Bev and Dutch and civilization. Right after breakfast, Bill drove into town to see his lawyer about a deed, leaving me to my own devices. Now was the time! A freak snowstorm blew up (typical Upstate weather), and I had to hunt up my galoshes. It was only a mile to the highway where I could flag down the Greyhound bus, but before I got to the crossroads, I was slogging in snow halfway to my knees.

My best friend's house was on the corner of the highway, and I decided I'd turn in there. She would probably talk to Bill for me. I walked up to her door and rang the bell. There was no answer. She wasn't home! By this time, I was cold, tired, and panicky. I simply couldn't walk another mile back home. As I stood forlornly beside the road, a neighbor drove up.

"Why, Mrs. Carr," he exclaimed. "What on Earth are you doing here on a day like this?"

"Well," I improvised rapidly (Mom had always cautioned me, "Never wash your dirty laundry in public."), "I got off the bus and I was to wait here for Bill, but something must have happened."

"We can't get down your road; the snowplow hasn't been through yet, but (and he glanced at my bedraggled clothes and my woebegone face) we can't leave you here. We'll take you to the village and the Sheriff can find Bill."

We rode to the village, and I was beginning to long for Bill to rescue me, when I looked up and saw Bill and his lawyer riding by in a car and laughing. The beast! I'd show him! There was a Greyhound bus about to leave and I got on. In the next city I could get a bus for New York City. At the terminal, I weakened and called Bill.

"Where have you been?" he demanded frantically. "I've called all over to find you. Where are you now?"

"In Rochester, at the bus terminal," I said.

"Now, see here," he said brusquely. "You've got no right to go traipsing around in this weather with my son! Young Lady, you get yourself back home right now. No, wait! Stay where you are, and I'll come after you. What's got into you?"

"You don't love me," I wailed. "You want me to have the baby in a field with a horse doctor!"

"Oh, dammit!" Bill exploded. "Are you crazy? You'll lose that baby for sure with all these shenanigans. Now you listen to me . . ."

I wavered. Maybe I was hamming it up, but still . . .

"Express for New York City," the announcer boomed over the loudspeaker. "Passengers boarding at Gate Two. Last call."

Fate had decided. I boarded the bus. I slept most of the way, and I felt a lot better when we drew into the station in New York City. I phoned Bev and Dutch and they came right down to get me.

"Jeez," Dutch said. "So, you finally came to your senses. Found out what these family types are like, huh? Now you leave everything to me. I've got a hell of a good lawyer. Get you a swell alimony. Beat you up, did he?"

"Shut up, Dutch," Bev broke in. "She's all tired out now. I'll put her to bed, and we'll talk about it tomorrow."

The next day over brunch, we plotted a strategy. "Get any bruises?" Dutch asked, hopefully.

"Well," I admitted, "it's just that . . ."

"Mental cruelty!" Dutch chimed in. "That's it! That's even better!"

"But she looks wonderful!" Bev pointed out.

"Yeah, yeah," Dutch agreed. "Put on a little weight, haven't you? Gotta make you look bad for the lawyer. Bev, slap some makeup on her. You know how to do it. Make her up for the part."

Between giggles, Bev went to work. Mascara (the cheap runny kind) an inch thick on my eyelashes. "Blink your eyes," Bev ordered. Presto! Two gorgeous black circles underneath. White powder under my cheekbones to make by face look gaunt. A shadow of black from my upper lip to the bridge of my nose to look like care-worn lines. No lipstick.

"Jeepers!" Dutch exclaimed admiringly when we were done. "Bev, you've done a damn fine job. She looks gawd-awful!"

So, when we went to see Dutch's lawyer, I was the very picture of a mentally-abused wife. I let Dutch do the talking.

That night, Bill called. He had known at once where I would head for. "I'm kinda lonely," he admitted. "When are you coming home?"

"Er, uh . . ."

"Keep 'im guessing!" Bev hissed in my ear.

"Oh, in a day or two," I said airily. "Maybe Thursday."

In the meantime, I was having a ball. The word spread, and all of my old customers came in to ask, "When are you coming back to dance?" and "You look more gorgeous than ever!" I lapped up all of the flattery like a cat with a saucer of cream. It was wonderful to be admired, to be flattered, to be petted. Thursday came, and I still lingered. That night Bill called again. He had had it!

"You said you'd come home today," he stormed. "And you're not here. I've written you a letter telling you how I feel. If you aren't home by tomorrow night, you can just forget it." He banged down the receiver.

Wow! He sure sounded mad! I had told Bev the whole story about the baby and all, and she said slowly, "Honey, maybe you better go back. This isn't the best time to make a break, and I think [and she turned my face up to hers] perhaps you really love Bill. Everyone has spats!"

Dutch, of course, was disgusted. "Dumb broad!" was his opinion. "Why my lawyer says . . ." But unexpectedly, he grinned. "If it's the real thing, Babe, enjoy. Enjoy!"

All the way home on the bus, I rehearsed my opening speech. "You must realize," I would begin, but when Bill and I saw each other, we rushed into each other's arms. There was no time for speeches. After that, it was business as usual. I kept watching for the letter that Bill had sent to me in New York City when he was mad. I bet it was a lulu! After a week had gone by, I tackled him about it.

"Look here, Buster! What happened to the letter you sent me?"

"What letter?" Bill asked, innocent as hell.

"You know what letter. Don't con me."

"Oh, that letter!" Bill said. "Well, I happened to meet the mailman on the road, and I kinda hinted you were expecting some mail and that I would hand deliver it, then I tore it up."

"William Carr!" I said scandalized. "Don't you know it's a federal offense to snitch my private correspondence?"

"No't ain't," Bill drawled. "Not when you've known the mailman all of your life, it ain't."

So, I went back to knitting pink booties for me and blue booties for Bill.

"Hmm, still plan to put a different color on each foot?" Bill teased.

I still spent most of my time wandering around the barns. I was in the huge middle barn one day after the men had finished unloading a truck of baled straw that Bill had bought. The men weren't working too hard; a lot of it is done by machinery. A rope was hung over a pulley attached to the roof twenty-five feet above; it worked like an elevator. So many seconds on the ground to give the men time to hitch the rope onto a bale, and then the pulley started and the rope hoisted the bale. At the edge of the haymow, about fifteen feet above, an iron bar swung out and metal teeth seized the bale and tossed it into the mow.

"Hey, Pat!" one of the men Bill just hired sang out, "Hang onto the rope for a second, will you? I've got to get something, but I'll be right back. Don't let go!"

"I won't," I promised, and I took a firm grip. Almost at once the pulley gave a click and the rope started to move. I stood on tiptoe and stretched, but the rope pulled me into the air. I looked down: ten feet to the ground, too far to jump. I looked up: the iron bar was swinging towards me with its jaws gaping. I screamed.

Bill came running. "You goddamn fools!" he roared. "She's pregnant! Let go, Pat! Slide down. Down!"

I slid down so fast that the rope burned my hands before Bill caught me. Then it happened. "The baby! The baby!" I gasped.

"Yes, Dear, yes, Dear," Bill kept saying over and over. 'We're on our way to the hospital."

I went to the local hospital after all, and the nurses were kind and considerate, and Old Doc was gentle and efficient, and Bill sat by my bedside all night. The whole wide world was kind and considerate, but the stork, alarmed by all the commotion, flapped its wings and flew away over the hospital, and it never came back to us again. Not ever. The baby was dead.

Bill wanted to store the baby things. "Plenty of room in the attic," he mumbled; but Old Doc advised against it.

"Best off to face it flat out," he advised.

So, we gave away the bassinet with the pink and blue flounces and the baby bed with the gay little ornaments, and the pink and blue booties (a color for each foot) that I had knitted with such care. We no longer spent our evenings hunched over the dining room table with papers and pencils planning how to make the library into a nursery.

"Those built-in shelves will be marvelous for her toys and her birthday gifts," I had exclaimed. "And the sunlight will pour through that bay window, and she can hear the birds chirping in the trees outside."

"And he can climb that tree when he gets old enough," Bill had chimed in. He was still hanging in there for a boy.

There was no longer any need to section off part of the woodshed for her tricycle or his football gear. Back to square one. Two people in a twenty-five room house.

Mom couldn't come up because my baby sister was graduating from college, but she phoned at once, when she got the news. "I know how you feel, Dear," she said. Mom's baby boy had died at birth. "But, you be a good girl. There's no use crying over spilled milk."

I waited until I was sure Bill had gone to sleep, then I cried into my pillow; but he always heard me. "Sweetheart, I blame myself for this," he said. "I should have taken better care of you. But, I didn't realize . . . . Perhaps it is all for the best. Perhaps . . ." And he gave a long, defeated sigh. "I really am too old to raise a child."

"Oh, no!" I protested, and it was my turn to comfort him.

Old Doc stopped in from time to time to see how things were going. "Miscarriages happen to a lot of women," he said gruffly.

"Yes, I know," I said, but deep inside I was thinking: Yes, but oh why, dear God, why me? Why hadn't I realized that the men were just joking when they told me to hold on to the rope? It was like telling a newcomer to the theater to look for the key to the curtain. Why hadn't I jumped at once? Why?

Later Old Doc said to Bill, "You've got to find her a new interest or her guilt will eat her up like an ulcer."

Then a friend of mine from the village called and said it was absolutely wicked for the two of us to rattle around in that house all alone when young people couldn't find a place to live and that she had a cousin going to be married next week.

"But, she's just a child," my friend said, "and we've talked to her and talked to her, but you know how it is when you're in love."

Yes, I knew . . .

"Do you suppose you could sort of 'share' that big house? I'll send her out."

"Well," I said doubtfully, "I'll ask Bill."

Bill agreed at once. Once more we got out the paper and pencils. What was the best way to do it?

"Only thing is, Honey," Bill warned me. "We can't spend much money. Looks like a bad year on the farm this year."

I learned early on that unlike Gaul with its three parts, all farming is divided into two parts: the Good Years, when we made a penny, and the Bad Years, when we lost our shirt. Feast or famine. That's us.

"Won't spend any money," I promised, and rapped on the table with a soup spoon. "This meeting will please come to order!" I announced. (Bill had appointed me the chairman of the board for the remodeling project.) "Now, the first item on the agenda is . . ."

"A kiss!" Bill asked, hopefully. The "eyes" have it!

"Order, order!" I insisted a few minutes later. "This board will proceed with due decorum. Let's get down to business. The front hall is a built-in divider. The east side will be theirs." We had to keep the west side because the driveway swung around to the kitchen and all of Bill's business callers came in that way.

"The east parlor will be their space. Paper the pantry, take off the door, and presto! A dining nook. For now, until we see how it works out, we can share the stove and the refrigerator. And, that's it!" I said, brushing my hands. "I hereby appoint William Carr an ad hoc committee of one to make the damn thing work! Meeting adjourned."

"Why do I always get stuck with the work?" Bill grumbled.

"Because you're so smart!" I said, and having thus buttered him up, I got to the gist of the matter. "Bill, please, can we put in another sink? Please? What if we both want to stack the dirty dishes at the same time?"

"Shouldn't stack dirty dishes," Bill said, virtuously. He was thinking of the time when we were first married and I said "Gobble that last piece of pie and come on. There's a marvelous movie downtown."

"Can't make it," Bill said. "Gotta do the dishes."

"To hell with the dishes!" I retorted. "Stack 'em in the sink."

Poor Bill sat through the whole movie with a bemused expression on his face. Obviously, stacking dirty dishes was not a local custom.

I did so want a new sink. Our old one was an antique, just like the stove. It was cast iron, a foot and a half deep, three and a half feet wide with a divider in the middle. The only thing it was really fitted for was to take a spit bath, and you couldn't even do that—the damn thing was set underneath a window!

"Well," Bill said, "if you've got your heart set on a new sink, I figger we better go see T.J."

"Who's T.J.?" I demanded.

"Theodopphilus Jeremiah Dillingham," Bill replied. "He's a very important person. T.J. is a plumber. The only plumber around."

"What's he like?" I asked, as we rode over to his house.

"You'll find out," Bill said, mysteriously.

"Does he do good work?" I persisted.

"Oh, my gol," Bill replied in shocked tones. "People don't hire T.J. to do their work, they hire him to listen to him talk!"

"Fine thing!" I said, indignantly; and I never said another word until we got to T.J.'s house. We parted in the driveway and a thing bounced across the lawn toward us. It had the coat of an Airedale, the body of a Great Dane, the coloring of a hound, and the tail of a German Shepherd.

"What on Earth is that?" I gasped, clinging to Bill's arm.

"Well, T. J. says it's a dog," Bill answered dubiously.

"It can't be," I retorted.

"Zombie!" yelled a voice from the porch. "Come here! Here! You know you're not allowed to chew on a cash customer!"

The thing trotted off, wagging its tail.

"Come in, come in, Brethren and Sistern," T.J. boomed from the doorway. "Ma," he yelled over his shoulder, "we got company! Oh, glory hallelujah!"

I rooted to the spot. Was this for real, or had I wandered into a Marx Brothers comedy act? "Move!" Bill said, nudging me, and I followed him into the kitchen.

Ma came bustling in. She was short, she was plump, she was round, she was firm, and she zinged with energy. She'd have to in that setup!

"T.J.," began Bill, "got a little business matter to discuss. Pat here wants a new sink. Don't need one; sink we've got's perfectly good; been in there for forty years; but she wants a new one. Do you think you could . . ."

"Take a look at the situation?" T.J. replied. "Ma," he yelled to his wife (she was standing right beside him) "got another yardstick? Zombie chewed this one all up." He hauled a splintered piece of wood out of his pocket. "Oh, praise His name! Let's go."

"Thought we'd leave the womenfolk here to get acquainted," Bill suggested. "Just you and I will go."

"Sure thing," T.J. approved. "Can't get no work done with women clutterin' things up. Glory hallelujah!" And off they went.

"Sit down, Dear," Ma said. "Cuppa tea?" she asked, hopefully, with the kettle in her hand (she was English).

"Er, uh, coffee?" I asked, just as hopefully. The world seems to be divided into coffee drinkers and tea drinkers and, like Kipling's east and west, never the twain shall meet. It's like cat lovers and dog lovers. Them as likes cats thinks that all dogs, including purebreds, are mutts. Them as likes dogs are allergic to cat hairs.

"Oh, sure, I've got coffee," Ma said cheerfully. "Keep a pot on the stove for T.J. He thinks I don't know he sneaks a little snort from the cupboard into his cup. Hah! Men . . . ," and she poured my cup. "I've been naggin' T.J. to bring me over to see you. New York City . . . Broadway . . . show business . . . you must have had such an exciting life."

"Well," I said thoughtfully, "I would think that living with T.J. wasn't exactly a rest cure! I'm curious. All that 'hallelujah' and 'Praise His name' stuff. Is he really all that religious?"

"Oh, my God, no," Ma snorted. "You see, Love, it's this way. T.J.'s father was a widower minister and he had six children. He married a widow with two children and she was a minister, too. And then they had two children (the Bible is strong on begetting) and T.J. said you had to put on a helluva good act to get anywhere in that family. When T.J. was growing up and his father wanted him to do something that T.J. didn't want to do, his father would say: 'But the Lord wants you to do it.' T.J. just figgered his father was ripping off the Lord for a backup and the Lord shoulda wised up and played it cool. No, dear, T.J. is not religious."

While we were talking, the men came back beaming complacently. "Rejoice, Sister Carr," T.J. said. "Reckon the Lord'll let me have that sink installed in no time. Anchor her right there by the door."

"Oh!" I protested. "By the countertop!"

"Well, figger the Lord won't object," T.J. said. "Cup of coffee?" he asked Bill, glancing toward the cupboard. Ma couldn't object to it if they had company. But, Bill knew T.J.'s cups of coffee.

"Guess we better shove off," he said. "Hard day tomorrow."

"Like, wow!" I said, when we were in the car. "He sure lives up to his advance billing!"

A few days later, the honeymoon couple showed up. She was a mousy little teenager who obviously adored her hunk of man. He was all American, all of seventeen years old, and very much the Lord of the Manor in front of his little wife. He inspected the rooms carefully and then said loftily: "Of course we'll be building a house of our own soon."

"Of course," I agreed solemnly.

"But, in the meantime," he said, as he glanced at this wife, "this will do."

Later, when Tina Louise and I strolled in the gardens, she confided in me.

"My husband just got his first job yesterday and we won't have enough money to take a trip and also move in here, but I thought that it was most important to have a home."

That sure put a load of responsibility on me. Imagine being a stand-in for a honeymoon! "Bill," I said, pleadingly, "those kids haven't got a thing except what they got for wedding presents. They are so in love, and . . ."

"Do whatever you want to, Honey," he said. So, we just left everything as it was on the east side of the house (all we took was our clothing), and I added stacks of bed linens and dishes, pots and pans, knives, forks and spoons, and even a bouquet of flowers on the table.

"It's beautiful!" Tina Louise exclaimed when she moved in.

Once more, I had the old familiar butterflies in my stomach of opening night. When, eventually, if ever, I stand before St. Peter, I should have perfectly gorgeous butterflies—I've had enough practice!

It worked out beautifully. (Thank you, St. Cecilia.) The young man, thank goodness, was a Republican, and he and Bill agreed on all points as to how the country should be run; and it didn't hurt any that he listened respectfully when Bill got going. Tina Louise, in spite of her air of fragility, turned out to be a whiz of a housekeeper. I had to spruce up my own place a little to keep top billing. She even showed me how to make gravy: hot grease and flour mixed, but the damn stuff still turned out lumpy for me. I became a sort of big sister and only once did I let her down, to my dismay. She had turned her radio up quite loudly so she could hear it while she was doing the dishes in the kitchen, and by some quirk of acoustics due to the high ceilings, it simply roared in my living room while I was trying to balance the books. Almost automatically I walked into her room and turned it down. I glanced up and she was standing in the door with tears in her eyes. She had thought this was her home, and I had made it obvious that she just lived here. I apologized and I damned myself for my thoughtlessness.

Since we now had two sinks to get plugged up, we saw T.J. frequently, and he always treated Tina Louise and me condescendingly. We were "Young Things."

"We'll fix him!" I said to Tina Louise. We plotted on a way to make him think differently of us. We rehearsed like it was opening night, and, the next time he came, we danced through the door with our arms around each other; did an "Off to Buffalo" shuffle which used to bring Vaudeville acts on and off the stage; dropped to one knee; and, thrusting our arms aloft, chanted: "Hail to the Chief!" Now, that should do it!

"My, my, my," T.J. said admiringly, looking us over from bended knee to up stretched arm. "Do tell. Word gets around right smart, don't it?"

Darn the man! He had upstaged us again!

After he left, we got a phone call from T.J.'s wife. "Sorry to bother you," she said, "but T.J. has lost his hat, and he's raising holy hell about it. That blasted hat! I wish he'd lose it permanently! He's had it since the War!"

"The Civil War?" I inquired sweetly.

Ma chortled. "Better not let T.J. hear you say that, or he'll plug up your sinks so tight they'd never come unstuck! He sure could use a new head piece. But, you know T.J., he never parts with a cent unless he has to. He's still got the nickel that they gave him for not squalling when he was baptized. That hat's so old, it takes two rolls of Scotch tape to hold it together! Well, got a few more numbers to call." She rang off.

Tina Louise and I had become such good friends that I felt I could scold her once in a while. "Stand up straight," I said one day. As a dancer, I was always conscious of how people stood.

"I can't," she said.

"Nonsense!" I retorted. "A young girl like you! You've been going around waddling like a duck. Suck in your gut!"

"I can't!" she said, desperately. "I've been trying to tell you for a month . . ."

"Oh," I said. "Oh! Tina Louise! How marvelous!"

"And, my husband and I have been wondering if you would . . . that is . . . we'd be so proud if you and Bill would be the godparents."

"We are the ones who would be proud!" I answered. Then I cried a little.

Not long after the affair of the missing hat (T.J. accused Ma of sabotage), we were invited to T.J.'s house for a coon dinner.

"Ugh!" I exclaimed to Bill when he told me. "I couldn't eat a coon! No way!"

"Now, Honey," Bill cautioned me, "it's like a command performance. Remember, T.J. is the plumber, the only plumber for miles around."

"It's all in how you fix it," Ma assured me when I confessed that I felt a little squeamish. "I soak it in salt water for forty-eight hours."

I had to admit that it tasted good, if I could just forget how the damn thing looked when it was alive! After dinner, T.J. fixed the coffee. I noticed that he ambled over to the cupboard with his back turned to us, but Ma just winked. And the coffee was delicious! Whether it was the coffee or the food, or both, we felt in a very friendly mood.

"T.J.," Bill started, "Pat here has been feeling a little down. Why don't you tell her about Old Doc's Poker Party?"

I braced myself for the worst. This wasn't just local humor, this was obviously local legend!

"You tell her, Ma," T.J. said, turning to his wife.

"Well," Ma went on comfortably, "T.J. and Old Doc and some hard-shell cronies played every Friday night. One night, Old Doc had all the luck. He raked in pot after pot. Then he suddenly jumped up and said, 'Got to check on a patient, sorry fellas.' And then he made for the door."

"So we all booed and yelled 'frame-up'," T.J. chimed in, "couldn't let him get away with that!"

"So, Old Doc agreed to one more game," Ma went on.

"No limit," T.J. added. "And the stakes was right high. Old Doc kept on raising the ante, and everybody dropped out, except . . ."

"Except my dimwit of a husband!" Ma informed me. "You know T.J.!"

"I had three aces!" T.J. said. "Pretty good, huh? But, Old Doc laid down . . . ."

"A full house," Ma said. "Oh, glory hallelujah!"

"So, Old Doc, he says to me," T.J. picked up the tale, "tell you what, old buddy. I'll make it up to you. You need anything in my line of work . . ."

"Probably thinking of a slight cold," Ma explained, "or (and she glanced sternly at T.J., who was glancing thirstily at the cupboard) a hangover."

"But, Old Doc, he says, snickering, 'T.J., if you every have a baby, I'll deliver it, free of charge, on the house.'"

Now, this was a double-barreled insult as T.J. was Bill's age, as Old Doc well knew, and T.J. said to himself, "I'll get you, you young whippersnapper! I'll fix your little red wagon!"

So, T.J. sulked and plotted revenge. Fate played right into his hands. His wife related the story to me.

Ma wanted a new refrigerator. T.J. sputtered until she started serving him warm beer, and then he tossed in the towel. They went to see Mr. Derrick, their neighbor who sold refrigerators.

"I picked out the one that cost the most!" Ma explained. "But T.J. told me not to get my knickers in a knot, that he would figger out a way to finagle."

In the meantime, Mrs. Derrick confided a delicate piece of news to Ma and asked her if she knew a good baby doctor.

"Old Doc's 'bout as good as anyone," Ma told her. Then Ma passed the news onto T.J.

"Oh, praise His name!" T.J. yelled excitedly. "I'll fix that son of a gun! Tell Mrs. Derrick to tell Old Doc that I sent her and that he'd go easy on the bill."

"So now," Ma said with a glance at me, "the scene shifts to Old Doc's office and Mrs. Derrick."

"Sit down," Old Doc said with his best professional air. "What seems to be the problem?"

"Well, it's not much of a problem, really," Mrs. Derrick said. "If I marked my calendar right, the baby should come in November."

"Ah, yes," Old Doc said, "And who referred you to me?"

"T.J. You know, T.J. Dillingham, the plumber? We live next door to him. He said you and him were pals, and . . ."

"We are," Old Doc admitted, warily. He was wading in shallow waters, but he could feel the undertow.

"T.J. said to be sure and tell you that he sent me and something about a promise and a full house," Mrs. Derrick continued.

"What?!" exploded Old Doc. "It's impossible!"

"That's just what my husband said," Mrs. Derrick remarked, in an aggrieved tone of voice. "Of course, I know I'm a little old, but . . ."

"Is your husband here?" Old Doc demanded. He had no desire to get tangled in the middle of a local scandal.

"Oh, my, no," Mrs. Derrick answered. "He didn't think it was necessary for him to come. This isn't the first time, you know."

By this time, Old Doc was grasping for the ropes. "What does T.J.'s wife think of all of this?" he asked.

"Oh, she's delighted! You see, she wanted a new refrigerator, and T.J. didn't want to give it to her, so they thought maybe you could help."

Old Doc choked. "Are you all right?" Mrs. Derrick asked, anxiously.

"Quite all right," Old Doc said. "But T.J. won't be when I get my hands on him! Now, Mrs. Derrick, there seems to be some sort of misunderstanding. At least, I hope there is! Would you mind giving me the whole story?"

"Of course," she said, cheerfully. "T.J.'s wife wanted a new refrigerator, and my husband sells refrigerators. T.J. didn't want to lay out all of that money, so he thought that by my seeing you, as you and he are such pals, that . . ."

"*Were* such pals," Old Doc corrected her.

". . . that if I said 'T.J. sent me', maybe your bill would be a little more reasonable and my husband would let T.J. have the refrigerator wholesale, and then everybody would be happy."

"I see," said Old Doc. After she left, he went to his cupboard and had a swig to calm himself.

"Old Doc came out to see T.J. the next day," Ma said. "Climbed up, down, and sideways all over him! Told him this is a small town and if the story every got out, he'd be sunk. T.J. threw out a 'praise His name' and told Old Doc that he hadn't had so much fun since his wedding night. Betcha that young son of a gun won't try to hornswaggle T.J. again!"

"Holy cow!" I exclaimed on my way home. "Bill Carr! Don't you ever let me catch you playing poker with that bunch of hoodlums!"

As time went on, Tina Louise grew bigger and bigger in her pregnancy. The result was that the hide-a-bed got rolled up less and less often. Her husband went to work before she was up in the morning, and, at night, it seemed like a lot of bother for just a few hours, unless they had company, to put the bed away. Of course, since it was out all of the time, it never got swept underneath. One day, I felt ambitious and said, "Come on, Tina Louise, let's get the damn thing up so we can sweep under it."

Lo and behold, we swept out a man's hat! None of us remembered seeing it before and we couldn't figure out how it got there. Disreputable old thing! So, we tossed it in the garbage. When we told Tina Louise's husband, he just shrugged his shoulders and said "gremlins". No wonder she adored him.

The next time we sent for T.J., his wife told me that he was in the hospital. "I hadn't heard," I said. "Is it serious?"

"Oh no," Ma said cheerfully. "Old Doc figgered he needed a little sawing. Be home in a few days. I feel sorry for the hospital!"

"Let's wait until he gets home," Bill advised. "If I know T.J., by that time he'll be thirsting for an audience.

Trust T.J.! He had gone to the hospital on his birthday. "Make a neat tombstone," he explained. "If I came in and went out on the same day. Of course Old Doc, he knew it was my birthday, so as I was being trundled down the hall all peaceful and contented like, I heard this god-awful noise. I reared up a little and opened one eye, and there was Old Doc and another sawbones tailgatin' on my buggy! They was both dressed in them white nightgowns they wear and they was singin' 'Happy Birthday to You'! It was kinda nice." T.J. went on, "Only both of 'em was a ways off pitch! Just to think," he mused, "if anything had happened to me, my last earthly recollection would have been two lousy tenors singing 'Happy Birthday' flat!"

"And, when he was able to sit up and take nourishment," Ma said, "I felt kinda sorry for him. Two days without a drink! So, I sneaked a little one-shot in my pocketbook. Not enough to hurt him, but the right Reverend Spellbinder came trailing in after me. As soon as he saw the reverend, T.J. slid the bottle under the sheets. The reverend trotted out all of his best bedside homilies, and T.J. kept getting thirstier and thirstier with every word. So, when the minister knelt by the bedside and said, 'Let us pray for this poor miserable sinner,' T.J. saw his chance. He got his teeth on the cork and yanked. Pop! The reverend twitched, but he stuck to his prayers, and T.J. raised the bottle to his lips. Glug! This time the reverend lost his dedication and glanced up just in time to see Ma wigwagging violently to T.J. to hide the bottle!

"Madam," the reverend gasped, "Are you ill?"

"No, no," she said, improvising rapidly. "It's just that your eloquence has moved me to the Spirit."

"I only hoped," T.J. put in, "that she'd have the sense enough not to get the gift of tongues!"

Being a holy roller by faith, the reverend bought this explanation. Once more, he knelt. "Dear Lord," he went on, "we can only hope that this poor miserable sinner will make good use of the extra time You have allotted him."

"And, he did, too!" Ma said. "T.J. knew the reverend was on the home stretch and he guzzled that drink as fast as he could.

"Amen," the reverend declared, and T.J. choked.

"Oh my God," the reverend said, horrified. "What's wrong?"

"Just the ether fumes," T.J. explained, in a weak voice, and the reverend trotted off, a sadly puzzled man.

Heartened by his success, T.J. had another little snort just before Old Doc made his rounds. Old Doc sniffed the air.

"T.J.," he said, sternly. "I give the orders around here. No alcohol!"

"Aw, Doc," T.J. said. "That there delicious smell is just the rubbing alcohol that the nurse used on me."

"Well," Old Doc snorted, "if she can make rubbing alcohol smell like that, then have her mix me one!"

About a week later, Tina Louise went to the hospital to have her baby, and her husband was the proudest father in town. He had figured out how to put one over on T.J., too; something that Tina Louise and I had never been able to do. He waited on the four corners until the streets were crowded with shoppers, and then he called out in ringing tones to T.J. across the street: "T.J.!" he yelled in clarion tones. "Get up to the hospital, quick!"

Heads turned, ears were cocked. An accident? A fire? A death? The street listened.

"Cashier in the maternity wing's got a bill for you. We just found out whose hat was under my wife's bed!"

For the first, last, and only time in T.J.'s whole life, he was speechless!

CHAPTER 6

"Ewe" and I

W hen Tina Louise came home from the hospital, we had, at long last, a baby in the house; and it was a baby girl.

"Pay up, mister," I said to Bill. "The pink booties win!"

Bill grinned and fished some money out of his pocket.

"Five'll get you ten," he said, pulling out a sawbuck, "that the next one'll be a baby brother."

Male chauvinism!

When the baby was baptized, Bill and I sponsored as the proud godparents, and, to my surprised delight, she was christened Tina Louise Patricia.

"Oh, my gosh!" I muttered to Bill. "Do you suppose she'll take after me?"

"Wal-l," he drawled, "reckon the poor little thing might do worse."

What, with learning to cook and how to dust (the Extension aide looked at my ceiling and said sweetly, "Five cobwebs?" At my horrified expression, she giggled and remarked, "Don't let it throw you. I counted three in my own bedroom!") and learning to cope with local humor, I hadn't had time to get involved with the farm. I wrote to Bev that I had landed the part of a pioneer woman, but I hadn't got my teeth into the damn thing. So, when Bill burst into the kitchen one noon yelling, "Pat, where are you? I need you! Quick!" I dropped the meat platter and ran.

"What is it?" I asked anxiously. "What's happened?"

"Sick lamb," he answered. "Almost dead. Have to work fast or we'll lose it. Fill the sink with hot water; put towels in the oven to heat; get the brandy bottle—it's in the medicine chest. Look!" He showed me a limp, dirty little body cradled in his arms. Its eyes were closed, its neck dangled at an awkward angle, and its ears lay flat to its head. It was a newborn lamb, the first I had ever seen, and a far cry from the snowy white symbols of innocence on Easter cards!

"Its mother wouldn't let it suck," he explained. "Just walked away and left it to die. Would have died, too, if I hadn't noticed it in a corner of the barn. It's pretty low, but it's still breathing. Maybe we can save it."

He dunked the lamb up to its neck in the steaming water in the sink and held it there until the warmth spread through its body. It stretched its neck and opened its eyes and gave a faint "baa." It was a miracle! It was alive. And, it was a baby. I was hooked.

Tina Louise heard the commotion and came rushing in. "What's going on? Oh, my God!" she said, when she saw how pitifully weak the lamb looked. Bill glanced at her and said reassuringly, "Human babies are a lot sturdier than lambs. Why don't you run along and let Pat and me take care of this?"

Tina Louise went back to the nursery and gazed thankfully at Tina Pat tucked snugly in her crib.

"The mother won't come near the lamb after we've handled it," Bill went on. "You'll have to bottle feed it. Run down to the drug store and get a baby bottle and a lamb's nipple. Be sure you ask for a lamb's nipple; lambs have long necks and deep mouths. Baby nipples are too short. Hurry!"

I broke all of the speed laws going through the village and prayed I wouldn't get picked up. When I got back, Bill rubbed the lamb dry with the warmed towels and he was ready for the moment of truth. Was the lamb strong enough to suck from the bottle? If it were too weak to suck, there was no hope. There was no such thing as intravenous feeding for a lamb. He dipped his finger into the brandy, forced the lamb's jaws open, and held the liquid on the lamb's tongue. For a second, the lamb lay still.

"Please," I begged St. Cecilia.

The lamb wrapped its tongue around Bill's finger and sucked. Bill smiled. "It's got a chance!" he said, "but we'll have to bottle-feed it."

"I'll do it!" I volunteered. "Please, let me do it!" I'd show Tina Louise that she wasn't the only one that could take care of a baby!

"Are you sure you want to?" Bill asked doubtfully. "Lambs have to be fed every four hours. It's not bad at ten p.m., but it's kinda rough to crawl out of bed at two a.m. when the house is cold."

"I'll turn the alarm clock up real loud," I promised. "And, you can stay in the nice, warm bed."

Bill grinned. He made the lamb a "crib" out of a bushel basket piled deep with straw. I planned to put a pink ruffle around the edge.

"I think I'll call her Belinda." I said. Bill gave me a funny look.

"Honey," he cautioned, "don't ever give an animal a name unless you plan to keep it as a friend."

I had never been around animals much. Mom wouldn't let me keep a puppy, but she did let me have a kitten with six toes on each foot. It soon wandered off; I think I gave it too much love. So, I was amazed to learn that all small farmers knew their livestock personally. Our junk man once told me that he had gone away for a weekend when he suddenly remembered that the food box in the horse stall was empty. "I turned right around and went back," he said. "I told that old mare that I was sorry. I apologized right to her face. Seems like when a man cares about something, he wants to take care of it."

When I repeated this to Bill, I looked him in the eye. "Of course," I said loftily, "you did bring me coffee that time when I was sick in bed."

"Had to," Bill grumbled. "You were driving me nuts."

I suppose when you feed and water and give fresh bedding to animals every day, you do get to know them. When I drove down to the orchard with Bill with a load of corn on the back of the truck, and a 125 young "feeder" pigs that had been rooting under the trees came rushing to the fence oinking like refugees when a Red Cross package of food arrives, I said to Bill, "My gosh; doesn't it make you feel important? Sort of like God or some such?"

"Wal-l," he admitted, "it is kind of a nice feeling."

Bill bought me a brand new alarm clock with an extra loud ring, and I crawled out of bed every morning at two a.m. Sometimes Tina Louise would hear me and come in, and we'd have coffee and compare the growth charts of our respective "children". I don't know which one of us was prouder. Belinda's formula was warm milk, never cold, laced first with a little brandy and later with syrup or some sugar for energy. Two a.m. is an ungodly hour to get up and shut off an alarm clock, but it was worth it. To cradle the little body in my arms, to see the little eyes look up at me so trustingly, to watch the wee mouth fumble with the nipple, to hear the soft slurping sound when it began to suck, and then to put the lamb gently back into its basket sleepily content, with its tummy full of the warm milk. Nice!

Belinda grew fast and became a "cosset"—a member of the family. She regarded me as her Mamma, and once when she was on the wrong side of an old-fashioned screen door that had netting all of the way down, she thought, "To hell with this crap," and butted her way through the screen and all to get to me. Oh well, as Mom always said, you can't raise a family without a little wear and tear.

We had quite a few orphan lambs that year. Mother ewes seem to only care for healthy lambs. If a lamb is too weak to butt the mother's milk bag and start the milk flowing, the mother just plain abandons it. It is something like the Spartan mothers who dipped their newborn babies into an icy spring so that only the hardiest survived. It is sort of a gruesome way to improve the species. Bill brought all of the weak lambs to me, and I faithfully kept to the feeding schedule. I wasn't always lucky, however. Sometimes I would find them so weak at the two a.m. feeding that they could only suck at my finger dipped in the brandy. By the six a.m. feeding, they would be dead. I would feel that I had been at fault, that there was something more I could have done or I had done something that I shouldn't have. I soon learned that there were booby traps in the feeding process. The size of the hole in the nipple had to be exactly right. If it was too small, the lamb would bleat in frustration, and the milk wouldn't come through fast enough. If it was too large, the milk would come out so fast that the lamb couldn't swallow it fast enough. If any milk got into the lamb's lungs, the lamb would get pneumonia and die. I was so heartbroken when I lost a lamb that Bill said sternly, "Now see here. If you don't stop crying over them, I won't bring another orphan into the house. I'll let them all die out in the barn."

So, of course, I cried even harder. Once he brought in two at the same time. "Fill the sink," he ordered, "and turn on the oven."

He dunked one lamb in the sink and popped the other one into the oven.

"Bill!" I shrieked, horrified. "What are you doing? You'll bake the poor little thing!"

"The oven is the best possible incubator," he replied.

Then I remembered hearing that my grandmother had been a premature baby so small that they had lined a cigar box with cotton, placed her in it, and put the whole works into the oven. She lived and went on to raise a family of six children of her own!

The mother ewes are absolutely adamant about twins, as if the twins could help it! They push one of the siblings to one side or else think "to hell with it" and saunter off, abandoning both of them, perhaps because there isn't enough milk for both of them.

"Nature is cruel," I said to Bill angrily.

"Sometimes," he said, and walked away from me. End of discussion.

When the lambing season was good and the ewes maternally inclined, the barns were a throwback to the time when the world was young. The babies wobbled at first, like human babies taking their first steps, but as they got stronger, they walked stiff-legged on their mother-of-pearl hooves like ballerinas on their toes. When the sheer joy of living overwhelmed them, they would jump up in the air, land on their front feet, and twist their hindquarters in a curving arc. They would certainly have taken a gold medal at the Olympics! I noticed that Bill found a lot of plausible excuses to spend time in the lambs' nursery. The lambs and the crocuses know more about spring than the calendar does!

Before the lambs are turned out to pasture, there are two alterations to their anatomy that must be taken care of: their tails must be docked, and the males must be neutered. Male "charisma" makes the meat strong in flavor.

"I could use a little help today," Bill said to me one morning after the lambs were no longer babies. "You don't have to do it, but Jim didn't show up today and I figgered on getting the lambs out to pasture."

"OK," I said resignedly. "You've twisted my arm. I'm a volunteer."

My job was to hold the lamb in my arms while Bill performed the "surgery". It was quite simple. The tails have one joint that is practically painless and, with one deft flick of the knife, the tail parts and the lamb, with only a small bleat of protest, jumps down and goes about its business. The neutering process involves slipping a tight rubber band around the base of the testicles. The rubber band cuts off the circulation and, in time, the testicles slough off. This, too, is relatively painless, although the lamb is justifiably indignant!

Every time one of the lambs gave a protesting bleat, I shut my eyes and winced. I shut my eyes most of the time, but held on.

"Good girl!" Bill remarked approvingly when we had finished and my knees were beginning to shake.

"Aha!" I said scathingly, "thought I couldn't do it, didn't you?"

"Wal-l," Bill drawled with a slight smile at the corners of his mouth. "I was just sort of, er, testing."

Lambs, unfortunately, grow up to become sheep. Why do cute little lambs have to grow up? Why does the darling two-year-old child turn into a three-year-old child who sasses you? Or a twelve-year-old who wants you to mind your own business? Or a teenager who instructs the Old Man about the facts of life?

Mature sheep are dirty and stupid. Ye gods, are they ever stupid! And stubborn! They are hell-bent on getting their own way!

"My goodness," Mom observed, "they sound somewhat like you!"

A full-grown sheep has nothing of the appealing, innocent look of a lamb. The eyes that gazed up at you so trustingly acquire the dull glaze of a dead fish. The lambs have a helpless look that made you want to pick them up and protect them, which disappears completely. Since sheep have very little means of protecting themselves, except for a few rams that have been allowed to keep their horns, they develop a horror of attack at the first sign of danger and huddle into as small a mass as possible. They reason (silly sheep) that a wolf or whatever will munch on the outer circle and slink away well fed before it can gnaw at those in the center. Consequently, every last sheep makes a try for the center, and they push and shove and haul so frantically that they actually smother each other!

I still clung to Bill's shirttail like a two-year-old, and I hung around the barns while he did the milking, although, Heaven forbid, I should shake hands with a cow! They are so big! Bill was short-handed again (there is always someone who doesn't show up), and he said casually, "Honey, why don't you go in and feed the sheep while I finish up the milking. Just toss a couple of bales of hay down from the mow and spread it in the feeding trough. You've watched us do it."

Me? Feed the sheep? I bit down hard on the bullet. "Yes, sir," I said, quaking, and went through the sliding door. The sheep barn was in back of the cow barn and, when I went through the door, the door slid closed in back of me, so I was alone. Alone in a sea of sheep. There were seventy-five of them, and they were milling around like the New Year's Eve crowd at Times Square. Every one of those seventy-five sheep was fighting mad! They were hungry. "Blaat," they cried. "Where is Bill?"

"Blaat," "Who is this funny-looking human?" "Blaat."

"Now, take it easy," I said to them and to myself. "Where there's a will, there's a way, as Mom always said."

Obviously, if I were going to throw hay to the sheep, I had to get the hay; and the hay was in the mow ten feet up in the air. I crossed to the wall and lugged the beat-up old ladder with two rungs missing over to the open edge of the mow. The hay was in bundles tied with wire, like a Gimbel's gift package without the bow on top. All I had to do was to lug a bale of hay to the edge of the mow and dump it over onto the floor below. I slipped my hand under the wire and tried to lift the thirty-pound bale. Ouch! I nearly cut my fingers off! "Think," I instructed myself, remember the sign over the desk in the President's office.

"Easy!" I tilted a bale up on one end, flopped it over, and I gained two feet. Repeat the process . . . Oops! One leg went out from under me, and I sat down hard. Inch by inch I straightened out the leg that I was sitting on, but I still had only one leg, and I needed both to navigate. I pawed around frantically in the loose straw and uncovered a gaping hole that had no right to be there. My other leg was dangling in midair! I hauled it out, looked it over, and tottered to the edge of the mow. If I pushed the bale over, would I go with it? I shut my eyes, heaved, and jumped back. Mission accomplished! I crawled down the ladder backwards and stepped onto the head of a sheep! The minute the sheep smelled the hay, they came running—all seventy-five of them—to grab at the bale. They were angrier than ever because they couldn't get to the hay as the wire was still tied around it.

"Aw, come on, fellas!" I pleaded. "Gimme a chance to untie it! Let me get my foot down!"

"Blaat," they answered. "BLAAT!"

I stood there marooned until finally I had a flashback to my New York City days. "Kindly step to the rear!" I bellowed. And they moved!

Bill had told me to put the hay in the feeding trough, so I lugged the damn stuff to the trough ten feet away, never mind my bleeding fingers. I staggered to the open end, seized the wire cutters, cut the wire, and the bale fell apart in clumps. I got a clump on the edge of the pitchfork, but what in hell was I gonna do with the hungry ewe clamped on to the end of it? Round one for the sheep. I grabbed another forkful and stepped into the trough with it. The men just tossed it in with the pitchfork. The trough had high sides to keep the sheep out and the hay in, and the sheep were supposed to poke their heads through twelve-inch spaced bars. They shouldn't complain, I've had less room for my elbows in a lot of fast food joints! But, they knew they had me buffaloed. They climbed up into the trough with me. I retreated. They pressed. I went the whole length of that trough backward until I bumped up against the planks at the end. Trapped! When one eager beaver reached out and licked a wisp of hay off my jeans, I threw in the towel and screamed. "Bill!"

He came running, and when he pushed open the door, saw me cornered and the sheep mad and the general air of a natural disaster, he doubled up laughing!

"Not funny!" I squawked. "I'm scared!"

He lifted me out and set me down in a corner of the barn.

"Honey," he said gently, "most of the time you're a big grown-up woman . . ."

"But right now," I admitted, "I'm just a little girl!"

Bill threw the hay down from the mow with no trouble whatsoever. He tossed the open bales into the trough and spread the hay out so that every sheep had an equal chance, and those damn sheep quieted down like ladies and chomped away peacefully.

The next day at noon Bill got a post card informing him of a lecture on artificial insemination for dairy cows. "Bill," I said excitedly, "please take me with you! Please? I want to learn all there is to learn about farming." (Small order!)

"Oh, my gol, no!" Bill retorted. "Women aren't supposed to go! Men can't talk straight out in front of women!"

"Ridiculous!" I snapped. Apparently, farmers could have sex as casually as the next guy, but it was not a local custom to talk about it in front of a lady.

The meeting was held in an orchard, but it had just rained, so the ground was a soggy mess. "Why didn't you tell me to wear my galoshes?" I wailed.

"Told you not to come," Bill said, and walked away. So, a perfect stranger took off his galoshes and offered them to me, while my very own husband pretended he had never seen me before. Strike one for the local custom. I spoke about it one day to the wife of the inseminator.

"Isn't it weird?" she observed. "Here I am, a married woman with four children, and I used to be head nurse in the delivery room. But, when the men call up and ask to speak with Jim and I say, 'He isn't in, can I help you?' they stammer and stutter and end up saying 'I'll call back when Jim is in.' Ye gods! I certainly know the difference between a penis and a vagina, but they back off as if I were a sixteen-year-old!"

But, the stories farmers tell at meetings! I went to a Farm Bureau banquet once where everyone was on his and her best behavior. The women all had new dresses and new hairdos, and the men had fresh haircuts and their shoes shined. All very prim and proper. The speaker of the evening was a senator or some such. When he began to lose the attention of his audience, he resorted to telling an amusing story. All orators lard their oratory with amusing stories.

"Talked to our first woman inseminator the other day," he said. (This was news!) "And we had quite a conversation. I asked her what they did if the bull was reluctant to give up his semen. 'Well,' she said, dimpling, 'I just reach over and yank a few hairs out of his head! That seems to get him going!'"

"Does it work?" someone in the audience asked.

"Well," the senator said with a broad grin, "ever notice how the front rows at a Burlesque show are filled with bald-headed men?"

Local humor.

A few weeks later, Bill came into the house and said, "Get your coat on, Honey. I've decided to get a registered ram to upgrade the flock. Bring in some new blood."

So, we went looking for a ram with a nice straight back and some evidence of natural ability. We found one that Bill liked and brought him home in the back of the pickup. Willie, our yearman, had turned all the eligible ewes into a pasture lot alongside the road, and we unloaded the ram into his new home.

"Come on," I said to Bill. "I've got things to do in the house."

"What's your hurry?" he asked. "Let's stick around a while."

The ram was raring to go. He knew his purpose in the scheme of things, and he was ready. As a matter of fact, he was randy! He raced up to the ewes primed for action. The ewes had all had lambs before, and they knew what it was all about. But, right in front of our eyes, they turned into convent-bred debutantes! They flitted their stumpy little tails in his face, and they ran. The ram ran after them. Around and around they raced at breakneck speed, and the ram raced, panting, after them. Those ewes were more coy than a reformed hooker! If the ram faltered, one of the ewes would cast a "come hither" look over her shoulder, and the ram would fall for it. We were parked alongside the road, and another car drew up and parked to watch the fun. Then another and another, until the state troopers stopped for a look. After all, they were being paid to supervise traffic, weren't they? Every man in those parked cars who had ever chased after a female playing hard to get wore a sheepish grin! Finally, the ram got mad. To hell with these flighty females! He stopped chasing, and sulked. At once, the ewes changed their tactics. They pranced up to him, they assured him he was the handsomest most ramly ram that they had ever seen, and they were all dying to get married. So, the ram started using his machismo.

"Wal-l," Bill drawled, "might as well go home. Show's over for the day."

The troopers waved the cars on and business went on as usual.

In spite of the fact that show business is cluttered with "meaningful" relationships, I was totally ignorant about sex in animals. I had never in my whole life seen two animals mate.

When the weather changed into the damp cold nights of autumn, Bill's asthma attacks got worse. He had to give himself hypodermic shots of adrenalin. It made my skin crawl to stand there and watch him plunge the needle into his arm. One night, when he had an especially bad attack, he said "Honey, I don't like to ask you, but do you think you could go out to the sheep barn and take a look around?" I sure didn't want to go as I wasn't feeling all that well myself; I had a headache and there was a lot of flu around. But, we had a rule in our family: either Bill got sick or I got sick, but never the two of us at once. Bill had beaten me to the punch, so I went.

I started down the lane with my flashlight. It wasn't too bad going down; the neighboring farmhouse still had their lights on, and I could hear the sound of an occasional television going full blast. But, when I turned the switch in the barn, I discovered, to my horror, that all of the lights had burned out except for a 60-watt bulb in the ceiling. The corners of the barn were thick with menacing shadows, and it was in those corners that rats lurked. I hate rats—their long slinky tails, their red eyes, their furtive air. Snakes I can endure, and I can see a spider without getting hysterical, but rats, ugh! As I stood there, I heard a terrified "Baa!" A rat had bitten one of the lambs! At the first hint of danger, the sheep stampeded. Around and around the feed trough they raced, and the rat tore after them. At the end of the trough, the first sheep and the last sheep met together and they formed a circle, like the covered wagon trains. The snake had swallowed its tail, and the hunter became the hunted. The rat was racing for its life. Its speed threw it high in the air, and, when it fell with a last blood-curdling squeal, it fell under the hooves of the sheep. The hooves trampled it into a squirming squishy heap. Still the panicky flock raced on: around and around, on and on. Senselessly, idiotically, I leaned against the wall of the barn and threw up until I gasped. Then I fled.

When I went back up the lane, all of the friendly lights had been turned off. All I had was the small arc of my flashlight. I stumbled over a stone and sprawled flat in a mud puddle, and my flashlight jolted out of my hand. I crawled on my hands and knees until I found the lane, and somehow I got back to the house.

"Why, Honey!" Bill said as I came in. "What's the matter? What happened? Are you cold?"

"No," I said, trying to keep from crying. "I'm not cold. My head hurts and I'm hot!"

Bill whisked me into bed and got the aspirin bottle, muttering to himself.

The next day, I had pneumonia.

CHAPTER 7

Buttercup

Tina Louise helped take care of me as much as she could when I had pneumonia, but she had Tina Pat, who was growing into a sturdy youngster, and her husband had been hired in a good position, so now they were poring over blueprints and choosing colors for the home they would build. Bill did the cooking and washed the dishes. He felt guilty that he had sent me to the barns, but to him, going to the barns at night, switching on the lights, and even kicking a stray rat, was such an everyday experience that he had no idea it would be such a terrifying experience for a "city" girl. I was a long time getting back my "oomph", but eventually it was spring. Who could stay moanin' low in the spring? Spring, that heavenly interlude between the blizzards of winter and the scorched earth of summer! I have always felt about winter the same way the small boy felt about pounding his thumb: It felt so good when it stopped! Hundreds of fragile white flowers were springing up everywhere, and the birds and the bees were stirring from their sleep.

"Want to run down the lane with me?" Bill called, as he drove up in the pickup truck. "Riverdale Dutch came up to the barn this morning. She's had her calf alright, but she's hidden it somewhere in the back lot! Gotta find it before it runs wild."

Riverdale Dutch is one of our registered Holsteins, known affectionately in the bosom of the family as "Rosie", but don't ask me why. Some day, when we strike it rich, Bill and I are going to have a Scientific Cow Maternity Ward, complete with whitewashed walls and all of the trimmings. But, since we're poor at the moment, Bill turned the bred cows out into a separate pasture down the lane and let them fend for themselves. They do a pretty good job of it, too. When a cow is "with calf" (farmers use the Biblical term), her udder dries up and she gives no milk. All of her energy goes into baby-building. "One thing at a time" is Nature's motto, so the farmer feeds a "dry" cow as cheaply as possible; hence the pasture lot.

I was glad Bill had called me. I am always glad to have an excuse to go down the lane. Trees grow along that lane as well as wild elderberries and bushes with strange blossoms. Down at the very end, a brook gurgles lazily. It was a super day; the sun was just warm enough and there was a slight breeze stirring. Every muscle in my body wanted to s-t-r-e-t-c-h and relax contentedly.

"Bill!" I exclaimed, tugging at his arm. "Look at that big tree over there by itself, with soft grass growing around it. Couldn't we stop and . . . er . . . . um . . . ," and I nibbled on his ear.

"Not during business hours!" he said sternly. "Now cut that out! We came to find a calf, remember? It might be quite a job!"

Newborn calves can wobble to their feet a few hours after they are born and they bump their mother's udder to start the milk flowing. After the mother cow has nursed her offspring, she starts thinking about all the "goodies" at the barn, and she warns her calf to keep out of sight while she ambles off for some "real food".

"The calf minds her, too," Bill said. "You can almost trip over a calf when it's lying down and never know it's there. Here's where she gave birth to the calf," he went on, showing me a circle of matted grass that the cow had trampled in order to have a smooth place to lay down. "Lord knows where it is now. If it jumped the creek and got in the woods, we will have a time of it!"

We tramped along the bank of the creek, but there were no hoof prints. "We'll go back to the truck, and I'll hoist you up onto the roof of the cab. Maybe you can spot her from up there." So, that was why he brought me along!

"Yep!" I yelled excitedly after he gave me a boost up there. "There it is!"

The calf was "playing dead," and the tall grass nearly hid it completely. Bill shot off after it leaving me to scramble down as best I could. "Hey! Wait for me!" I hollered. "I'm the one who found it!"

The calf was a beauty, three or four days old, and as big as a deer. He acted like one, too! When we got near him, he reared right up in the air and was off before Bill could latch onto him. There were fences in his way, but he sailed right over the first one and took the next one in his stride. Then he hit the lane, hesitated for a second, then tried to get back into the field, but put his brakes on a little too late, skidded into the fence, and rammed his head between the rails. His rear end waggled free in the breeze, but the harder he shoved, the tighter he jammed his shoulders in the fence. Bill was on him in a second and threw him flat on the ground. "Get the rope!" he yelled to me. "It's in the truck."

"Must have lost it!" I yelled back, "there's nothing here!"

"Have to go to the barn for another one," Bill decided. "Can't handle him bare-handed. Here! Grab ahold of him and hang on until I get back. Don't let him get away." He yelled as he drove off.

I flung my arms around the calf's neck. He reared up and threw me off. I grabbed his legs, and he started to kick. I latched onto his tail, but he flicked it away and swatted me. When he fell over on his side for a moment, I sat on him. I braced my feet against the fence rail, grabbed the upper rail with my hands, and hung on. He was pinned, but so was I! When he heaved, I heaved. When he thumped, I hit the earth. Talk about bull-doggin' a steer! One minute I gazed at the sky, the next I ate dust from the lane! Where was Bill? The calf began to get mad and let out a bellow. There were ten dry cows peacefully grazing at the other end of the field, but at the first bellow from the calf, they came tearing up to his rescue. Tons and tons of cow-flesh on the hoof, and all galloping hell-bent straight for me! They sniffed at the calf's head and when they decided he wasn't hurt, they started feeling sorry for me thwacking up and down. One sympathetic soul reached through the fence to my side and licked my face! "BILL!" I shrieked. I heard the truck stop and Bill get out. He stood still for a moment while he took in the scene.

"My, my," he said admiringly, as he gazed at the cows, the calf, and me. "You folks been getting acquainted with each other?" he asked. Then he laughed!

"T'ain't funny!" I yelped, as the calf gave a final heave. "Shut up and get me out of here!"

He tied the rope around the calf's neck and disentangled us. Then he hauled the calf onto the back of the pickup. "My, my," he said again as he got into the cab. Considering my recent martyrdom, I felt this was a totally inadequate comment.

"Bill," I said, as soon as I could use my breath for anything besides just breathing, "Bet you were surprised I could hang on to him, weren't you? Bet you didn't expect to find us both together, did you?"

"Oh, yes," Bill said judiciously, "I expected to find you both together, all right. The only question in my mind was how far I would have to go to find you!"

In view of my heroism, I felt that I had earned the right to name the calf. "Let's see now," I pondered. "Mmm . . . 'Buttercup' has a nice ring to it. I think I'll name him Buttercup."

"Buttercup!" Bill said, scandalized. "Honey, he's a boy calf."

"Oh, in that case," I said loftily, "I'll name him 'William, Jr.'"

Bill knew when he was licked.

Buttercup didn't mind. In spite of his name, he put on weight and broadened out. In a few months, Bill decided to take him to the stockyards with some "cull" (nonproductive) cows. "Not Buttercup!" I wailed.

"Now, now, Honey," Bill said. "We need the money and veal is bringing a good price right now." At the word "veal", I sniffled louder than ever.

"You don't have to go along," Bill offered. But of course, I wanted to. The new truck was in for repairs, so Bill loaded up the old truck.

The old truck was quite a character. It was five years older than dirt and it was a local legend. Nobody could drive that truck but Bill. Absolutely nobody. It was so temperamental that Bill called it a "her", and so stubborn that I called it a "him". When cornered, Bill pronounced it was "Sh-im-aphroditic" thereby achieving one of the most complicated double puns on record. He was really proud of that one! But we both knew she was a Jezebel! One door was off completely and the other wouldn't open. The cushions were ruined, and the driver had to sit on the gas tank, which was under the steering wheel. The truck was so noisy that a horn would have been gilding the lily. It had no brakes, no horn, and the starter was shot. In order to stop, you went through the following ritual:

First, cut the gas to "idle" and shift the floor stick to "neutral".

Second, cut the ignition.

Third, turn the key back on in seconds so as to catch the spark (no starter, remember?) No one wanted to have to get out and use the crank!

And, for goodness sake, don't park on a hill!

The driver had to use both feet on the clutch in order to shift. Talk about split-second timing! And Bill was going to drive this thing into the stockyards sixty miles away with a load of cattle! Not even St. Cecelia could field this one!

"You're crazy!" I told him. "Wait for the new truck to be fixed!"

"Got a check out," Bill said briefly. "And the bank won't wait."

I was all aquiver about going to the stockyards. Buyers come from all over the county for their needs and brokers handle everything. There were holding pens for cows, calves, young bulls, hogs, sows, shoats, and anything that squealed, grunted, mooed, or walked on four legs. Since the price depends on supply and demand, the going rate varies from day to day, and a difference of even a few cents a pound makes a big difference in the farmers' profit. Bill had a feel for the market that was almost uncanny, and other men envied him. I asked one of the stockyard brokers if he could forecast the price. "Pat," he said, "I dabble at farming, raise a few hogs. Last week the price of hogs was high on Monday, low on Tuesday, and way up on Wednesday. Know when I brought my own hogs in? Tuesday!" We both laughed.

Bill had a hunch that the market would be high on this particular day, and besides, there was that check at the bank, so old truck or new truck, we were going. Willie and Bill loaded the cows and tied some rope across the back (the tailgate was gone, naturally). Then they crowded Buttercup in the front, right against the cab window.

"You can keep an eye on him in case he tries to get out," Bill told me.

"Bill," I warned him, "you know how that calf can jump."

"Oh, he'll be alright as soon as the truck starts moving," he said, carelessly.

Of course, I had balked at the idea of selling Buttercup. I had earned him, hadn't I? But Bill was firm. "Can't raise him for breeding," he said. "It's bad to have the herd in-bred. Plus, a mature bull is a walking time bomb."

I felt a little like a Judas, but obviously papa knew best.

In order to keep an eye on Buttercup, I had to twist my body halfway around and my neck the other halfway around, and it was darned uncomfortable. I'd have curvature of the spine and/or a dislocated neck long before we got to the stockyards. Oh well, into each life some rain must fall.

For a while, Bill and I chit-chatted about this and that, and every four or five minutes or so, Bill would ask, "Is Buttercup OK?" and I would say, "OK!" But, when we were about halfway there, somehow we got switched onto the subject of new drapes for the living room. This was a red hot issue and proved to be a tactical error.

"Don't need 'em!" Bill insisted.

"Do, too!" I retorted.

In the heat of battle, I forgot that I was the official lookout. During a lull, I glanced back. "Buttercup's gone!" I yelled.

"Can't be!" Bill said (wishful thinking). "He's probably stuck behind one of the cows. Look again."

"Nope," I reported. "He's gone. What do we do now?"

"Keep going. The stockyards close at noon, and if we get there too late, we'll be charged for a stall and feed over night, and we won't get the check for a week. I've got to make a deposit today!"

Getting a deposit today was a way of life.

"We'll stop on the way back and look around. Stop worrying."

But, I worried about Buttercup all the way to the yard. He had jumped out on the edge of the Tonawanda Swamp, a desolate area that was just what its name suggested: a swamp; dank, muddy, overgrown with small trees that rotted and fell to the soggy ground.

"What will he eat?" I asked Bill.

"You're going off cross lots a little in your thinking, aren't you?" Bill pointed out dryly. "If Buttercup had gone to the market, he wouldn't be eating at all for very long!"

We kept to the back roads and the deserted bypasses going in, and I was smart enough not to comment on that fact. Otherwise, Bill would have driven right down the main street in Buffalo just to show me how foolish it was to be a jottery female. We got to the yards before noon, and our broker gave Bill a nice fat check. Somehow Bill always hits the top price. "Gotta keep the bank happy," he explained.

We started on the trip back, and, after a while, I noticed a car was trailing us. "Bill, do you think . . . ?" I asked nervously.

"Might be an unmarked patrol car," he agreed. "Figures he can trap the old truck and earn himself a ticket."

There was only one traffic light between us and home, and, on the trip in, it had been green (thank St. Cecelia). But, with the car behind us, as we got near the light, I started biting my fingernails. The light was on green and Bill speeded up, hoping to make it. The car behind us closed in, almost tailgating. "Red!" I shrieked. Bill changed gears, coasted, and turned the ignition on again in three seconds. Wham! The car that had been tailing us crashed into us! At once, a cop in uniform appeared. Where had he been hiding?

"Saw the whole thing," he announced sternly. "Saw that car crash into your truck. Anybody hurt?"

"Not to speak of," Bill said, magnanimously. "Guess it shook my wife up a bit." (This was definitely the understatement of the year!)

"Are you hurt, Dear?" Bill inquired solicitously.

"N-n-n-no," I managed to stammer through chattering teeth.

"If you had had your car under as good control as this gentleman had his truck, this wouldn't have happened!" The cop said to the driver of the unmarked car. "Ought to give you a ticket, I ought! Watch yourself!"

We drove straight ahead, the unmarked car made a right-hand turn, and the officer strode off. Whew!

When we came to the swamp again, Bill and I got out and looked for signs of Buttercup. No luck. We drove to the General Store and Post Office, left the old truck idling, and went in to inquire.

"Saw a calf looked like that," said one of the men leaning against the counter. "Down the road apiece in front of that house that Jim lets. You know, the one with ten kids and ten window lights busted out."

"Well," said the store owner, "if you saw that calf in front of that house, ain't no use looking any further. Next time you see it, it'll be on their table with them kids digging into it. Them folks is mean!"

I worried about Buttercup, and Bill fussed about the money he had lost. We went on home. When we arrived, it was chore time, when the animals are fed and the cows are milked. We told our yearman, Willie, about losing Buttercup.

"Ah'll git 'im!" Willie volunteered.

"Our Willie" wasn't the same as the "seasonal help", where field workers were employed only for the growing season, about six months out of the year. Willie was employed full-time on the farm and was considered part of the family. The farmers in our area have a strong, almost clannish, extension-of-the-family relationship with their yearmen. In return, they got loyalty, possessiveness, and an occasional rebuke. Once, Willie knocked off early because he was sick. In my impatience to finish the field, I put another man on the cultivator. Not having Willie's expert eye, the other man "cultivated" out a row of plants, right by the road, where everyone could see!

"Young Lady," Willie said sternly when he came back, "does I git sick, y'all lets thet field be. Ah got meah mouthin' frum mah friends, like 'Hey, Big Boy gittin' so old yuh cain't see?' Sheesh!"

I stood rebuked.

And, once, when I went to see a friend of mine, and Miss Laura's Arrie D. was dusting, I said, "Arrie D. I love those chairs. Where did Miss Laura get them?"

Arrie D. said "Us bought them at the auction."

I had a special respect for Willie. He was intelligent, hard-working, and competent, even though he couldn't read or write. He could scrawl his name in capital letters, and that was all. He had been born in an isolated shack in Florida and his mother had had thirteen "chilluns". In between birthing and washing and taking in laundry and trying to keep food on the table, there was no time for raising the children. One by one, the older children had been pressured into helping out. It was not that Willie had been denied an education, the school was there; it was that no one had the time or the concern to make sure that a little black boy went to school. When he was in a good mood, Willie sometimes told me about how things were when he was growing up down South.

"Down there," he said, "iff'n yuh is walkin' on the sidewalk an thuh Cap'n sez 'Good mawnin', boy', yuh tetches yuah cap and sez 'Good mawnin', Cap'n', an yuh gits right off'n tha sidewalk." Willie chuckled as he told me this. He wasn't aggrieved or indignant, just proud that the Cap'n had noticed him at all. To Willie, Bill was "Mistuh Bill", but I was plain "Pat" or "Young Lady", depending on the mood he was in. So, when Willie said he would bring in Buttercup, I would have bet my last dollar that he would.

After the work was done, when we thought Buttercup might start thinking about the good grain he used to get and wishing he were back home, instead of going in for our dinner, Willie, Bill, and I got in the truck and went back to the spot where Buttercup had jumped out. Willie adored Buttercup and pampered him. Not too far away was a small plot of ground that someone had cleared for a garden, and Bill spotted hoof marks in the soft ground. We thought that we saw the calf peering at us from behind a tree, but although Bill and I called and cajoled, Buttercup refused to come out.

Then Willie called: "Sugah! Heah, Sugah!" And Buttercup came sauntering out, stuck his head in the pail Willie held, and started to eat. The men slipped a rope around his neck and hoisted him in the back of the pickup, and Buttercup rode home in style, with Willie as his personal bodyguard. I had learned to communicate with the livestock, but Willie communed with them.

When we had Buttercup safely in a stall, I said to Bill a little timidly, "Don't you think it would be cruel to send him to the stockyards after he tried so hard to escape?"

"Wal-l," Bill said slowly, "maybe you're right. Darned little cuss sort of earned his life."

So, the calf was turned out to pasture, but Bill warned me sternly, "Never let me catch you going into that field alone."

Farmers have a healthy respect for bulls, even young ones. They know that a bull calf fed by hand, petted, and trained like a dog will, when it becomes mature, turn on its owner without warning; a half-ton engine of destruction aimed at the nearest human being. Even the calves are handled with caution. Our veterinary tells about the time he was called to castrate a bull calf. The farmer had hold of the calf by a rope run through a ring that had been inserted through the bull's nose. When Doc started about his business, the farmer got so interested, he forgot about holding the calf and let the rope slacken. The calf bolted and made straight for Doc. That calf knew who was wrecking his machismo! Doc made for the wall, but there wasn't a toe-hold in sight. All there was was a slippery chute leaning almost straight up against the wall. "Here goes!" Doc yelled. He took one look at that young bull at his heels and walked up that slippery chute like it was a ladder with rungs. Then the bull came snorting and pawing right after him. The farmer loped after both of them with a pitch fork in his hands. He rescued Doc, of course, but I had this delightful picture of Doc and the bull suspended in mid-air chasing each other through all eternity. So, I wasn't really tempted to dilly-dally through the fields with Buttercup. I knew my limitations!

Doc took care of our dairy cows, too, and I learned that many of the veterinarian practices are startling and barbaric to a city person. Usually the cows have their babies with no problems, but Daisy Mae had been lying down and groaning for quite a while when Bill finally came in the house and called Doc.

"I'm afraid she's in trouble," he said.

Doc came at once and knew immediately that the calf was dead. Daisy Mae would die, too, unless Doc reached inside of her, inserted a hacksaw, sawed through the dead calf and, attaching a rope, pulled the carcass out in sections. Daisy Mae lived!

Along with learning how to drive Jezebel, I learned how to drive the tractor in order to haul stones off the field. I climbed up on the seat and looked over the field and the brook. Bill was about to deliver lesson number one. "This," he said, standing alongside the tractor, "is the clutch." I drew in a deep breath. "You push it down when you let the clutch out, and you let it up when you put the clutch in." I exhaled. "Got that, Honey?"

"Uh huh, I see," I said, with an air of intelligence. I am a good actress! I wondered where the clutch went when it was in or out, and what it did when it got there, but I felt that that piece of information could wait. Surely that came in lesson number two.

"This," said Bill, pointing out a handle, "is the gear. You push the clutch out like this," and he pushed it with his hand, "and then . . ."

"But, you pushed it in," I said.

"I did not," said Bill, "I pushed it out."

"But you pushed it down in," I said. "I saw you."

"Well, sure," said Bill. "You push it down in to throw it out."

I could see this was going to be harder than I thought! "It doesn't make sense to me," I said. "However . . ."

"At the same time that you push your foot down, you pull the gear handle down towards you for low gear, through neutral ahead for second, high is through neutral ahead on the other side. Got that so far? Alright, then, down toward you to the right is reverse. Now, go ahead. Don't be nervous. Nothing to it. All my kids could drive tractor when they were four years old."

"Those darn Whiz Kids, again!" I muttered, and pushed out the clutch; or was it in? I yanked at the gear handle, and it slid through neutral down into reverse. Well, perhaps "slid" isn't the right word.

"Damn it!" roared Bill, who jumped for his life. "Damn lunkhead!" he yelled, rubbing his shin. "What's the matter with you? Don't you know your left from your right? You could've broken my leg, backing up like that! Coulda broke it easy! What makes you so dumb?"

Well, add attempted manslaughter to the list of things I have done to Bill! "You're the one who's dumb!" I said, smote to the quick. "First, your directions are all backwards and opposite, and, furthermore, you've got the whole darn field to stand around in, and you parked right there in back of me!"

"I wouldn't have been right in back of you if you had gone ahead when you were supposed to have," Bill replied logically. Damn him! "When we want to go ahead, in this neck of the woods, we go ahead, not backward. It's a local custom. I've always done it that way, and my father before me. Maybe it's different where you come from. What's the matter with you, anyway? Want to collect on my insurance? Ain't you ever drove nuthin'?"

"Sure ain't, Bud," I said. "I was brung up on taxi-cabs. I'm used to going both ways."

"Well, happy hunting!" said Bill. "Don't forget lunch." And off he went about his business, rubbing his shin. "And try and call a taxi to do your tractoring some time!"

I was supposed to pick up small, medium, and immovably large stones; load them on the "stone boat" (two flat, reinforced planks of wood joined together); and haul them off to the gully. From my vantage point on the tractor, I could see stones all over the joint. I wouldn't have any problem getting a "boat full". I loaded up, drove down the steep slope to the gully, and unloaded. Coming back, I got almost to the top of the slope when the engine sputtered and began to conk out. All of a dither, I started to shift from high to low gear. I got as far as neutral, and, while I hesitated with the clutch out trying to remember which was low, the tractor started to roll backward. Well, I knew what that was: "Reverse," I thought frantically, as I gathered speed. "When you go backwards, you go in reverse." I never thought of the brakes—not me! I kept on rolling. There was nothing—absolutely nothing—between me and shattering destruction in the gully below except one lone tree. This looked like the end of the road for old Pat! I looked backwards and steered toward the tree, thrusting my right arm out rigidly behind. I would halt the tractor! I jammed my arm against the tree trunk. "Saved!" I breathed, afraid to move an inch.

After I hung there a moment, I realized something wasn't quite right. I began to figure that if I was holding two tons of tractor immobile against a tree with nothing but my good right arm, either my muscles were improving or else there was no hill at all and it was everything else that was crooked. I looked down. The crossbar was braced against the tree. "Whiz Kids! Four years old," I muttered, gritting my teeth. "How I loathe them!"

I started up again and rode in low gear. There was some stone on the slope that I had left until last. I was stymied and I knew it. I didn't know how to lock the brakes. The stone was so big, I couldn't lift it onto the stone boat, but had to hook the chain around it to drag it. "Oh well, I could probably manage it," I thought.

The chain was short and fastened to the tractor. I pushed the brakes down with my hand, sprawled across the tractor, and tried to reach the stone and hook it with my other hand. I was about an inch too short. This was maddening! Every time I reached the stone, my hand slipped off the brake and the tractor rolled. I didn't dare shut off the motor; Bill hadn't showed me how to start it. I was sort of trapped. I wriggled and turned and said "Damn, damn, damn; a trouper never gives up!"

I heard a snicker from behind me. I turned and there was Bill, seated comfortably on a rock, watching me struggle. "How long have you been a sports spectator?" I demanded.

"Oh, a right smart spell," he admitted. "Say, lookit, Pat, why don't you charge admission? I'd be willing to sell lemonade!"

By a stroke of luck, I was able to redeem my slightly marred reputation a few days later. Bill and I and a salesman were going over to Jamestown to look at a used truck. On the way, we had a flat tire. Bill and the salesman struggled to get it off; one of the lug nuts had stuck. The men tried and tried to unscrew it until they were disgusted. Cool and composed, I looked the situation over. Casually I inquired, "What's the matter boys? Left-handed screw?"

The men looked at each other and then at me respectfully, and took off their hats. I could tell Bill was proud of his little lady. For days he told and retold that story. Duke cornered him one day.

"Bill, was it a left-handed screw?"

"Well, no," admitted my husband, "but it might have been!"

After this display on my part of Whiz Kid material, I was promoted to drive old Jezebel.

I was constantly learning that farming is not the placid existence I had always thought it was. When I was shopping in one of the stores in the village, I saw a girl four or five years old, beautifully dressed, but with a long ruffle sewed to the end of her sleeve. "Such a pretty child," I said to a friend, "but why does she have those long ruffles for cuffs?"

"Oh," said my friend, "when she was younger, she reached through the bars of a pigpen with an ear of corn in her hand, and the sow bit off her hand at the wrist."

Farm machinery is dangerous and treacherous. I was introduced to a middle-aged farmer, a "mucker", who raised onions. He didn't offer to shake hands as he had two steel claws instead of hands. He had been running a "topper", which is a series of knives that cut at lightning speed as the onions pass on a belt, and somehow, one of his hands slipped and got caught. Instinctively, he tried to free the caught hand with his other one, and both of them were mangled so badly that they had to be amputated.

There are many horror stories, so safety precautions are as important on a farm as anywhere else. But, farmers are always pressed for time, and familiarity breeds contempt. Bill teased me about being a worrywart, but sometimes you just have to worry.

I went down in our hay field one day when the men were baling, and I suddenly heard them shouting and running towards the tractor. Then they stood in a circle around someone or something on the ground. "It's Willie!" someone yelled. "Got caught in the power take-off!"

The power take-off is a large revolving piece of metal that has grooves cut in it like a giant cork screw. The grooves are at an angle, and Bill had warned the men never to attempt any repairs until the take-off was shut down. The take-off was attached to the back of the tractor and picked up the power of the engine and transferred it to whatever tool was attached to the tractor. There was a sleeve of smooth metal that fitted over the take-off like a shield, but it was a bother to adjust it, and it was tempting when the tool fouled to just lean over the take-off and attempt to free it. Apparently, Willie had tried to do this and now he was lying on the ground.

"Our Willie?" I shouted as I raced towards the circle of men, but the men yelled, "Don't come over here! Willie says not to let you come over here!"

I braced myself for a terrible accident. An arm wrenched off? A leg torn off? I grabbed one of the men as he ran by. "How badly is he hurt?" I asked.

"Aw," he said, laughing. "He ain't hurt a'tall! The power take-off ripped his pants right off'n him! He ain't hurt! Just hell-bent you ain't gonna see him with his pants off!"

Living on a farm has its moments.

As Buttercup got older and heavier, Bill began to mutter about getting rid of him, but I teased to let him stay. I loved to stand outside of his pasture fence at sundown and watch him silhouetted against the western sun.

"Don't want to let it go too long," Bill said. "Don't want anything to happen."

I couldn't believe that Buttercup would ever turn on anyone. Not Buttercup! But, one noon, when we were eating lunch, the phone rang.

"Help!" screamed a woman's voice. "Our bull has my husband pinned in the barn!" It was the neighbor down the road. Bill, Willie, and I jumped in the car.

"You stay inside with his wife," Bill told me (she was an invalid). "The bull has gone back into the pasture. We'll go in the barn and look around for Art."

They found him crumpled up in a corner, unconscious. "Call the ambulance," Bill yelled into me. "He's hurt bad!"

At the hospital, they told us that Art would live, but he would never walk again without using canes. His hip had been smashed like an eggshell.

"Never dreamed that bull would come after me," Art said, when he was convalescing. "Gentle as a lamb until he made for me, all of a sudden. Crowded me into a corner and like to have killed me! Would have killed me, if I hadn't grabbed a pitch fork and run it through his nose. That cooled him considerable. Why, I hand-raised that bull!"

The next day, Bill sold Buttercup.

"The Pillar Farm Barns (facing east) circa 1957"

"The Pillar Farm Barns (facing south) circa 1957"

CHAPTER 8

Cucumbers Are Green, Like Me

I was so busy running errands for everyone else that I hardly ever got down to the village anymore, but when I did, I always stopped in at the local diner called the "Lunch Room". This was one of the favorite places for just sitting and socializing. Whenever I walked in the door, the Lunch Room coffee pot rises and pours itself.

"Black, no cream. Thanks, Lucy." I said as I carried my cup over to the booth where Freddie Gage was sitting. "What's new?" I asked, taking a seat across from him. The Lunch Room was our central clearing agency for news.

Freddie leaned over, looked all around suspiciously, and lowered his voice to a whisper that carried to the front door. "Cukes!" he said. "Cukes are the hottest things in town. Been hot right straight up the line. Cukes."

I knitted my eyebrows. "Cukes?" I asked. "You mean those horrid little green things soaked in brine that pucker your mouth?"

"Shhh!" hissed Freddie, waving his hands. "You want everyone should hear? You're speaking of my bread and butter. I buy those things!"

"Well, buying them isn't so bad as eating them," I said. "That's where I draw the line. And stop breathing garlic in my face. This is a small town."

"I don't want you to eat them," said Freddie. "I just want you to grow them."

"What for?" I asked practically.

"Oh, Mamma Mia!" said Freddie, waving his hands around. "I'm trying to help you! I'm trying to give you a tip! They're hot! You'll make a lot of money. You wouldn't mind making a lot of money, would you? You don't have any objection to that, do you?"

Visions of cancelled notes danced through my head. "Well, twist my arm." I said, and went right home to tell Bill. "You've got to put in cucumbers!" I babbled. "We'll make scads of money! We'll be rich! They're hot! I can own two pair of silk stockings at one time! Freddie Gage says . . ."

"Whoa," said Bill, "back up. I don't like cucumbers. They stink!"

"Oh," said I, "I don't either. I mean to grow them, not to eat them!"

"Oh, they're a tasty dish, all right," said Bill, looking at me.

"Oh, Bill," I blushed, "do you really think so? Well, Freddie Gage says . . ."

"Are you married to that joker?" asked Bill, with a trace of scorn.

"Of course not," I said, scandalized. "You know perfectly well to whom I am married!"

"And who's going to pick those cukes? That's what else I'd like to know," he retorted.

"I'll find the pickers," I said.

"Where?"

"Oh, here and there," I said airily, gesturing with my hands.

"We'll see about that. I don't know though. I'm still not sold on the idea. Every damn time I put in cukes, I lose money."

"But not this time," I said. "Freddie Gage says . . . . I know, I know," I said hastily. "I know to whom I am married."

"You'd never guess it," said Bill. "I won't do it."

Well, eventually I talked him into it, and it meant more work for both of us. We bucked out five acres of old apple trees, and we planted cucumbers; a new variety that was square on both ends and had a good "paint job". They could have been used for a centerpiece in a pinch. They weren't a pickling cucumber, but a slicing cucumber. Sliced cukes don't make me pucker; in fact, they make me sick to my stomach. It was a very new variety; so new that I couldn't locate it by mail but had to use long distance telephone. Bill turned green when he saw the phone bill—I am nothing if not a "maker-turner-greener"!

When the vines started to grow, they were so thick and shiny that the Farm Bureau sent the Future Farmers of America (all nice, young boys) to our place to see how the vines look when they are growing. This was encouraging. The lecturer pointed out that that was how vines should look when they are growing and the boys, who were all farmers' sons, looked very closely in order to learn so that they could go home and tell the old man how vines should look when they are growing. Bill finished off the afternoon by telling them why those vines were growing and when they ought to be producing (they can't do both at once). I was so proud that I decided to go see Freddie.

I went down to the Lunch Room and had two cups of coffee, one right after the other; black, no cream. Freddie called me over.

"They're hot!" he hissed, after looking everywhere but under the salt and pepper shakers. "Keep 'em under wraps. I'll let you know when the time is ripe. Trust me."

I paid for my coffee and went home. "Freddie Gage says . . ." I started to tell Bill.

"I'd rather buy his column than take some of his advice," Bill said. "That way I could tear it up or wrap the garbage in it."

"Freddie says that when the time is ripe . . ."

"It's the cukes that get ripe," said Bill, "not the time."

"Freddie says, when the time is ripe, we can trust him to . . ."

Bill raised his had in protest. "Pardon me," he said, turning up his hearing aid. "Did you say 'trust'?"

"You'll be sorry," I said.

"We'll both be sorry if you keep listening to Freddie Gage!"

Our neighbor Betty had put in cucumbers that year, too, only hers were for pickling. "Cukes" are cucumbers and pickles, but "pickles" are not cukes. Now that makes sense, doesn't it? Betty and I pored over the farm journals together.

"I dust mine with lime," she told me.

I called Bill immediately. "Bill," I said, "Betty puts lime on her cucumbers. Couldn't we put some on ours? Please, Bill?"

I could hear him sigh over the phone. "You tell Betty that lime stunts the vines, and, how did I farm all of these years without the two of you?"

Betty made a pot of good strong coffee. "I know just how you feel, Dear," she said. "I'm married, too. Men are all the same."

Pretty soon the vines started to blossom. Blossoms are apt to be frustrated unless they have bees to carry their "love letters".

"Please, can we get some bees?" I pleaded with Bill. "The bee man says you can have them for free if you'll give him the honey that they produce."

"Honey," Bill frowned. "It's been a long time since I've heard that word; ever since Freddie Gage has been buying you coffee . . ."

I shook my locks indignantly. "I buy my own coffee," I said. "Don't you think the bee man is bee-ing nice? I told him to bring four swarms."

"Remind me to farm without you next time," Bill retorted.

Betty called me up the next day. "Oh, Pat," she said, "it's terrible! I went down to say 'goodnight' to my cukes last night, and they were beautiful; but I went out this morning and the field was almost completely gone! I can't imagine what happened. The vines were yellow and drying up. They'll be completely gone by tomorrow. When the leaves are gone, the cukes turn yellow. I did everything the *Farm Journal* said to do!" she sobbed. "Maybe I didn't put enough lime on them."

"I'll be right over!" I said, pausing only to don a black dress.

"See," she said. I looked across her field. The dead vines were already crumbling back into the earth.

"Did you call the Farm Bureau?" I asked.

She nodded. "It's verticillium wilt. That was their professional diagnosis. There's no cure for it."

"Do you want me to ask Freddie Gage?" I asked.

"For Heaven's sake!" snapped Betty. "Do you know that little squirt?"

"Just a couple of cups of coffee worth," I said.

"If he pays for it, that's all you'd get anyway," she said. "I don't know why I ever listened to him. Don't tell me you listened to him, too!"

I went to look at our field, and I drew a deep breath. Smug with my own safety but mindful of my manners, I called another neighbor, Jean. "Go right out and look at our cucumbers. There's a verticillium wilt that's sweeping the country. It's liable to kill off all of our cucumber crops. It killed Betty's right down to the ground. She used lime, too!"

I could hear Jean gasp. Then she went to the window to look and came back. "Safe," she reported, "but I better call May. They've got fifteen acres planted."

"You'd better," I said. "I'll call Joe."

When the cuke crop was ready to be worked, I went to see Miss Anne, the crew leader, who immediately began her calculating.

"Le's see now," she said, counting on her fingers. "They's Miss Grace an' John's wife an' Pork Chops an' 'Not Guilty Blackie' an' Buster an' the lil chiluns. Reckon us can do it." She had raised fifteen children; I felt I could trust her with my cucumbers.

A solid camaraderie existed between Miss Anne and I. We were good friends. She knew her business and I didn't, so there was no nonsense. I just turned the field over to her and paid her when it was done. After all, she was an expert. I ran the errands: a loaf of bread, 10¢ worth of luncheon meat, five packs of cigarettes, a can of salmon, a big bottle of "Orange Squeeze", and a Coca-Cola at four o'clock.

Bill came out and saw the happy family group. He raised his eyebrows.

"An afternoon break is very refreshing," I said. "All the labor experts advise it. I didn't invite you," I added, "because I knew you had work to do."

Bill bridled at that crack. "Thank you," he said.

"How did you ever run this farm before you had me?" I asked.

"That's not the question," Bill answered. "I think you've got it ass-backwards, as usual."

Jerry Kovack, who is the fieldman for a cucumber buyer, came out to look at the field. Jerry is little and he has come up the hard way. He often tells me things right out that other people would love to tell me, but are too polite to do so. Jerry walked around and through the vines. He was impressed with the cucumbers. He brought his boss out to look at them.

"Nice piece of property you've go there," said his boss, Francis. "Mind you, I wouldn't say you could retire on it, but it's a nice piece of property. Make sure you take care of it, now."

Well, that was just the tonic I needed. I was so proud! We cultivated and we hoed nine and ten hours a day. I tried to hoe, but I gave up. I chopped all of the plants off! We sprayed to kill the insects. The 500-gallon spray tank filled with poisonous chemicals rumbled across the land. We looked for rain showers and we looked for drought. We told the bees to get busy. The cucumbers grew. We picked the first scattering harvest. The price was right and the quality was A-1. I was so proud! For once, I'd gambled and won over Bill's objections; or so I thought.

Then came Labor Day and the High Holidays; the market collapsed. You couldn't give cucumbers away! "Freddie says . . ." I began, and ended lamely, "what do you think about the cucumbers?"

"Why, thank you, Baby," said Bill, kissing me. "It's nice to be back in the family again!"

"You've never been out of the family." I responded.

"Wal-l," said Bill, "I think we ought to put them in storage until after the holidays. The price'll zoom up then."

It was a wonderful idea. "Oh, Bill!" I begged. "Let's do them real fancy! I mean, why not make 'em look nice? I just love fancy, high class things, don't you?"

"How much will it cost?" asked Bill, and then added, "I love you."

I could tell he was proud of me despite the recent developments.

Betty and I went shopping for packaging material. We found a beautiful purplish shade of shredded tissue paper that made the cukes look a little gangrenous, but "The Trade" recommended it, and who were we to dispute them? We bought brand new bushel baskets. We made nests of shredded purple paper. We packed the cukes in tenderly and faced them in neat, orderly rows. They looked like soldiers in there, orderly as they were. We pulled the shredded tissue paper up around the top. We bought fancy liner with a scalloped border to fit around the inside of the cover and, the crowning touch, a heavy rubber stamp that stamped "WILLAM CARR, EXTRA FANCY SPECIAL" for all of the world to see. Then we stepped back to admire our handiwork.

Bill took them down to the cold storage and engaged rooms for them. I began to get a few qualms. "If you make a better mousetrap . . ."

In that case, why wasn't there a path beaten to the door of that cold storage? Or was it asking too much? Bill hired the locker for first one week, then ten days.

"Hadn't you better go and look at them?" I asked.

"You women!" cried Willie, who was doing the milking. "Always fussin' over somethin', aren't they, Bill?"

"Sure are!" said Bill. "Wouldn't mind if Pat was fussing over me that way! She thinks I don't know what I'm doing."

Finally, I got so worried that I blew my top. "I want to see those cukes!" I said. By this time, they must've become tired of hearing from me, so Willie and Bill went down and pried the lids off of ten baskets out of the one thousand that we had stored, and brought three cucumbers home.

"See?" Bill said. The cukes were perfect. When the market really got hot, at $5 per bushel, Bill shipped them all to New York City.

He was busy the afternoon that the trailer truck picked them up, so he sent me down to sign the Bill of Lading. The owner of the cold storage drew me to one side. "Pat," he said, "let me warn you of something. I really shouldn't say anything, it's none of my business, but there's dry ice on that truck and your cukes won't carry well. The dry ice will heat them."

That made sense. I figured this was a case for the Judge. I called up Bill, but he was nowhere to be found. I called the truck owner.

"Now, don't you fret," he said cheerily. "That dry ice will only stay on there for an hour or two, and then I'll shift trucks and put on fresh ice. There's a good insulating wall between the ice and the cukes, anyway. You can bet we'll take good care of your stuff."

The cukes were supposed to hit the Sunday night market in New York City, usually the best one of the week. If I pulled them off of this truck, we wouldn't be able to get another one.

"She's always fussing, isn't she?" I could hear Willie saying, and Bill answering, "She sure is."

"OK," I said, "let 'er roll." All $5,000 worth of cucumbers went rattling off down the highway.

We went to the movies that night and, when we came home, Leslie's light was still on. He came running down the steps from his apartment.

"Telegram!" he cried. "Then another telegram and two phone calls—collect!"

"Trouble?" I asked, knowing the answer already.

Leslie is a trucker who knows all about "hot" cargoes. "Trouble," he agreed.

We read the first wire. "Cukes are 75% rotten. Please advise."

The other wire said the same. The collect phone calls were from the driver.

There was only one thing to do. "Dump them!" we wired back.

Later we were to be given an extra bill. It cost 25¢ per basket to push them into the East River. Even the water must have turned green!

"I know now," Bill said, "how Mr. Hughes must have felt when he went to bed on election night as Mr. President and came down to breakfast the next morning as Mr. John Doe."

"The dry ice," I thought; the fancy shredded paper, the damp air in the storage, and the proud stamp of "WILLIAM CARR" for all the world to see. Now all of it was at the bottom of a river. There were cucumbers around the barns that we had just tossed out on the ground when we were packing the others. They were still fresh and firm.

"A better mousetrap . . . ." I mused.

I called up Betty. "Make room on the mourner's bench," I said. "I'm coming over."

"I heard," said Betty. "I'll put the coffee on."

Pretty soon the two of us were sympathizing and crying together.

When it was time to pick again, Miss Anne didn't show up. It was Saturday, and, well, Saturday is Saturday in all parts of town. Sunday is "the Lord's Day". Monday I began to come to. Tuesday I went over to see her.

"Us cain' wuk no moah," said Miss Anne reproachfully. "School's stahted an' de big chilluns got to go, an' de lil chilluns needs us. Us cain' wuk now."

Well, this was a fine mess. "But where will I get help?" I asked desperately.

"Ah doan know," Miss Anne said, closing her door. She would have no further interest in me until she wanted a job, next spring. Then she'd be around, you could be sure of it.

"Try Davis's camp," suggested one of the farm hands. "He might have someone."

I drove along the canal and over the bridge to the old Stonecipher house. Four or five men stood in the yard forlornly holding their hands out over a fire made from broken baskets. The men crowded around the car. They volunteered their services to me.

"You want help, ma'am? Us'll come. But, please, ma'am, you pay us; Davis, he don' give us nothin' out of wat us eahns."

I went up to the house. The porch had no steps, just an up-ended crate. The floor sagged and there were big holes in it. Davis was in bed. His "bed" consisted only of two quilts on the bare floor. He was lying there coughing, while his baby son crawled over him.

"Ah gits thuh money foah mah men," said Davis.

"I won't do it that way," I said. "We pay our workers directly. Some of your men are coming anyway. They've already said they would."

"I'll take you to anuthah camp," said Davis.

He drove his truck down the road and I followed. We circled around for a while and then ended up back at Davis's camp.

"Ah dun fergit wheah that road at," said Davis.

The men I had spoken to earlier had disappeared, except one. He fingered a fresh bruise under his eye.

"Ah ain't comin', ma'am," he said, quite matter-of-factly.

Monday it rained; Tuesday it rained; Wednesday it rained. Cukes worth $5 per basket grew to the size of jumbos worth 25¢ per basket. Thursday, a truck stopped and five men got out. They were workmen.

"Brought you some men," said Freddie Gage, waving his hands. "Found 'em using up good chair space in the bus depot. Can you use 'em?"

"What a lifesaver, Freddie!" I said. "Since I'm not married to you, I can only hug you!"

"Don't mind if you do!" said Freddie. He deserved it. The new crew picked 500 bushels of cucumbers that had grown to the size of squashes and fed them to the pigs. The pigs were rapturous. They'd not had any meal that good in their whole piggish lives!

After that, we got down to business and had a pretty good crop. When we made out our income tax, I decided to beat Bill to the draw.

"See," I pointed out. "No tax to pay."

"Daddy's little helper," said Bill. "You wanted to raise cucumbers!"

I told our neighbor, Mr. Zerner, about it. Walt is eighty years old and he's been married for sixty years. He is a gentleman. He laughed until he cried. He shook his head over and over.

"Do you think Bill will ever forgive me?" I asked.

"Forgive you?" he replied. "He's probably tickled to death! Just think, you'll never dare to bawl him out for anything again, as long as you both live! Don't I wish I had something like that on my wife! Why, she'd never hear the end of it! God, woman, I would never let her rest!"

CHAPTER 9

Lo! I Am A Solomon! Or Am I?

After the harvest slacked off, I had more time to think about the house. Think? Think. "Think big!" the posters advised us. Well, if that was the way they wanted it.

Our first fling at being landlords had been successful. Both Bill and I missed Tina Louise and her family, especially the baby, Tina Pat; so why not tackle the upstairs for another apartment? Of course, it would involve a little remodeling, a handful of nails, and a spare board or two, but . . .

When I mentioned it to Bill, he was a little leery. Bill had developed a tendency to be a little leery of all of my new ideas.

"Just think how wonderful it would be!" I pointed out. "Not to have to clean or lock up the spare bedrooms upstairs when the Ladies Aiders came for lunch!"

"Well, Honey," he answered, "since it's your idea, you will have to find a carpenter. I'm too busy with the farm."

There was a war going on somewhere or other (as usual), so there was no spare manpower. None. All of the young males were either in the Army, the Navy, the Air Force, or working for the government at astronomical wages. I looked everywhere and finally came up with Jeremiah.

"Make a good choice?" Bill asked skeptically when I told him about Jeremiah.

"Well, he says he's seventy years old," I announced dubiously.

"That's good," Bill agreed. "Won't get caught in the draft."

"And he used to be a sheep shearer. He gets $10 an hour." I added.

120

"He's a carpenter, all right," Bill said. "Hire him."

Jeremiah showed up the next morning clad like the lilies of the field. He wore a bow tie, a flannel shirt, woolen pants, and boots. He had on everything but his false teeth, which he couldn't find. I started him off painting the ceiling. As the heat rose from the floor and the sun heated up the house, Jeremiah heated up, too. Sweat covered his forehead and dribbled off his chin. First, he undid his tie, then he unbuttoned his shirt, and in a last burst of desperation, he hauled off this shirt and flung it to the floor. Wow! There stood Jeremiah clinging to the ladder and glowing like Rudolph the Red-Nosed Reindeer's nose—he had on red flannel underwear!

"Poor man," Bill remarked sympathetically when I told him about it at lunch. "Why don't you let him take his pants off, too?"

"Ye gods, no!" I yelped. I felt that the sight of Jeremiah's skinny old legs in red flannel long-johns would really drive me around the bend. At times, I would attempt to give advice or orders to him, and he would jabber back at me. (Why didn't he look for his teeth?) Finally, after the umpteenth time that I said, "Sorry, I didn't understand you," he jumped up and down in a frenzy.

"You don't lishun!" he squalled. "You jush don't lishun!"

But, that afternoon, when he cut my last bit of cherished mahogany to fit around the left side of the mantelpiece instead of the right side, *I* jumped up and down in a frenzy. Few kind words were spoken and I paid him off.

That night at dinner when I reported to Bill, he was angry. "Where are you going to get anyone else?" he demanded. "At least he could drive a nail!"

"Not straight," I retorted. Period.

The next day, I went down to the bus station and grabbed the first unattached male that got off a bus. It was Andre. He was French Canadian, and he had twelve children to support (so he said), and he was a gorgeous hunk of machismo with his dark skin and coal black hair. And, he was looking for a job! I carried him home triumphantly.

"Ever do any carpenter work?" Bill asked him.

"Yes, sir!" Andre averred. "Built my own house in Messina."

A friend told us later that it was built from railroad ties and tin cans squashed flat and you could "throw a cat" through the cracks in the walls!

"Had to build it," Andre continued, "got twelve kids to bed down."

Bill was impressed, either by Andre's carpenter skills or his stud ability, I'm not sure which. Anyway, he hired him. When Andre showed up the next morning, Bill said, "Well, I have to work in the back lot. I'm sure Pat can tell you what to do." And off he went down the lane.

I had planned to tear down a partition between two bedrooms in order to make a kitchen dinette and living room. Bill had dug up two wrecking bars, and we set to work. Wham! Bang! Thunk! It was glorious. The plaster cracked. Bang! The dust rose. Crack! The wall collapsed, and Andre and I ran to the window for a breath of fresh air.

"I'm glad it's over," I said, when I had finished gasping. But, when I turned around, instead of the lovely open space I expected to see, there was a forest of studs! Studs are two-by-four pieces of lumber that go from the floor to the ceiling, and since they are nailed in two feet apart, the whole wall looked like a cage in a zoo.

"What'll we do next?" Andre inquired.

"Well," I said, stalling for time. "Let's smoke a cigarette and think."

We smoked a cigarette.

"You are the carpenter," I said.

"Yes, ma'am," he said. "I am a carpenter, but I ain't no miracle worker."

We smoked another cigarette and thought some more. The pause lengthened. Finally, I had an inspiration.

"I know!" I said, snapping my fingers. "I know what to do! I'll go ask Bill!"

Poor Bill! He got "ask-Bill-ed" a number of times that day, but it made him feel sort of important to rescue the damsel in distress. When he went downtown that night, he remarked to one of his friends: "Those two are kind of a funny pair. They get everything all torn up and then they holler for me!"

While Andre and I were struggling with the upstairs, Dottie and her son, Russell, moved into Tina Louise's rooms. Dottie was a carefree, outgoing twenty-nine-year-old that greeted the world with an all-out zest; and the world responded in kind. Her young man was overseas, and she and I soon developed a sister-like relationship. Because Dottie had no other family, she "adopted" Bill and me as hers. Once, right in front of me, she ran up to Bill, threw her arms around him, and kissed his smack on the lips!

"Aren't you jealous?" she asked, when I didn't react.

"Of course not!" I said. "I know you don't mean it in 'that' way!"

"How do you know I don't?" she retorted. Talk about the understudy taking over the lead!

Finally, Andre and I (and Bill) got the upstairs finished. The last nail was driven and the last curtain hung. The farmer across the road, on hearing (from Andre) how expertly he had done our carpentry work, told Andre that he could have his tenant house rent-free if he would fix it up. The tenant house was a charming authentic Colonial "salt box" that had been allowed to deteriorate.

"Yes, sir!" Andre agreed. He moved his litter of twelve children and their mother down from Messina. Time passed. The summer waned. The windows remained broken, the clapboards were never replaced, and, when the farmer discovered that they had chopped up his solid oak staircase for firewood, Andre departed. By request.

After much thought and prayers, (Please, St. Cecelia, a nice tenant!), Dottie and I wrote out an ad: "Country apartment. Ideal for small family." We sent it in to the city newspapers. We were swamped with responses!

"You really will take children?" one caller asked in astonishment.

"I like children!" I said firmly.

Dottie and I held a summit conference.

"I'll leave it to you girls," Bill said.

We finally chose a young veteran with a wife and a two-year-old boy. (Please, St. Cecelia, make it the right choice!). The wife and son had been staying with the husband's mother 500 miles away while he looked for a place to live.

"I'll telephone my wife tonight," he said as he paid the rent. "She'll be on the bus by midnight!"

"But she hasn't even seen the place yet!" I said, shocked. "What if she doesn't like it?"

When I told Bill that night at dinner, I saved the good news until last. "And they have a two-year-old boy!" I said. "Now, that should please you."

Bill gave me a quizzical look. "Honey," he said, "you don't know what you're letting yourself in for. Have you ever raised a healthy, active, two-year-old boy?"

"Of course not," I answered indignantly. "You know darn well I haven't."

"Just asking," Bill said hurriedly. "Then you'll find out!"

I did, too! Our new brood arrived the next afternoon. Bill and I stood in the front hall to welcome them. Bill had taken time out from the chores because, as he put it, he "figgered he ought to take a look at what we were getting into".

It was a cold day, and, when I flung open the door, in strode a young man carrying a bundle that was three feet high, three feet wide, and at least three feet thick. Layers of padded snowsuit, layer upon layer of wooly scarves on one end; fluffy boots of fur on the other end; and, a crowning gesture, a white bunny cap. Little Mike sure had that "layered look" down pat! All I could see of Little Mike himself was a pink button nose and two wide-awake blue eyes that cased the joint. Trailing after Little Mike and his papa came Little Mike's mama wearing a hip-length jacket, sheer silk stockings, and boots with three-inch heels.

"I expect you're tired from your trip," I said, handing them the keys, to their new apartment. "Your rooms are at the head of the stairs and the doors are open."

Bill and I had turned to go when a horrid thump caught us in mid-stride. Little Mike's father had set him down while he fumbled with the keys and his mother had strode to the balcony to admire the French windows. Little Mike had made a break for it. He toddled to the top of the staircase, lost his balance, and pitched head-over-heels down the stairs! There were twenty steps in that staircase, and Little Mike bounced off every one of them. He gave a double bounce off the last one, rolled over, caromed to a stop at Bill's feet, and came up fighting. His papa came tearing down after him and, anxious to gloss over this somewhat shaky episode, picked Little Mike up and held him out towards Bill.

"Kiss the nice man. Kiss Mr. Carr." He urged.

Little Mike puckered up, changed his mind midair, and kicked Bill in the stomach instead!

"That's quite a young man you have there," Bill remarked thoughtfully. "Yes, sir, quite a young man."

Little Mike's papa fled and his mama giggled.

Little Mike soon had the run of the whole house as if he owned it! His shrewd little baby mind soon figured out when Bill and I had lunch, and, like a puppy, he reasoned the best food was the food you went out and hunted for. In he would trot when Bill and I sat down to eat.

"Bill," I protested as Little Mike stood there with an "I'm starving" look, "I know his mama just fed him!"

"Oh, well," said Bill cheerfully. "A little glass of milk never hurt anyone. C'mon, Pardner."

Bill would pull up a chair, pile on the city telephone book and the *Home Veterinary Guide* on it to bring Little Mike up to the level of his peers, tie a bandana around his neck for a bib, and set a glass of milk in front of him. I looked away for one second and CRASH! The glass splintered, and the milk poured onto over as it the floor. I mopped up the mess and Bill poured a second glassful, a little less cheerfully.

"Now, young fella," he said sternly, "you drink this one!"

Little Mike carefully raised the glass to his mouth and paused.

"Careful, now," Bill cautioned him.

For a second they gave each other the "hairy eyeball", and then Little Mike proceeded to pour the milk on the floor!

"Oh, boy," I cried. "You'll get it this time!" I thought as Bill started towards him; but when Bill got close enough to swat, Little Mike opened his arms wide and, with his most cherubic grin announced: "I WUV you!"

Bill picked him up and hugged him, then said reproachfully, "Little Mike, you pack one helluva punch!"

Everybody loved Little Mike, but the only thing that really made him bearable was the fact that his parents realized he was a pint-sized demon.

"He can visit you," his mother said, "if you treat him like he was your own. If he's bad, swat him."

He came home bawling one day when I was having coffee with his mama. "I don't know what you got," she told him, "but I bet you deserved it!"

When they moved away (it seemed like people were always moving in or out), Bill put on his slippers after dinner and sighed luxuriously. No more Little Mike to grab his newspaper or demand a hobby horse ride on this knee. Darby and Jones sitting by the fireside—that was us. But, after about half an hour or so, Bill jumped up exclaiming: "All this peace and quiet is too much now that Little Mike is gone. Let's go to the drive-in movie!"

Dottie moved into the upstairs apartment. "Closer to Heaven," she cried with a giggle. This left the downstairs apartment free. I was cautious about selecting the new tenant because, although our living quarters were separate, Bill and I still had to share the kitchen with this family. We ended up renting to a married couple, Katie and Clarence. Katie tried to upstage us. She and Clarence had come down in the world financially, but they still had "connections". The first thing Katie did was to order vellum stationery with "The Pillars" engraved on top. She used this to write to her friends who were vacationing in the Bahamas or the Greek Isles, or wherever. She looked down her nose at Dottie. Me she tolerated because she had been in show business herself at one time. She had been a "hoofer", a most inelegant term. She was charming to Bill; because of his twenty-year term as a judge and town councilman, she figured Bill knew the "Right People".

"Social climber," Mom sniffed, when I told her. Poor Katie! She would have looked elegant on a pleasure yacht toying with a cocktail. She would have been photogenic at a soiree toying with a cocktail. She would have graced a governor's reception toying with a cocktail. As a matter of fact, Katie would have been at ease anywhere toying with a cocktail. She was rarely seen without one. When she was slightly "lit", she would make the most devastating comments. Then, the next day, she would apologize.

"You know, of course, I didn't realize what I was saying," she would declare. The hell she didn't! Once I overheard her saying to Dottie, "I will be so glad when Mrs. Carr lets us have the whole downstairs. There is just something about Pat's tea towels!"

Katie's husband had come from an excellent family. His father had been a prosperous businessman and Clarence had inherited the business. Unfortunately, the factory burned down and Clarence didn't have enough "umph" to get back on his feet. So now he was on his "genteel uppers". Once, with great diplomacy, he had asked Bill for a sizable loan. Katie and Clarence had been invited as house guests for a week at some upper-class home, and of course there would be the servants to tip and the occasional tab to pick up on the nightclub route. And, since Bill was in politics himself, surely he could appreciate the contacts Clarence would make. Bill gave him the loan over my protestations.

From time to time, Clarence brought up the subject of their "taking over the whole downstairs so that they could entertain", but it was always "whenever it was convenient", so there was no hurry.

CHAPTER 10

Whose Apartment Is This, Anyway?

One morning, just after I'd finished my after-breakfast chores, the phone rang.

"Do you have anything available?" asked Mr. Cronin, the local real estate agent. "I've got a personal friend down here in my office who's stranded. She just got out of the hospital, got a van-load of furniture on the way, and the apartment she was supposed to have isn't ready yet. As a matter of fact, they haven't even started on it and she's about at her wits' end for a place to stay."

"Oh, dear," I replied, "I haven't got a thing."

"Well, suppose I send her over. I really feel sorry for her," he said.

"But, I'm filled up!" I protested.

"Let's see now, how would she get there from here? Route 98? She can reroute the moving van and be there in three-quarters of an hour," he continued.

"I can't!" I repeated.

"OK, fine, half an hour, then. Her name's Herta Marlowe," he said and hung up.

"Well," I said. Mr. Cronin has done me quite a few favors, but there was nothing I could do. I had absolutely no room for a newcomer. The upstairs was full, and Bill and I were living in the western half of the downstairs. Clarence and Katie were on the eastern side. We shared the kitchen, which ran straight through from east to west, and we shared the bath. Of course, there was the "woodshed" hitched onto the whole works, and we had talked vaguely of "someday" turning that into an Early American where Bill and I could lead a quiet life. Actually, it was pretty "Early American" as it was now; all we had was the wooden plank floor, scarred from woodcutting of five generations; the overhead beams; and a strip of leftover yellow paint around the window.

There had been some talk between Katie and me about letting her have the whole downstairs—both the eastern and the western sides—as one apartment, but the plot had been simmering all winter without coming to a boil. Katie didn't really need the whole downstairs; she's one of those women who can take a Five-and-Dime coffee mug and stick a piece of trailing ivy in it, hang up a pair of ruffled white curtains, and make a home out of a clothes closet. Her husband is only now beginning to appreciate her for this.

Clarence stood off to one side and listened to all of our chatter about this "one apartment" project, but whenever I asked him about throwing the two sides of the house into one, he would say: "Oh, whenever you get around to it; there's no hurry. You enjoy sharing the kitchen with us." And he would grin.

He liked to put things off; besides, he enjoys cooking for us. Clarence is a marvelous cook. Every time he makes a mutton with a dash of garlic, I drool so obviously that we usually get invited to share it. On the other hand, when Clarence drools for the lend of our car, he usually gets it. It sort of evens out.

But my housekeeping must be a trial for Katie. Her apartment is always immaculate: the glass shines, the curtains perk, the floors are waxed. Three maids working in relays could never keep my apartment looking like that, but to this gal, it's as easy as pie! I just don't have the "gift". I belong to the school of thought that believes that everything that goes into the washing machine comes out all pure and shining, so I was not above snatching a tea towel as the handiest weapon to use to dust off a chair when Mrs. Reverend Hamlin dropped in unexpectedly.

"I know how it is, Dear," Mrs. Hamlin would say affectionately. "I used to be artistic myself."

After one of these bouts with the tea towels, I sort of halfway noticed that they didn't quite wash up like everybody else's, but I didn't appreciate the full extent of the social chasm until I stood in the upper hallway painting and overheard a conversation between Katie and Mary Lou where Katie remarked very loudly: "There's something about Mrs. Carr's tea towels."

"I know what you mean," said Mary Lou.

I could almost *hear* the look that passed between them. I slunk down the stairs.

"Bill," I said, "please give me some money. I'm going downtown to buy some tea towels."

He started to ask me why I didn't just clean the ones I had, but one look from me and he was silent. I certainly struggled with my housework, but there were times when I blew in so sweet and it came out so backwards! I hadn't realized that after the honeymoon was over, the days are twice as long as the nights are.

"Oh, glory hallelujah," Dillingham, the plumber, has said on millions of occasions.

So, the more I thought about unloading the sprawling apartment that Bill and I lived in and moving into the Early American woodshed and the quiet life, the more I was convinced that it was the perfect fade-out. It would be the ideal place for us to grow old together. The jukebox would play "Hearts and Flowers" while Bill relaxed in his immaculate one-roomer; Katie would be spared the sight of my tea towels; and I would move Mr. Cronin's friend, Herta, into our apartment with Mr. Cronin patting me on the shoulder and saying: "Well done, thou good and faithful servant!"

I decided to seek advice with regard to this new arrival, so I went scouting for Clarence. "Clarence," I said, when I found him, "I've got a female in distress on my hands. She's got no place to live, a van-load of furniture on the way, and Mr. Cronin is sending her here. Would you and Katie be willing to share the kitchen with her? Any friend of Mr. Cronin's would be a marvelous housekeeper. Would it be alright?"

He nodded without hesitation; "Why, of course," he said. "I'd help any female in distress, although you understand, chivalry comes easier if she's an attractive female. I'll square it with Katie, no sweat."

"She looks just like me," I said, and ran to answer the doorbell. It was Herta. She didn't look a bit like me—she had disconcertingly direct blue eyes and blonde hair just beginning to turn grey and the impersonal gaze of a trained nurse. Her girlfriend was with her, a stout forthright person who had a boyfriend in New York City and thought Herta was nuts to come so far away from the bright lights. Where had I heard that before? It sounded like a broken record.

Herta took one look at the apartment and burst into tears. She was just convalescing, and it had been a hard trip and a difficult day. "It's what I've always dreamed of!" she cried. "My antiques in these high-ceilinged rooms; my chaise longue here; my Renoir copy on that wall over there; and my andirons, that I've had in storage for years, in use again in the fireplace! These doors! My Persian rugs on these beautiful knotty pine Mission style floors! Oh, this house needs me! And my cat—General Mac Arthur—on those lawns, catching mice under those magnificent trees!"

"And catching hell from Petie, our dog," I thought to myself, but I refrained from comment. "Well," I said out loud, "I'm so glad I could arrange to offer it to you. I thought you'd like it. I have a few items to clear away. I'll get my things moved out right away. You go sit out in the yard, and I'll bring you some iced tea."

I herded them outside to the garden chairs, then I marshaled my plans. I may be a lousy housekeeper, but I'm fast on the draw. "Hot plate out of the barn; carry water from the cellar; extra bed out of the attic," I started a list in my mind. I flagged down Jimmy and Willie. "Get the bed first," I told them, "then the chairs. I'll move the piano. Don't get the sheets dirty. Grab ahold of the table. Of course it'll go through the door; it's got to!" And, of course, it did—taking only a little of the wood with it.

I caught my heel in one of the planks in the Early American floor and sat down on the bedclothes I was carrying. "Sounds like Miz Katie's sure mad," said Willie, grinning from ear to ear. "I done come by her room on the way down from the attic an' she soun' powerful mad. She kep' sayin' they ain' no bedstead up there an' nothin' but a mattress and some springs in the attic."

I thought, "Well, that isn't anything to be excited about." I said to Willie, "Get some of those cement blocks Bill got for the chimney and put the springs on them." And then I thought: "Oh, yes; I've forgotten to tell Bill!" As I went out the door, Herta called me from Katie's living room.

"Mrs. Carr, please come here," she asked.

I went in, expecting to find everything under control. "Oh," I said, noting the cocktail shaker and the row of empty glasses, "I see you two have met already. Katie, this is Herta."

"Mrs. Carr," said Herta, with a cold-storage smile on her lips, "there seems to be a slight misunderstanding here."

"Oh?" I said, all unawares.

"There certainly is," said Katie, sitting on the edge of the Victorian sofa. She was every inch a lady with a cocktail in her hand. "There certainly is. That's MY apartment she's trying to rent. Pat, dear, have a drink, if there's any left."

I sure needed one, but edged toward the door instead. "Not just now," I replied. "I need all of my right mind. I've got to get Bill transferred before dark. Incidentally, dear, that's MY apartment Herta's just rented; past tense."

"It's MINE!" Katie cried, with just the teeniest lurch.

"Well, if it's yours," I said, striving for the whimsical touch, "my husband has been sleeping in your house!"

"Hah!" said Katie, almost crossing her eyes in an effort to concentrate on the Maraschino cherry in her glass. "She can't have it!" she said, draping her arm across the back of the sofa.

"It's mine, dammit! It's mine!" I replied.

"MINE!" said Katie, stonily, "and if that old biddy rents it, I'll lock the bathroom door and never let her in!"

Plunk! Went her cocktail glass on the coffee table. I thought the cherry would fall out, but it just bobbed up and down comically.

Herta finished her drink. Katie poured another. We sat there brooding.

"It's mine!" said Herta suddenly, banging her fist on the coffee table

Katie picked up her cocktail protectively. "It's mine and wild horses won't drag me away from it."

They glared at each other. "OK, girls," I said, "cut. We've got a helluva second act!"

We reached some sort of temporary compromise. Herta went to a hotel for the night. Katie retired to the attic. I fried Bill some eggs on the hot plate. Clarence disappeared.

"What else could I do?" I asked Bill. "Herta was in a tight spot. We're supposed to 'do unto others' and it was almost an act of charity . . ."

"Have you ever heard," Bill said intensely at two a.m. as the cement blocks tipped and he rolled off onto the floor, "have you ever heard that 'charity begins at home'?"

I jumped out of bed and helped him put the springs back on. "Honey," I said, "we'll be damned lucky if charity is the only thing that begins around here tomorrow!"

Bill kicked me in the shins at the crack of dawn. "Arise and shine, little Florence Nightingale!" he said, "and brew me an egg in the coffee pot." He was still groaning from his sleeplessness. Bill had had a rough night. He put a foot down on the wooden planks and ran a sliver in his toe. Mom had always warned me that even good marriages had their bad days, but she never told me they came in bunches, like bananas!

"I'll sand it," I said hurriedly, and ducked under the bedclothes giggling. Bill didn't think it was all that hilarious. He sat on me. Hard.

That made him feel better. "Gee whiz," I said, crawling out of bed, "you've squashed me flat!"

"Well, you're always complaining that you're getting too fat," Bill replied; "it's a cheap way to reduce."

After four cups of coffee, my eyelids came unstuck and my brain cells started to function. I was worried about Katie. Katie's solution to all of life's problems was to get drunk. I tried to keep an eye on her, but she was like a two-year-old: right under my nose one minute and gone the next. Spirited away, most likely.

Pretty soon the combatants began gathering for Act Three. Herta arrived in a swirl of polite friendliness, two hired men, a van-load of furniture, and a roomful of local aunts and cousins. They were delighted with the house; it was just the thing for her. The furniture was uncrated. Her chaise longue was mahogany, lovingly hand-rubbed. It fit perfectly in the corner where Herta had pictured it. The silvery-pink Renoir copy gleamed against the American walnut woodwork. Her rosewood gateleg table stood between the windows, with a lovely brocaded ladies' and gentlemen's chair drawn up by the fireplace. Her carpets were dark and glowingly patterned.

There was a great deal of bustle as they unpacked. The cousins unwrapped dishes and fluttered. Herta filled her brass samovar and poured tea. I beamed and fluttered a bit myself. Maybe this would show Mr. Tell of the Farmers' Mutual that the house was a good solid substantial project catering to the backbone of the nation and the First Families of Ferndale. I hoped he had picked today to drive by.

I looked up from my teacup in time to see Dottie violently wig-wagging to me from the doorway. "Such beautiful doors," murmured Herta's cousin, the stout one with the cane.

"Aren't they?" I murmured back. "You don't see work like that nowadays," I added and sighed. "The Old School Tie"—that was me. Dottie coughed and wig-wagged again. "Excuse me," I said, and practically backed out curtsying. "OK," I said as soon as I hit the door, "what's the pitch?"

"Shush!" hissed Dottie. "Have you seen Katie?" she asked.

"No," I replied, swallowing the lump in my throat. "Do you think she's where I would want to go?"

"I don't know," said Dottie. "I've been trailing her all over the house, but I can't find her. There's something mysterious about it. There's a pack of cigarettes and an empty beer bottle in the attic; an empty coin purse and a bottle of wine in the cellar; and a fifth of scotch and a few hair curlers in the corn crib; but no Katie. I can't figure out where she's hiding or what she's up do."

"It sounds like you're getting warm," I said, "keep trying. Have you looked in her place?"

We went there and found the cocktail shaker empty, but still wet. "So are the glasses," said Dottie, squeezing a few drops out of one.

"Well, it's a good thing it's empty," I said, "the way I feel; otherwise, I'd probably drink a shot as fast as any man downstairs!"

"Oh, Mrs. Carr," called Herta, "do join us for a cup of a tea. These cups were my great-grandmother's. The angel food cake, of course, is mine."

I re-adjusted the smile on my lips and went in to the angel food cake. "So glad you like the beamed ceilings," I murmured, "so in keeping with the time period."

"And the view from these windows," added Herta, "those Lombardy poplars and the meadows and cows."

"Exquisite," I agreed, restraining an insane impulse to remark audibly that I preferred the purple cow.

Herta offered me a tray. "Do try these wine drops," she said.

"No, thank you," I replied. The very mention of the word "wine" made me shudder. Where was Katie?

Dottie hove into view at the kitchen door. "Excuse me," I said, "telegram."

"What is it?" I hissed.

"I found her!" she hissed back. "C'mon!" I muttered my apologies and an "excuse me" and departed hurriedly. We went up the back stairs to Dottie's apartment.

"Well?" I asked, going into the living room. Darned if I could see Katie.

"You won't believe this," said Dottie, going into the bedroom, "but this is where I found her."

Katie, our own little Katie, was under the bed! I tried to haul her out of there. "Katie," I said, "what nonsense is this? Come on out of there!"

"Go away," cried Katie.

"Katie," I replied, "that is a very unflattering pose. Get up."

With a dignity I wouldn't have believed possible under the circumstances, Katie arose. She marched to the sofa and sat on the very edge—perched there like a canary.

"IT'S MINE!" she yelled, "I saw it first! I could see my loveseat in the corner and my mother's portrait over the fireplace. I could see white curtains and figurines placed around, and doorstops. HER taste is horrible! It's MINE! I can't let you do this!"

Then Katie slid gently to the floor. Dottie helped me get her up again. "Katie," I said, "you gave a marvelous performance, but for Pete's sake, don't get carried away and do an encore. All good actors know where to draw the line."

"I shall hang myself," said Katie in the tone used by Lady Macbeth faced with the "damned spot". "I shall hang myself in the barn. From the rafters. Hang myself. And you'll have to cut me down. Get me a priest!"

"Holy Cow!" I said to Dottie, "let's get her downstairs."

"Well, sure, Pat," replied Dottie, "but how?"

"Katie," I said, "if you fall down those steps, I'll tell Bill."

"I'll walk down," she replied, "don't worry about me." She did, too, and into the kitchen.

"Oh, Mrs. Carr," called Herta, "my cousin, the one who lives next door to Mr. Tell of the Farmers' Mutual, knows your husband's eldest son. She's told me all about him. What's more, she is SO anxious to meet you. Is that dear Katie with you?"

"Work fast!" I told Dottie. "This is it: Now!" We shoved Katie through the kitchen and got her into her bedroom. I locked the front door and started to lock the bedroom door.

"Wait a minute!" cried Dottie, "you aren't leaving me in here with this nutcase, are you?"

"Call the rectory," I hissed, "they're open now. Maybe the priest can handle her. Maybe she'll really hang herself. If she doesn't hang herself, maybe I'll do it for her! Coming!" I caroled to Herta and went back to Studio One. "No lemon, thank you. I always take my tea straight. Clear, I mean, clear," I amended hastily. "So, you know Mr. Tell of the Farmers' Mutual?" I asked Herta's cousin. "We bank there."

"I know you do," said the cousin, "that's why I don't see why Mr. Tell disapproves so of your renting. I think it's wonderful. You share this beautiful old home, and you have all of these delightful people around you."

"Yes, we're always entertained," I replied. "What delicious cake!" Through the window I saw a car coming up the driveway. I wondered who in the world that could be. Then I excused myself to get to the driveway and waylay the good Father and cushion the shock for him. By this time, I was groggy myself and I felt that if anyone suggested a sanatorium, I would order a room with two beds—I needed a good rest.

"I-I-I wanted to explain," I began; but it wasn't the understanding middle-aged priest I had hoped to see; it was the young Father who was strict on discipline. "I, er, well, this is her apartment," I said and unlocked the door and shoved him in. He looked around puzzled, then turned to me as if demanding an explanation.

I took my radio in to Herta. "Just till yours comes in," I said. "Wouldn't you like to plug it in now, to see if it works?"

"How sweet you are," said Herta. "Dear Mrs. Carr, I am so upset. The man who moved my barrels of dishes let them slip and tore a jagged gash in your beautiful knotted pine floor. Even though it was an accident, I feel so bad about it."

"Oh? Oh, yes, of course," I said, looking at a four-inch jag. "Don't give it another thought. I can sand it down."

"How nice you are," she replied, "and how marvelous about such an irritating episode."

"Well," I said, "you get that way in this business. Nothing bothers you; not even breathing. You learn to roll with the punches."

The priest stood in the hallway. I was positive I had locked him in, too. "This woman," he started sternly, "is not my province. Did you know that she is inebriated?" And with that, he strode off. Boing! There went the rest of my sanity! Finally, St. Cecelia got into the act. Katie passed out. Herta retired to her rooms to contemplate her grandmother's highboy.

Bill came in for dinner and found me stretched out on the mattress on the springs on the cement blocks. "Oh, Bill," I said, "it's been one of those days when I just can't cope. I can't cope!"

"Now, now," said Bill, patting me, "charity begins at home, Florence Nightingale. Remember your philosophy, O Angel of the Battlefield!"

The next day, Katie took some of her ivy in to Herta and Herta gave her an antique perfume bottle. By the end of the week, they found that they had a lot of things in common, among them Herta's car. That Saturday, when I was running a few things through the laundry, Katie came down. "Look, Honey," she said, "here's some 101. Let me do your tea towels." I was getting pretty famous for those grimy things! The dove of peace was once more in residence at The Pillars.

Herta thought that Russell, Dottie's son, was such a little gentleman. "You know," she confided in me, "he even picked me a bouquet of wildflowers the other day. And washed my car. And he's so nice to General MacArthur; he never teases him as other young boys often will."

On one horrid occasion, General MacArthur stayed out all night and Herta was very much upset. I got a glimpse of him up in a tree and we finally got him down with cat food and honeyed words. "There he is," I said, handing him over. "There's your night-prowling dissipated feline, General MacArthur."

"Oh, no," said Herta, as she spanked him lightly on the rump, "that's Private MacArthur—he's been demoted."

Russell was a nice lad: considerate, polite, and rarely in trouble. I was taking a bubble bath in our bathroom one day when Russell walked across the porch. Our bathroom had been cut out of the original kitchen so it faced on the porch, and, since first things come first, we had to get the tub and the sink and the john paid for before we could dabble in such luxuries as changing the seven-foot window that went from the rim of the bathtub to the ceiling. That promised to be quite a chore. My sister delighted her PTA with the story of sitting on the porch in a rocking chair and talking over the night's plans with me while I soaked in the tub. We used to pull down a heavy, gloomy green shade, but it made it too dark inside to see if you were clean, so we just posted that window "Off Limits" and forgot about it.

I guess Russell did forget about it and I was soaking in the tub when he came out of his door; walked past the bathroom window, eyes straight ahead; clicked his heels in front of the kitchen door; did a quarter turn, and, as he went into the house, said cheerfully, "Good Morning, Pat!" I was glad I hadn't spared the bubbles.

That bathroom played a very important part in our social life. It was between Herta's and Katie's kitchen and our studio apartment. It was a direct route for Dottie to come down her private stairway, come into our studio, go through our bathroom, and—surprise, surprise—be in Herta's kitchen. Everyone always took the most direct route in our house; this was a lot easier than going from Dottie's stairs to the porch, walking six steps, and going in Herta's door. The bathroom was the common meeting place of the clan: Herta would stand in her doorway, and Dottie would stand in mine; and poor Bill suffered untold cramps before he learned not to be diffident, and, after some time, even he adjusted. At least once a month the girls wandered through the bathroom when someone was in the tub. She either would usually have gone unnoticed since they were always intent on going from one door to the other, and, if the bather would just keep still, no one would have ever noticed; but, it was humanly impossible not to squeal, and then, of course, the person walking through would squeal in answer. That made for some interesting sounds. I have often wondered what we would have ever done if we had an introvert in the house.

Bill offered to partition off the bath so that there wouldn't be a passageway for the girls from door to door, but I refused. I had some rights in this house. Besides, I sort of liked the community spirit of the whole thing.

Since Bill and I ate, slept, held court, and ran a $40,000 a year business in one room, our reflexes sped up considerably. I would frequently be dressing and answer the phone, call upstairs to someone to come down, open the closet door, step behind it to finish dressing, carry on a conversation with someone, keep track of the phone conversation that was none of my business, and step out from behind the closet door all in sixty seconds with my brassiere hooked and my respectability intact. As my voice teacher used to tell me: "Everything is grist for the mill."

Everybody tried to "help" Bill because of the extra commotion, and one day they all pitched in and cleaned up the cellar. They scrubbed the concrete around the base of the water heater, and, although no one realized it, some of the scrub water splashed on the electrodes and they shorted out. When the furnace went on again, the oil poured, but the arc didn't close. I was standing by the motor, and I leaned over to see what was wrong. WHOOSH! At that exact moment the arc closed, the surplus oil ignited, the fire doors burst open, and I got the flame full in my face. I backed away with my hands outthrust. My coat collar was on fire, my glasses were charred, and my eyebrows were singed. Once more, I was rushed to the hospital in town. My face was bandaged like a mummy's with only a small hole for my nose and mouth. My lips were so swollen that my upper lip touched my nose. One of my friends (a conservative WASP who believed that a lady should never show her emotions in public) came to see me. She walked out of my room and fainted.

The doctor told Bill that I would be blind.

CHAPTER 11

Poor Little Thing

The nurse was standing by my bed. "Pat, dear," she said, "its twelve o'clock and we're going down for lunch. I've put a 'tap' bell on your bed stand. If you start to choke, just hit the button. Someone will hear you and come to help."

She walked to the door, and then I heard the echo of her footsteps in the hall.

My hands were bandaged, my eyes were bandaged, and there was an ice pack around my neck. The blast from the furnace had seared the inside of my throat and, when the swelling thickened, it was agonizing to suck air into my lungs. If I started to choke, I would have to fumble for the button, paw at the "tap", and hope that someone would come before I asphyxiated. Not exactly "fail-safe", but I was too beat up to care. Listlessly, I drifted into the world of the newly blind. I heard doors open and shut; I knew the nurses by their voices; and I could tell morning from night by the breaks in the routine.

Bill spent every minute he could spare (and a lot that he couldn't) at the hospital with me. He had never given up hope for my eyes, and as soon as I became more alert, he asked for a consultation. Several days later I heard a strange voice in the room.

"Open your eyes," the new voice ordered. I couldn't. They had been bandaged shut for so long that the words triggered nothing in my brain.

"Open your eyes," the voice insisted. This time my brain got the message. I opened my eyes, and I could see! I saw Bill and a new doctor, and the village doctor next to him, and the nurses all crowded in my room.

"You'll be all right," the new doctor said, matter-of-factly. "Second degree burns on your face, neck, and the backs of your hands. Do you realize, young lady, how lucky you are that only the backs of your hands were burned? If it had been your palms, your fingers would have twisted into claws. Just don't ask for a mirror for a few days yet," he said smiling. "You don't look very appetizing right now."

They filed out of my room talking excitedly; every last one of them pleased as hell that I could see. As soon as they left, I wobbled to the bathroom and looked in the mirror. The specialist from the city sure was right. I didn't look very appetizing. My cheeks were puffed out like a chipmunk's, one side more swollen than the other. My eyebrows were burned off (my glasses frames had been charred, but the lenses had saved my eyes), and there was a lump here, a lump there, lumps everywhere, and each one was an angry red. "St. Cecelia!" I whispered aghast.

"Be patient, My Dear," she murmured.

That night, when Bill came in, I was crying. "I know you married me for 'better or worse'," I sobbed, "but I guess you're stuck with worse now."

"Whoa, now," Bill said gently. "You've been awfully brave so far. Hang in there a bit longer."

I kept hoping that Mom would come up. She called every night, but my baby sister, Mary, needed help with her kids. After I had gone home, my skin started to heal and the ugly dead layers peeled off leaving my face fresh and glowing.

"T'ain't fair," Bill grumbled. "All your wrinkles have peeled off!"

"Bill," I said curiously, when I was well enough to talk about it, "how did you feel when they told you I was going to be blind?"

"Wal-l," he said slowly, "I thought about how hard it would be for you." Then he added indignantly, "Nobody but a damned fool would stick her head in front of the fire doors when the furnace was about to explode!" That's my Bill!

Judy and lived with us for two and a half years. So did her husband, Leslie, and her three children: Marti, aged three; Marjy, aged 2; and Timmy, who was born here. The family group was completed by Brownie, their wretched little cocker spaniel that was always mistaking the hall balustrade for a fireplug. When Roxanne lived in the downstairs apartment, she would come to me one a day and point out that there was the funniest smell in the front hall. I would sniff around, ferret out the trouble, and clean up after Brownie. Then we would sympathize with each other.

One day, Judy came to me bug-eyed. "Oh, is Leslie ever mad!" she said. "He went out the front door in a hurry and he slipped. Oh, is he mad!"

"Oh? Am *I* mad!" I replied. "That Brownie! I could murder that dog! I could fry it over an open fire and sandpaper it raw! Oh, am I mad!"

Brownie heard me yipping and came down the stairs, wriggling every one of her twenty-two inches. She lay at my feet, rolled over on her back, and cut her eyes around until I picked her up. She was so soft, warm, and silky that I had to hug her. Brownie had a way of making up my mind.

Brownie had never been spayed, so she lived in all the glory of her doggie womanhood. At "certain" times, male dogs from the four corners of the land would congregate under our windows and howl. It was quite a convention. They woke up Clarence one night and he went out on the porch and fired a gun into the air. We finally asked Judy to consult with a vet.

Once every few weeks thereafter, Judy would come down and ask "Who's the best vet, Pat?"

And I'd answer: "Why Doc, of course."

"Well, do you think he would fix Brownie?"

"Don't see why not."

"Oh dear, she's so little," Judy would say.

"Well, you can't wait until she's a mother," I'd argue.

"How much does he charge?" she asked.

"Judy," I replied, "for Heaven's sake! Call him up and ask him!"

"But she's so little," Judy would say.

"She has big ideas!" I added.

Once in a while, Judy would change her tune to: "Leslie won't give me the money to have Brownie spayed, and will he ever be sorry."

Another six months would go by, and Brownie would once more be confined to quarters. On these occasions, our own dog, Petie, would go half mad with unrequited passion. He would pant and heave and walk the floor all night. During one of these "Mad Dog Scares", he was almost done in. Brownie would sneak down the stairs to our place, and she and Petie would commune audibly through our closed door.

"I can't stand this," I told Bill. "Why on Earth doesn't Judy do something about it? Or, at least, keep her dog in the cupola? Honestly, I feel sorry for Petie."

"You never felt sorry for *me*," my husband said, and rolled over. "Let Petie out into the hall."

"But Judy doesn't want her bred," I said. "Do you want any more puppies around this house?"

Everyone who is too softhearted to take care of unwanted puppies gives them to us.

"All I want," replied Bill, "is to be able to go to sleep before 6 o'clock in the morning, when I have to get up. Petie isn't making half as much fuss as you are."

"I can't sleep with that racket!" I cried. "What'll I do?"

"Put Petie in the hall," repeated Bill. "Let 'em breed."

"The vet said those two dogs couldn't breed." Petie is a lusty collie-shepherd mix. "He said not even Nature could solve that one."

"Maybe not," said Bill, "but they'll be a lot happier trying. Go ahead, let him out there."

Nothing in the way of formal courtship took place in the hall, but they sure learned a lot about each other. The next day, I was working in the kitchen, and I glanced out the window. "For Heaven's sake," I said, "what are those two dogs doing?" Petie was on the bottom edge of the porch and Brownie was on the step above and they were . . . . "Oh no! Bill!" I yelled, "Hurry, get in here!"

Judy carried on stinking, "Doc says it'll kill Brownie," she said. "The puppies will be as big as werewolves and they'll kill poor little Brownie."

"Will they?" asked Bill? "T'ain't very likely. Nature's been in this business a lot longer than Doc has. Where there's a will, there's a way, even if it's puppies."

We all watched Brownie anxiously. The puppies arrived on the back porch. They had Brownie's size and Petie's coloring. Brownie only yelped once while she was having them. Judy named them "Improbable", "Impossible", "Unheard Of", and "Accidental".

I had been warned about getting sunburned, so I stayed indoors a lot and, unfortunately, it was my job to answer the phone, since I was nearest to it.

"Pat, dear," the caller cooed. I was beginning to get a little leery of conversations that started with "Pat, dear"! Usually it was the lead-in for a soft touch. Sure enough, there was a zinger to it!

"Pat, dear, could you possibly help us out? I have a client (the caller was a friend of mine who worked for Social Services) with three small children and no place to go. She says they've been sleeping in somebody's car. She's such a brave little thing. And the kids are dolls. It's really pathetic. I'd consider it a personal favor (I winced) if you could take her in."

"NO WAY!" I said firmly.

"We'll be there in ten minutes," my friend replied. "You'll love the kids!"

"We're filled to the eaves!" I shouted, but she had hung up. Eaves . . . eaves . . . of course! There were servant's quarters up under the eaves in the back, but they had been boarded up for years. There was a lavatory, but no bath. Would the toilet still work? No refrigerator, but was the gas stove still connected? A car honked in the driveway. The driver of the car (smart gal) kept the motor running and pushed out her passengers.

"This is Marleena," she said, pointing to the mother.

As soon as the girl stood up, I knew I had been flimflammed. "Poor little thing" like hell! She was three inches taller than I, her shoulders were muscular, and, although she managed a frail droop, her hair was spun gold straight out of a Grimms fairy tale by way too much bleach, and it fell to her waist. Her eyes had the wistful look of a hound dog that had been kicked once too often, and her voice had the concentrated pathos of all the burdens of the world.

"Oh, you poor little th . . ." I started impulsively, until Judy swatted me.

My friend (?) tore out of the driveway as the three-year-old tugged at my jeans and gave me a slobbery kiss. The baby started to squall and Judy picked him up to hush him. Willie came trotting up the lane, picked up the two-year-old and the bundles and solicitously held open the door. Jeepers! Men may marry brunettes, but they sure do wait on blondes!

I introduced Marleena to the rest of the group. Clarence played the role of the Ivy League gallant; Herta and Katie were graciously condescending to a member of the lower class ("You mean they were snooty, don't you?" Mom remarked when I called her to tell her about our latest additions.); and Judy and I kept our fingers crossed.

That night, when Bill came up out of the field, Marleena went to him. "Mr. Carr," she said in a sticky-sweet little-girl voice, "I need a job. I want to work and take care of my babies."

"Why, of course," Bill said, expansively. "Any little girl as brave as you can always get a job. Come down to the field at seven tomorrow morning and you can join the hands hoeing."

Later he said to me, "Pat, we should really try to help her. She's in a tough spot. Three children and no husband. Poor little thing!"

I wanted to clobber him, but I refrained. It wasn't that I minded, you understand, but a lady does like top billing on her own stomping grounds.

Marleena reported promptly the next morning with her little brood in tow. She turned the three-year-old and the two-year-old loose in the field, and the ten-month-old was in a pram that she had scrounged from someone's attic. Bill assigned each worker a row and they all started out together. The other hands soon outstripped Marleena so that when they got to the end of their rows and started back on the next one, someone would turn back and finish Marleena's row so that Bill wouldn't think she was being "lazy". In the meantime, I had gone on an errand for Bill, but, as soon as I got back, I drove down to the field.

"Things will go better if you take a look around once in a while," Bill always said. So, I took a look and a then a second look around. The toddlers were yanking up the plants by the handfuls! Marleena heard me squawk and came running. She could move fast when she wanted to, and she could think fast when she had to.

"Oh," she cooed to the children, "you're picking a beautiful bouquet for Pat! Give her the pretty flowers."

The "flowers" were presented with another slobbery kiss. "Thank you," I said gravely.

That night, as we sat at the table eating our dessert, I was remembering how awful my cooking had been when Bill and I first married. "How did you ever stand it?" I asked Bill.

"Wal-l," he drawled, "you were so proud of it that I made my mind up that I'd just quietly go on eating until you improved or I'd died of indigestion, whichever came first!"

Marleena came in then. "Jimmy just threw my last pack of cigarettes down the toilet," she said and looked meaningfully at my pack. Automatically I tossed her my pack and then realized it was my last one. Holy cow! Now she had me doing it! There's just something about those eyes that glistened with unshed tears and that damned little-girl voice . . .

The next morning, Marleena showed up an hour late to the field. "The baby threw up and I was awful worried," she explained.

Marleena did love her children, but her idea of raising them was to coo at them when they did anything bad. She and I stood at the foot of the stairs talking one day when the three-year-old started to tease at her to come upstairs. He got madder and madder when we kept on talking and finally he unzipped his zipper and pulled out his little peapod, leaned over the banister, and peed on his mother's spun gold hair!

"Now, dear, you mustn't do that," she cooed.

I haunted the local library for days over that one, but no child psychologist had had the guts to do a confrontation with that issue.

Marleena came to work later and later, but Bill stuck it out. When we planned to have the field sprayed by a helicopter to kill the bugs, I said to the hands, "If the helicopter comes over while I'm in the village, I want all of you to clear the field at once and stay out of it for thirty minutes. That spray is dangerous!" Sure enough, the helicopter came while I was gone, and, when I got back, the hands were all huddled in the lane. Marleena and the three kids were sitting in the field placidly eating their lunch, and the baby was sucking on a bottle nipple that had been lying uncovered!

"It seems like a lot of bother to wheel the pram over to the lane for just half an hour," Marleena explained.

Since the spray didn't do a damn thing to the bugs, I guess it didn't hurt the kids!

Marleena came to work later and later. "The alarm didn't go off." "I couldn't find the baby's diapers." And so on, and so forth. Finally, she came to Bill with those beautiful unshed tears glistening on those long eyelashes. "Mr. Carr," she said bravely, "I know you're counting on me, but I have to quit. The babies need me."

"Thank God!" Bill said to me afterwards. "Maybe we can get some work done now! The men are two days behind schedule in their hoeing."

Marleena's next confrontation with the commercial world was a part-time job in a bakery. The hours were from 10 p.m. to 4 a.m. That way Marleena figured she wouldn't have to worry about the babies because they'd be asleep. Well, maybe she didn't have to worry about them, but I went to bed every night with our bedroom door wide open. At one a.m., a baby hand tugged at my pillow, and a little voice wailed, "I want my Mommy! I want my Mommy!"

Bill grunted, turned over, and went back to snoring. I got up, staggered to the kitchen, warmed a glass of milk, put an extra pillow and a blanket on the couch, and at five a.m. (farmers get up with the sun) carried the little stinker back upstairs to his mother, who was sleeping soundly.

The baker picked Marleena up, took her to work, and brought her back home. She was supposed to quit at four a.m., but she got home later and later as time went on.

"Where do they go?" I asked Bill. "The saloons close at one a.m."

"Every gin mill in town has a back door for the night crews," Bill told me. "And the Police Chief says there's a lot of traffic in that old gravel pit. Half the kids in town have been started in that old gravel pit!"

One night, when the baker came to pick her up, she wasn't home. She wasn't home the next night, either. The baker was a practical man. He figured that fun was fun and a romp in the gravel pit had its rewards, but a man has to earn a living somewhere along the line, so he fired her.

"Hey," Bill said the next morning. "How long has it been since Marleena paid her rent?"

As a matter of fact, she had never paid any rent!

"Better speak to her about it," he told me.

So, *I* should speak to her about it, eh? Instead, I called my friend at Social Services, Lois, who was the one who dumped the poor little thing on me.

"Lois, dear," I cooed. "I would consider it a personal favor if you'd see that Marleena came across with some rent."

"Turn-about is fair play" is my motto.

Between getting back in the swing of farm work, keeping an eagle eye on Katie, and popping in to admire Herta's antiques, I never seemed to get up to see Marleena. When I dashed up the three flights of stairs with a new toy for the baby, I ran smack into a young man I had never seen before.

"Who are you?" I demanded.

"I'm Marleena's boyfriend," he answered.

This was something new! None of Marleena's previous intimate relationships had been live-in affairs.

"Pat, dear," Marleena said, as she came out of the lavatory, "this is Jim. He's . . ." she paused to count on the fingers of both hands (she was never very good with arithmetic), "I almost sure, he's the baby's father."

Since all of the kids had different fathers, it was gratifying to know that at least one of them could be identified.

"Uh . . . you wouldn't have a cigarette on you, would you?" the young man asked casually. "I'm fresh out and I go nuts if I can't smoke."

"I know how it is," I said sympathetically. "I'm a chain smoker myself."

I divided my last pack. He seemed like an amiable never-amount-to-much young man, but he was quiet, and, between the two of them, they could keep an eye on the children. Famous last words!

That night, we were sitting out on the lawn, and Marleena barged over to "borrow" a cigarette leaving Jim to mind the children. We heard a loud cracking, a faint wail, and, when we looked up, there was a gaping hole where the upstairs window screen had been.

"My God!" Bill cried. "The baby's on top of that screen!"

We all raced with our arms opened wide hoping one of us could catch it, but the baby and the screen plummeted down like a parachute that had failed. Down, down, down, the baby rode the screen like a sled. At the edge of the lawn, the screen struck the shrubbery, bounced once, and gently came to rest. While the rest of us were shaking, the baby cooed and clapped his hands. It had been such fun! I almost went to the emergency with cardiac arrest, and Bill had to take a shot of adrenalin.

Bill began to complain about the cartons of cigarettes that showed up on our grocery bill.

"I'm not smoking any more than usual," I protested. "It's Marleena and Jim that keep 'borrowing'!"

"Well, tell them to buy some of their own for a change," he grunted.

Ever since the furnace exploded, I had a horror of fire. If I were downtown and the fire whistle blew, the cops would assure me that it was at the other end of town, or the clerks would call the station house to find out where the fire was and report the whereabouts to me. I was ashamed of my hang-up, but I sure couldn't shake it. So, when Marleena came in one night and said: "Pat, I know how uptight you get, so I wanted to tell you not to be alarmed if you smell smoke. I was cleaning out my stove and the rag caught fire."

I was pleased at her thoughtfulness. Usually Marleena didn't give a damn about other people's feelings. I heard her knock on Katie's door, and then Herta's. Judy was on a late date, so Marleena left a note for her. When Bill came in after a last check on the barns, he wrinkled up his nose.

"Smell smoke, Honey?" he asked. Bill was very alert to the possibility of fire. All fires are terrifying, but in the country, with no adequate water supply, it was even scarier. Bill had seen too many farmhouses and barns go up in flames.

"Not to worry," I answered. "Marleena was cleaning her gas stove, and her cleaning rag caught fire."

"Oh," was all Bill said.

Judy came home around midnight and two minutes later she was pounding on our door. "Mr. Carr!" she screamed. "There's smoke drifting up past my window! The house is on fire!"

Bill jumped up, grabbed the fire axe he kept hanging above the door for emergencies, and ran up the stairs.

"Don't turn in an alarm yet until I check," he yelled to me. All too often, Bill listened to the girls talking about "rats with tails a foot long" that had turned out to be itty bitty mice to trust any tenant's report; and woe betide any farmer who turned in a false fire alarm at midnight! He found the "hot spot" halfway up on Judy's wall and chopped through as high up as he could reach hoping to cut off the fire from above, but the flames had already raced beyond him and were eating their way to the attic. He opened the attic door and the smoke billowed out. He plunged in and his asthma smacked him. Clarence heard him staggering around, yanked him out, and forced him to go out onto the lawn. Downstairs, I was frantically jiggling the telephone receiver.

"FIRE!" I babbled to the operator.

"At once," she said. "Is it bad, Mrs. Carr?"

"I don't know," I said.

"Wake Tony," Bill wheezed. "Firemen . . . need . . . his pond."

I groped my way across the road to our neighbor Tony's. A gale wind had come up and rolled in a fog that was thicker than pea soup. I beat on their door, and, when there was no answer, I threw my shoe at the window.

"Coming!" Tony called as their lights snapped on. "We heard the siren. Your house? Be right over! Show the firemen where to plug in their hoses!" He added.

I went back across the road. All of our tenants were huddled on the lawn. Clarence, Katie, Herta, Judy and her family, Marleena and her three kids, everyone except Jim. Jim had disappeared. "St. Cecelia," I begged. "I don't care about the house. Honest. Just don't let anyone get hurt. Please!"

We could hear the fire engine's siren, but we couldn't see it in the fog. The fog was so thick that the volunteer driver, who knew the roads like the back of his hand, had overshot our road and wasted precious seconds finding a space in which to turn around. As soon as they got to us, they ran up ladders forty feet in the air, broke the windows in the cupola, snaked hoses up the banisters, and, within ten minutes, the fire was out.

"You're sure a lucky man, Judge," the Chief said as he slapped Bill on the back (they served on the Town Board together). "Another five or ten minutes, and we'd have been too late. You'd have lost it for sure if they hadn't built this house so damned well! There was a ten-inch beam across the opening in the attic where the inner and outer walls come up. Held it back just long enough so we could reach it! Everything's safe now. How'd it start?"

"Dunno," Bill snorted. Herta had given him a hypo of adrenalin, and his asthma had let up enough so that he could talk.

"Looks like it must have started pretty high up."

Suddenly the Chief spotted a sofa pillow still smoldering on the ground. "Where did that come from?" he demanded.

"Upstairs on the balcony," one of the firemen answered. "Looked like it was smoldering so I tossed it over the railing."

The Chief turned to Bill. "If I was you," he said, "I'd kinda look into this."

"I certainly intend to!" Bill said, grimly. "And, thanks, Art."

The Chief sounded the "all clear" and they drove off, but slowly because of the fog.

Wearily, but thankfully, we trailed back into the house. There was no use going back to bed—we were all too excited. I put the coffee pot on, and we sat around the dining room table.

"Now, about this sofa pillow," Bill began.

I turned pale. It was the pillow from Marleena's sofa. Bit by bit, the story came out. Jim had been drinking; he had also been smoking. He had lain on the davenport and passed out. The cigarette dropped out of his hand. Marleena smelled the pillow burning, poured water over it, and then, anxious that no one should find fault with her Jim, she carried it to the upper balcony and leaned it against the wall to air out. But, it was an old-fashioned pillow, crammed tight with crumbly foam rubber. The spark had eaten deep into the center of it and was smoldering. When Marleena stood it up against the clapboards, the gale wind sprang up, fanned the spark, and the clapboards caught fire.

I was furious. What if Bill had been trapped in the attic? What if the firemen hadn't made it in time? What if someone had been hurt?

"That woman goes in the morning!" I snarled. As one, all of the other tenants turned on me! You'd have thought I was the prize bitch of the year!

"Now, now," Clarence said. "Accidents do happen."

"Beer always makes one sleepy," Katie said, virtuously. "That's why I never drink it."

"I'm sure Jim will be more careful," Herta chimed in.

"Where would the babies go?" Judy wailed.

"After all, there wasn't much damage," Bill said. "And, with that no-good young man for a boyfriend, Marleena's more than got her hands full. Poor little thing."

"Aw, nuts!" I exploded. "I'm going to bed."

For a few weeks, Jim tiptoed around the house with his halo on straight, but it didn't last long. Nobody expected it would. Once more, our garbage bin filled up with beer cans. Judy, our official "Harbinger of Woe" flung open the kitchen door when we were eating lunch one day.

"Can't eat a meal in peace and quiet," Bill commented.

"Bill! Come quickly!" Judy screamed. "Jim's trying to kill Marleena! Honest! And he's got the door locked."

We could hear Marleena screeching clean down in the front of the house. It sounded as though Jim was chasing her around the table. Resignedly, Bill climbed the steps.

"Open this door!" he commanded. "Young man! You open this door, or I'll kick it in with one foot and you out with the other!"

Jim opened the door. Marleena was clutching her throat with both hands and Jim was hanging onto a butcher's knife that was big enough to do extensive damage.

"She stayed out all night!" Jim began.

"Never mind that," Bill retorted. "Marleena! Go down to our rooms. Pat! Call the Sheriff! I've had enough of this nonsense!"

I called the Sheriff. The Sheriff and I had a sort-of ongoing relationship. He would often call me. "Pat, do you have a farm hand called 'Pork Chop'?"

"Maybe," I would say cautiously. "Clue me in."

"Well, he says he's out of cigarettes, and . . ."

"Got the message," I agreed. "Be right down. But you tell him that I'll work the price of a carton out of his hide when he gets back here!"

As I was talking to the Sheriff, Jim had slipped by Bill, staggered to the top of the stairs, fallen down all twenty steps, and lay at the bottom in a drunken stupor.

"Well, ma'am," the Deputy said to Marleena, when he arrived. "He ain't doin' no harm lyin' there. Do you want to charge him?"

Marleena looked at Bill, but Bill just glared. So, the Poor Little Thing bit the bullet. "I'll charge him," she said, and burst into tears.

In addition to my other chores, I now added a daily trip to the jail so that Marleena could take cigarettes to her beloved. Our jail was sort of a cozy arrangement. Originally, it was a private residence, just like the hospital. It was built of hand-hewn stone and resembled the medieval castles that perch on the banks of the Hudson River, or hide in splendid isolation on private islands. The "front" room was the reception center, the visitor's room, and the charge room. The Sheriff lived in his own quarters upstairs. It was run along the lines of a "home away from home", and, since the only requirement for admission was to commit a slight felony, many of our workers, when jobs were slack in the wintertime, were pleased to accept the free room and board. Most of the work around the place was done by "trustees" and, more than once, when I was waiting in the visitor's room toting cigarettes as usual, a familiar voice would say: "Hey, Pat! Heist your feet! I gotta mop the floor!"

When Jim was brought before the local Justice of the Peace, that worthy man phoned Bill. "Bill," he said (they were in the Masonic Lodge together), "kinda wanted to get your idea on this young man, Jim. Looks to me like one of those husband-and-wife spats. Figured maybe a good stiff warning?"

"Wal-l," Bill drawled, "that butcher knife was downright sharp."

So, Jim was invited to remain in residence for a while. Marleena came while we were eating (she always seemed to catch us when we were eating). "Mr. Carr," she said, mournfully. "Jim's planning to break out of jail tonight!"

"My God!" I exclaimed. "Do you think we should call the Sheriff?"

"Guess not," Bill said. "They've got some pretty sharp guys down there. Marleena, you've been watching too many crime shows on television."

It was an excessively hot night, and Bill was sleeping in the nude. However, I had that faint prickling at the back of my neck that usually meant trouble was brewing, so I wore pajamas. Around midnight (the bewitching hour?), I was awakened. Someone was tossing pebbles at the windows. Then came a violent pounding on the front door and Jim yelled: "Marleena, Baby! Let me in! They're after me!"

Bill rolled out of bed suddenly, realized he was au naturel, and dove back between the sheets. "You go!" he hissed. "You're the only one who has any pants on!"

I dashed to the front door and collided with Marleena, who was fumbling with the night latch. "Over my dead body!" I said furiously. "You let him in and I'll boil you in oil!"

Lights flashed on all over the house and doors were opened. Everybody gathered on the staircase. Clarence was resplendent in a royal purple smoking robe. Katie was clutching the ever-present cocktail shaker. Herta was in curlers. Judy was barefooted. Bill was in back of the curtain peering out of the window. What a picture for a candid newsreel!

The moon came out from behind a cloud, and, for a moment, Jim was silhouetted against a pillar. The Sheriff's car came streaming up and they pounded on the door demanding admittance. In the confusion, Jim darted across the porch, dodged between the trees, sprinted down the driveway, and ran smack into a Deputy who had been stationed on the road. Our local police weren't all that dumb!

Bill, by now decorously clad in pajamas and robe as befitted a Deacon in the church, opened the door to the Deputy on the porch.

"Glad you could come," he said. But, as the young man was leaving, I grabbed him.

"Look," I said fiercely, as I gazed at our various stages of disarray. "Don't you dare let this get into the papers!"

"I sure won't, ma'am," he assured me. "I've only been married two weeks and my wife is kinda funny about some things."

150

The next day, when I was talking to my friend Lois at Social Services, I confided. "It's really embarrassing . . . an escaped convict and all. What will our other tenants think?"

"Think!" she snorted. "I'll bet they enjoyed every minute of it! Hell, I'd raise their rents to cover the floor show!"

The Sheriff was slightly miffed at the way that Jim had thumbed his nose at our little facility. He had waited until the dumbwaiter brought up food from the kitchen, hung around until it was empty, climbed in, pulled the ropes, dropped to the basement, and slunk out a basement door that was unguarded. Et voilá! As the French say. So, when Jim arrived back at the jail, they went over him with a fine-tooth comb. They asked a lot of questions, like: "How old is he? Why isn't he in the Army?" They made a few phone calls, and they came up with a few answers.

Jim was a draft dodger. Upon finding this out, he was reported and the MPs personally escorted him to a boot camp. With the minimum of training, he was shipped overseas. Three months later, he was shipped home in a closed casket. He had stopped a napalm bomb.

With a final burst of conscience, he had made out his GI insurance to his girlfriend. Marleena was rich! With her new found wealth, she was able to pay the rent for an apartment over a gin mill and moved at once, with appropriate sorrow.

Poor little thing!

CHAPTER 12

We Put In A New Heating System—In Pieces

W hen the cold weather set in in earnest, the question of heat in the house for the tenants began to rear its chilly head. It's not that our place was a slip-shod job—the house was well-built; but it was right out in the open—nothing for miles to break the wind. And, what Bill considered adequate heat and what the tenants considered adequate heat differed by quite a few degrees, inevitably to Bill's disadvantage.

The furnace was twenty years old, anyway, and dying a lingering death. The chimneys were good, but the fireplaces and the furnace were hitched together so that you couldn't use both at the same time. This posed its share of problems: part of the house was hot water heat and part hot air heat. With one of those flashes of cerebration which have convinced my husband that I am only slightly sub-normal, I came up with a solution.

"Scrap the furnace!" I said. "Scrap the hot air! Tear out the hot water heat! Put in steam! Get new radiators, a new furnace . . . !"

"A new chimney," said Bill, catching fire. "Oil burner . . . let's go!" He sobered up. This is wartime, Little Big Shot, just where are you going to get all these things?

"Leave that to Mother," I said.

"Andre and Dillingham can do the work," said Bill.

I reeled at the thought. Andre and TJ? Together? Oh goodness, we'd better get our eardrums insured! We got the last furnace left in Buffalo; we got the last oil burner left in Western New York; and we got the last chimney bricklayer known to man. All we had to do was fit them all together.

About this time, TJ began to turn up missing a few mornings. We didn't say anything at first, but he finally offered an explanation.

"I start out on time," he said, "but the steering wheel on that 'Old Nag' of mine just gets right out from under me and takes off for Al's Place."

"Does Ma Dillingham know about this?" I asked.

"Oh, praise the Lord," replied Dillingham, "Old Nag and my wife aren't on speaking terms!"

"I don't doubt it," I said. I knew that Ma was a little banty rooster as far as her TJ is concerned, and, when Old Doc says "No Beer", Ma has been known to plunge into the depths of the local tavern and haul forth her beloved, who usually has to be literally dragged out. Al has an 1850 rifle with an eight-foot barrel tacked up on the wall with a placard reading: This is the rifle that Ma used to chase TJ clean back to Dillingham Landing. Hanging right next to it, just to make it good, is a cap with a bullet hole in it labeled "TJ's".

One especially exasperating morning, I went over and routed him out. "I'll drive in back of you," I offered, "then you're sure to get to work."

"Oh, now, Pat, you don't want to do that. Old Nag'll only do twenty miles an hour," he replied.

"TJ," I said, "twenty miles an hour is all right with me, as long as it's in the direction of our house. That's the important thing."

About this time, I moved right over into TJ's class myself. I became known as THAT Mrs. Carr. She gets things done. I never thought I would be put into a category as exalted as TJ's.

"If we're going to put in a new heating system," said TJ, "we gotta have radiators, and, if we're gonna have radiators, we gotta have pipes. Miles and miles of pipes. Oh, Glory, praise His name. There isn't a piece of pipe to be had in the land. Let's forget the whole thing."

"TJ," I said, "how much pipe?"

"Oh, miles and miles of it."

"When you two get done romancing," said Bill, "I'll measure it up. What TJ means," he added, "is that he needs more pipe than you'll ever find. Everything is on 'priority', and there's no use going on, Dear. You're licked. We might just as well give up."

"Oh, praise His name," I said, "I'll find it!" I went to every listed and unlisted place in Rochester and Buffalo.

"Sorry, not a piece of pipe on hand. Sorry," was all I heard.

On the way home from Rochester, right on Main Street, we saw a little hand-printed sign. It was the answer to our prayers. It said "USED PIPES IN BACK". We bought out the place. "Da-da-dee-DAH!" I cried. "We now have . . ."

"Bricks," said Bill. "We need bricks for the chimney. We'll see if you can get them as easily."

"Have them there for you by next Friday," said Andre.

"OK. Bricklayer, bricklayer, bricklayer. Who's got the bricklayer?" I asked.

Bill had the answer for this. "Used to go to school with Jed Evans. I'll try him."

The old, one-room country school alumni association triumphed.

"At one o'clock on Friday," I told Jed when he called. "The bricks will be here then."

When the bricks weren't there by noon on Friday, Bill was good and sore at me for getting Jed. He thought Jed would be mad at him for coming on a wild goose chase. I left hoping Jed would be late arriving and went to see Andre. Andre almost had apoplexy at my berating, but I got the bricks. They were waiting for Jed when he arrived, right on time.

"We'll put in the oil burner, if you have the chimney hooked up by Wednesday afternoon," said the Dorff Brothers. We did. They never thought we'd do it!

"Well, we did," I said, "and, I'll remind you every fifteen minutes!" I added with a smug note.

"How do you do it?" said one of the Dorff brothers when he inspected the job. "I can't get these things done. Of course," he added, looking at my outfit, "I'm not a female!"

Da-da-dee-DAH!

"Radiators!" cried TJ. "We need twenty-four of them."

This one was really tough. I started talking in my sleep. None in Rochester; none in Buffalo; none in the whole world, most likely. It looked like we'd hit a snag.

Bill sent me to Batavia on an errand, and I was walking across the street with three-year-old Marti fastened to my coattail, when I glanced up casually at the red traffic light. In the line of vehicles was a truck with "Wrecking Company" printed on the side. "Boing!" On went the light bulb in my head. There's the answer! Wreckers! I grabbed Marti in my arms and jumped onto the running board of the truck.

"Radiators?" I asked the driver.

He nodded.

"How many?"

"Yardful."

"Hold 'em!" I yelled. The light changed. The trucks in back of us started to honk their horns. Marti wriggled out of my arms. I made a grab for her and carried her to the curb. I looked back in time to see that God-given truck with the yardful of radiators vanishing out of my life forever. I hadn't asked for the name of the company!

I ran into the hotel on the corner. "Do you . . . could you . . ." I babbled, while Marti squalled.

"Yes, Madam," said the desk clerk cautiously, the model of efficiency and kind service. "A glass of water, perhaps? Baggage Boy!"

"No, no," I stammered. "There's a truck with no racks and a dark green door. Some wrecking company. Do you know whose it is?"

"Oh," said the clerk, "that's probably the Charlotte Wrecking Company."

"Where are they?" I asked.

"Five miles north of town," he replied.

"That's just what I needed to know. You're a dear! Where's the phone? May I have change for a dollar?"

I called Bill. "Drop whatever you're doing and come right over! I've got a yardful of radiators under my belt!"

We hitched up the chimney and the pipes, the steam and the radiators, the oil burner and the drums, and it all worked! We would have a new heating system.

Oh, praise His name, Andre was marvelous. He carried a half a ton of radiators up and down the stairs without a puff. He brought his fifteen children down from Messina on the wages that he earned from us. About this time, Andre's good friend, Georges, came to work on the farm for Bill. He and Bill became quite friendly.

One day, Bill said, "Hear Andre's got a house that he built for himself up in Messina. Hear it's quite a house." Georges roared with laughter.

"Oui, oui. Andre has 'ouse. She's ver' cold up nort'; thirty degrees below! Andre, he cut young tree in de wood. He has de pole. Nail tin alongside de railroad on de pole. Swing cat t'ru de timbers; no cellar, no window. Bad boys, she tip ovair, and Andre, he nevair get it straight agin. Board of Healt' say 'Clean up'. Andre, he move across de road. Huh!"

"My, my," I said to Bill. "How fortunate we were to find Andre. Canadians like him don't come along every day!"

The steam heat worked, though, and man and boy, we fired her up before the first snowfall. It felt heavenly all through the house.

After the first snow did fall, Bill found himself relying heavily on my background of barefoot dancing. I can practically walk through fire and over stones barefooted. I've almost had to do it in some of my more exotic acts. Consequently, when the furnace would go out at three a.m. on a winter's morning and someone would have to go outdoors and around to the back cellar, Bill would poke me in the back and say, "You go, Dear. You don't have to bother with your shoes and galoshes. Just steel up your feet and go to it!"

Bill has another "cute" trick. When he wants me to do something for him, he says, "You do it, Dear. You're younger than I am." This is accompanied by an admiring look. It was quite awhile before I came to; the carrot dangling before this poor donkey's nose was the vanity of women, and what a carrot that is, too! Bill was very bright sometimes.

When we were sure that the heating system was in working order, we started to unload the bathrooms that were shared. We have had neat couples, but never the twain shall share a bathroom. There's always a slob in the works somewhere. This is always one couple that mops twice a day, and one that washes out stockings and drapes them over the tub. I find myself dashing up twenty-five steps four times a day to see how perfectly awful Jean leaves the bathtub.

"Oh, Dear, I didn't mean for you to scrub it," the informant would say lamely, as I wielded the brush, "I just thought you ought to know about it." So I, who loathes housework, found myself doing janitor service for five renting families. By now, I guess you could say I'm used to it and just chalk it up to human nature.

Fired up by TJ's success with the girls, Andre developed a pretty turn of intellectual wit. One day he gave me a real start. I went up the back stairs to the old servant's quarters, which was now a darling little apartment with four rooms and a bathroom. I pulled open the bathroom door to see if Andre was working and . . . .

"I beg your pardon!" I squawked, as my face turned beet red, to see Andre seated on the toilet.

"Har, har, har," Andre roared. "Fooled you, didn't I! Had my pants on and the seat down. Har, har!"

"Well," I said. "I didn't look closely enough to take in all of the details, but that's not funny. It's sick!"

"Yes, ma'am, Mrs. Carr, ma'am," replied Andre, sounding only half apologetic. Then I found myself sneaking around the corner so I could see the expression on the face of his next victim. I just about laughed myself silly at the next blushing "intruder"!

TJ and Andre set up as big a clamor about the soil pipe situation as they had over the radiators. We found ourselves shushing to a whisper when we even mentioned the stuff. We got a haul once, though, that we heard of through a fortunate event. Someone with priority had placed an order for nine feet of soil pipe with a friend of mine who tipped us off. We bought the old pipe before it was even dug up. Soil pipe was being made right in Medina, ten miles away, but we couldn't get priority, so this was quite an achievement. The manager was very sympathetic, and I got the impression that if the pipe came up missing some morning and the list price was found on the cash register, no one would call the FBI; besides, they'd never find us out here. But, I didn't quite dare. Our family lawyer always told me that he expected to find me in jail someday, anyway, and he was always giving me good advice about how to stay out. I told him that all anyone wants a lawyer for was to get them out of jail when they are in, and I was willing to wait for that day as long as he was.

Andre came up with the idea that we should just cut a hole in the kitchen ceiling and let the overhead bathtub drip, but Doc Draper was a health officer and he wouldn't OK that idea. A foot here, a foot there, eventually we got the soil pipe we needed to connect up the bathrooms. Well, this was something, anyway. With six families and ten children, everyone was rooting for us to get those bathtubs in quickly, before it really got cold outdoors.

We found Andre was of special value as the tenants began to move in. The original door keys were lost and there was no skeleton key that would fit. We were afraid everyone would be locked out of their rooms. Andre was the only man in the area who could file those keys down to fit. He certainly had some peculiar "talents"! We never found where he'd picked them up. Long after he left us, I would drive to wherever he was and say, "Andre, we've got a sick cow and the vet has given up. Can you save it?"

He would always have a remedy: a hot mash, some wild herbs. The Canadians had a knack for it, alright.

Getting the fixtures was as much of a headache as finding the soil pipe. The whole thing wasn't without its silly and melodramatic moments. Someone did actually sidle up to us in a restaurant and hiss out of the corner of his mouth, "Want five bootleg bathtubs?" We never did go the black market route, although some of our stuff may have had a slight tell-tale gray tinge.

TJ and Andre used to get themselves so tangled up in their pipes that Bill would have to come and pry them out. TJ would swear he'd not been drinking. After they got all done, Bill went around and took out about half of the pipes that turned out to be unnecessary. However, the important thing was that the bathtubs worked, and the tenant families were pleased. So, we rubbed our hands with satisfaction.

"You're like Santa Claus to me," said Pauline, our new tenant. "We've always lived with my mother. She doesn't like my husband and tried to tell me how to raise the baby. You're like Santa Claus!"

"I refuse to grow a beard," I replied.

When things simmered down a little, I started to go to the local library for some good books to read. TJ's sister is the librarian. Before you wonder about that, let me tell you that Mary isn't a bit like TJ. Her eyes are blue, but they hide behind glasses. I'm sure that she scrubs her face with Ivory soap and I'm almost sure that she wears white under-things with embroidery and blue ribbons. In short, she's like a muslin doll.

"Mary," I said, looking over the books. "What's good? I'm so tired out from this house racket, I could die. Pick me out a book."

I just didn't have the time or the energy to pore over books. Mary handed me The Lotus and the Wind. It fell open at a well-thumbed paragraph. I read aloud: "He ripped off the sheet at the fearful ecstasy of her cry, 'Robin'. He sprang on her, fierce as a hunter at her shriek. She struggled with him all night, with teeth, nails, and flesh, until, in the first light, she fell back, open-mouthed, bleeding, insensible and triumphant."

I looked at Mary, who was peering over my shoulder. "Oh, my," said Mary admiringly. "How do you find those places so fast?"

Before I was married, I belonged to that staunch little group of gals who went around humming "Anything you can do, I can do better", but not anymore. Not me. Because, the few brains I do possess flatly refuse to work when they come in contact with plumbing, electricity, machinery, and hammers. All of these things were unfamiliar to me before I was married, but since then, my world has been bounded by plumbing, electricity, machinery, and hammers.

After TJ and Andre left, I decided to open up the blocked bathroom sink. All by myself. This would give me something to do. I stopped up the overflow and the kitchen sink, which was on the same line, the bathtub, and the bathtub overflow. I got the plunger and I plunged and I plunged, but I didn't budge a thing. I tried once more. Just once, I struck pay dirt in the shape of a sudden overflow of sewer water, dark and smelly from the pipe. The next thing I knew, it was running all over my kitchen sink full of dishes. Bill finally got his electric drill and cut through the solidified mess of home aids I had poured into the pipes.

About this time, there grew up around the house an informal fan club called "Let's Help Pat". You can bet I didn't start it! It was one of the most delicate periods of my life. Refrigerators that were just mildly out of tune were adjusted and readjusted by enthusiastic laymen. Doors that stuck slightly were taken off of their hinges and then, naturally, wouldn't open at all. True, I was usually responsible, at least for the ideas. Volunteers ran up and down twenty-foot ladders with ten-foot storm windows while I sweated. Finally, our repairmen laid down the law.

"If anyone monkeys once more with that float, I won't come back." The plumber sounded furious and I was good for a whole three days after that. One night, when someone shut the water off completely in the house by turning off the wrong faucet ("Let's try all of these little wheels down here, maybe we can fix it ourselves!"), we hunted and hunted for several hours, inspecting depth of wells, pumps, etc. before we discovered it. Bill took me to one side and put his arm around my shoulder.

"Pat," he said, pleadingly, "couldn't you manage to look a little less pitifully courageous?"

CHAPTER 13

Six Families Need A Lot of Water

Whoever said that "a change of trouble is as good as a vacation" must have had our place in mind, because we had the equivalent of quite a few vacation changes. After Andre and TJ got six bathrooms, six kitchen sinks, and a laundry room hooked up, we found ourselves with all those lovely miles and miles of pipes and only one well. This was something we hadn't bargained on. Of course, we did have two enormous cisterns that caught rainwater as it dripped off the roof into the eave troughs, but the girls took one look at its yellowish color and said, "Oooohh, we don't want to wash in *that!*"

We were undecided. Bill was justly affronted. "Upstaters" are proud of their rainwater: it's softer than any chemically treated water could ever be.

"Dang little dumb clucks!" Bill said. "Don't know enough to appreciate good honest rainwater! Detergents here, synthetics there; somebody ought to get folks a synthetic brain—especially some of the folks around here that I could name!"

When the house was built in the 1840s, there was a storage tank in the cupola of the barn. They pumped all of their available water up there, and gravity took care of the water pressure. But times change. That was when the Squire and his Lady bathed in a 14-karat gold-trimmed iridescent gold luster wash basin and got a bath by the pitcherful. I have the gracefully fluted walnut stand that they used for a towel rack in my living room, which I use for a bookstand. My dear spouse considers it an eyesore; Bill shudders every time he passes it. I showed him a picture of a prize-winning flower arrangement in an antique chamber pot, but he threatened divorce, so I dropped the subject. Since civilization has snatched the towel rack and the chamber pot from their daily use, it takes a heck of a lot more water to achieve the same results. The fields had water standing in puddles where we wanted to plough, but we found ourselves in the uncomfortable position of "water, water everywhere, but not a drop . . . ." in the house! We weren't lacking in pipes, at least. TJ and Andre had left such a maze of pipes in the cellar that we were thinking of looping vines from pipe to pipe and calling it "The Jungle Room".

Instead, Bill came up with a better idea. He put a rotary pump in the well and a plunger in the cistern. However, the rotary ran so constantly that it was always burning out its motor, and the plunger hiccoughed like a drunken machine gun! Poor Herta slept right over that pump. I didn't envy her location in the slightest; and since that was the pump that fed the hot water tank, I was driven into hoping that those who rolled in at two a.m. would go to bed unwashed, if not unshaven. We tried tying the cisterns and the well in together for the laundry room, but if someone forgot and left a faucet on, or just one of the toilets leaked, the pipes would run dry. Period!

We tried putting up some of those impersonal little signs like: Please Conserve the Water, and THIS MEANS YOU! It didn't help a bit. I was always being torn in two directions. Every time that Pauline washed her clothes, for instance, the water went off. Every single time! We began to wonder. One by one, everyone confided in me in the strictest confidence: "You know why, don't you? You know what she does?" I would assume a completely uninformed expression.

"What does she do?" I would ask.

Naturally, just trying to be helpful, they would tell me. It seems that Pauline had had her first baby when she was twenty-seven years old and, since Pauline's husband was a traveling salesman and on the road a great deal of the time, the baby was Pauline's whole universe. And, for the most marvelous baby in the universe, nothing but the best would do. Obviously. Got the picture? In this instance, it meant turning on the faucets, all three of them, full force, and holding the washed diapers under the running water until they were as pure as the driven snow. I'm sure that if I had had a first baby, I would have done the same thing. If only she wouldn't do it when Dottie was trying to get breakfast! No water for the coffee was a little annoying; not to mention the early morning washing, shaving, etc.

Carla, who had just moved in, had been a professional Beauty School Graduate, and she turned on all of the faucets full tilt to rinse her girls' hair until it squeaked. I liked my hair done that way, too. If only she wouldn't do it while her husband, Eddie, was trying to shave! So, you see, there were personality differences here.

I began to get a split personality. I knew just how convenient it was to use the electric heater to dry hair in a hurry, and how diapers could be damp dried in front of the gas oven, but I also had to pay the bills for the gas and the electricity, as well as balance the books, so I was unsure as to what to recommend. The girls would start to confide in me about some little thing they didn't exactly want the "landlord" to know, and then realize with a start that I was the landlord! Finally, I found a way out.

"Look, kids," I said. "You can tell 'Pat' anything—she's a good egg, but don't let 'Mrs. Carr' know. I hear she's a regular old harridan!" This always restored their confidence in me. When the summer drought hit us and the farm pond dried up, the cows had to come up to the barns and the situation got acute. Two or three times a day, the clarion call would echo form the halls and the laundry tubs: "Pat! The water's off!"

At this call to arms, I would crank up Jezebel and go roaring down the lane, bouncing through the woodchuck holes, yelling: "Bill! Bill! The water's off!"

You can imagine what the neighbors thought. I tried going on foot one day, but I had to get right up to him before he heard me.

"Thought it was a little sea gull crying," said Bill, who was mostly deaf. Even Bill could hear Jezebel coming!

"The water's off again!" I'd yell, and toss the torch to him. Leaving the land unturned and the furrow unploughed (albeit with a curse upon his lips), Bill would leap into Jezebel and dive into the fray. He'd speed to the cellar and prime the pump as if he were on an ocean-going vessel, while five females, who had been ready to snatch me bald, would stand around and coo.

"Now, Bill, did Pat take you away from your work just for *that*?" And Bill would grin and say, "OK, girls, now you gotta wash the dishes, then we'll be even—that's fair enough!"

This priming-of-the-pumps was a formula so complicated that I was never allowed to learn it; either that, or else Bill knew darn well how important it made him and he determined that this was a secret that might conceivably be handed down from father to son, but *never* from husband to wife. Oh, that would be unthinkable! Of course, whenever Bill wanted a bath, he just primed the pumps beforehand and ran the pressure way up. He had another secret, too; perhaps he feared I would do the same, if I had the knack. He knew that out in the well house, away from all the pipes, the water came out of the ground cool and pure and thirst-quenching. I caught the dog and him there one hot day guzzling.

When the summer drought kept up for two or three weeks and the water started going off regularly, I began to get a little rattled. It didn't faze Bill a bit; he was able to adjust to any of nature's moods. He would sidle up to one of his favorite tenants and say: "Now, I don't want everyone to know this, but I know that I can trust you. You know where the washing machine is?"

"Yes," the trusted tenant would answer.

"You know where the laundry tubs are?" Bill would continue.

"Yes," the trusted tenant would answer.

"You know where the pipes go in back of the tubs around the corner, and where that straight pipe goes up?"

"Yes."

"Below where the overflow in the cistern is?"

"Got it!" the trusted tenant would reply, making notes, and waiting for Bill to reach the punch line.

"There's a pipe there—put it in myself—with a faucet in the lower third. Get a pan full of water there when there isn't a drop in the pipes."

The trusted tenant, overwhelmed by this display of confidence, would thank Bill profusely and, the next time the water would go off, he would think the matter over, test all of its ramifications, and then, in a moment of supreme decision, would bellow down to me: "Pat, get Bill! The water's off!"

Civilization has certainly softened us up. Once, I believe, somebody did actually end up at that faucet, but by that time, he was so tired, he just barely had the strength to hold the tea kettle under the tap. Instead of turning the tap, he used his last spurt of energy to holler up the stairs: "Pat, get Bill! The water's off!"

The pumps broke down once when Bill was at a Conservation meeting. All I could think of was to send Willie to the neighbors with the ten-gallon milk cans and have him fill them with water and pour it into the cisterns. He set off, but he had a number of farms to visit. It worked all right with the water, but it didn't with Bill. It had taken Willie and the truck all afternoon to do the hauling.

"Next time," said Bill, "just dump Coca-Cola into the tubs—it's a lot cheaper."

Eventually, even Bill admitted that six families with ten "little ones" needed more water. Lots of water. Probably a lot more than we had.

So, we went to the Lanz Brothers to locate the site and drill the new well. One brother has the "gift" of divining. He takes an elbow-length peach branch, shaped like an inverted "V", and walks with an end of the "V" in each hand until the tip of the "V" points to the ground. "There it is," he says, matter-of-factly. "There's your underground stream." Nine times out of ten, he's right. Our New York City friends, who without question use the daily miracle of water from White Plains, thirty miles away, look at this other "miracle" with skeptical eyes and say "Do you believe in that stuff?"

I don't know. The truth is that I've seen it work a good many times, and that's made me something of a believer. In this hard-bitten, realistic community, where people are careful about their money, everybody pays the Lanz Brothers a nice sum to find their wells. I've seen the peach branch bend when Mr. Lanz holds it, and I know that there's no monkey business because it won't do it for me.

The ideal site for our new well was at the intersection of two underground streams, so we had a good chance. The Lanz Brothers were booked up weeks in advance, but they agreed to help us. No red-blooded male could withstand the sight of five beautiful young mothers and ten beautiful, but dirty, children. Since the Lanz Brothers were both red-blooded males, it was a foregone conclusion: they rearranged their schedule. I also pointed out to the elder Mr. Lanz, who was a family man himself, that if those diapers didn't get rinsed out right away . . . , well, I could just tell he understood.

They came the next week, asking only that the beautiful young mothers be scattered on the lawn in sun suits and admiring attitudes. The drilling began. Pretty soon I saw what the damage would be. The truck dug ruts in the lawn, they sawed off some limbs of the maple tree that grew outside my window so that the drill could go straight up in the trees, and they dredged up gobs of mud that ran all over the grass. However, the babies loved the noise and their mamas loved the excuse to drop their housework. Well-drillers work by the foot. Either they find water, or you run out of money. Either way, the deal is declared a draw. You hate to quit once you've started. I stood by with my checkbook in one hand and my hopes still high. The workmen stared at the sky, the drill, and the sun suits. All the while the drill went deeper and deeper into our little cash resources. Water at twenty-five feet? No. Fifty feet? No. Seventy-five feet? Nothing. Was it a desert we lived in? Shale, sledge, rock, and an unknown black substance that no one had ever seen before (Bill tried to rent a Geiger counter and screamed "Eureka" for awhile), but no water. It was like a day at the races. Go home broke or make one last bet? At 100 feet, Bill and I flipped a coin. At 120 feet, the long shot came in. She came in slow and trickling, but she came in wet. We acted like we'd hit oil!

We bought a third pump and put that one under the ground floor bedroom on the east side. It gave late sleepers the impression that a mess of hornets was moving in right under their pillows. When that apartment was vacant and we showed it to prospective tenants, the girls used to stop using the water so that the pump wouldn't kick in, otherwise we'd never rent the place. Later they would say to the startled newcomer "Didn't you hear it before you moved in?" I kept a spare bottle of aspirin for these cases.

Since this well was 120-feet deep, it was a trifle salty, so the girls all ganged up on Bill and said "Ooohh, we don't want to drink that!"

Bill just frowned good-naturedly. "Wal-l, now," he would drawl, "what you miss is the flavor of that canal water they drink in town. You just pour a bottle of your scrubbing disinfectant in it and catch some of those little minnows to put in there, and you'll have 'good' tasting water to drink—just like the kind you're used to!"

"Ooohhh, Bill," the girls would say in unison.

The state geologist thought that if we went down fifty feet farther, we might strike natural gas, but we were a little afraid. What would we do with natural gas? Between that and the steam in the house . . . besides, we were now broke.

"Wal-l, now," said Bill, "there really is enough water in the wells, but we can't pump it out fast enough for everybody to do everything at the same time. If everybody would just be sensible . . ."

"You're pretty optimistic," I replied. "When did you ever find a houseful of women to be sensible?"

"No reason they couldn't be!" Bill said triumphantly. "Talk to them. Make out a schedule. Easy! You can do it!"

"Yep," I replied. "It's easy and I can do it. Phooey! I could just see Carla washing her hair at ten a.m., Herta washing dishes at noon, Pauline washing diapers at one p.m., Katie taking her shower at two p.m., and me galloping up and down the stairs with a stopwatch! 'OK', I would be yelling. 'Change sides and turn off the faucets.'"

I'd as soon think of ringing the bell for curfew at five a.m.! Better not mention it lest Bill come out in favor of it!

Bill retorted, "If we could just get by until the plowing was done!"

So, I tried. The girls said, "Well, of course, if it would help Bill!"

Carla drew the nine a.m. spot so she could do her hair. Pauline could do her laundry at ten a.m. Judy could bathe the baby at one p.m. Herta could do her dishes at two p.m. Katie could shower before the men got home from work at four p.m. No one mentioned buying a whistle, and of course, Bill and I could go dirty. We got so used to saving the hot water for the tenants that we used to go to a hotel on weekends and reserve a room with two bathrooms. Then we'd scrub down and both feel clean for the first time all week.

To return to where I was before I wandered off to a hotel to take a bath, we agreed on a schedule. Famous last words. We should have known better. Carla had a date one evening and she had to wash her hair before she went out. Pauline ran out of diapers before it was her scheduled time to wash them. Katie got back late from her shopping and missed her bath. And Eddie—good old Eddie—took the afternoon off and came home to get a shower; he probably didn't even know about the schedule!

So, each person in his or her own little bathroom, in his or her own inimitable way, turned the faucets on full tilt. Five minutes later I dashed out of my own bathroom yelling for Bill. "Honey! Come quickly! The water's off!" It was the same old familiar cry.

I was all dewy-eyed with gratitude when Clarence drew me to one side on day and said confidentially: "Now, Pat, you know nobody in this house has been actually hurt by the lack of water this summer. Now, seriously, have they? I know the girls complain about it, but you don't take that seriously, do you? They're just building up trifles, like women do. But, when you come right down to it, there's never been any actual hardship now has there?"

I felt myself drawn to Clarence by a bond of understanding. He had formerly owned property. He knew all about taxes, depreciation, and interest on mortgages. He was quite knowledgeable about financial matters. He had had money; he still had charm, although, along with his charm, he was one of the few men I have ever known who could raise hell in a stylized fashion. He should have lived in the "Days of Old" when men were bold, although I can't quite visualize Clarence in armor on a prancing horse. I would cast him more as, say, Keeper of the Privy Purse. He usually had a faintly indignant expression. It was easy to see him as a child explaining to his mother that he was *not* involved in the present mishap; someone else had done it. But, on certain subjects, he was a fountain of logic. On this occasion, Clarence and I were discussing the water.

"Why, I agree with you, Clarence," I said. "I don't believe there's been any downright serious inconvenience." Fine for me to say that, but there was some truth in it. Too late I remembered the Chinese custom of belittling our virtues lest the gods be jealous. Believe me, the next time I'm going to depreciate those wells right down to zero, for that was the day of "The Famous Shower".

Clarence had an important engagement that evening and he had Katie lay out his clothes while he took a shower. He was very excited about the upcoming event. Clarence was fastidious anyway, but this was a hot summer day and he outdid himself. Sportsman perfume, shaving lotion, discreetly scented soap. Ah! The soap. Straight from Santa Claus, firm, easily lathered, the type that hands around one's neck for convenience in the shower. How he was enjoying his rub-a-dub-dub! Slippery and shining, full of love for his fellow man, and considerations for Bill—poor, overworked Bill—Clarence turned off the faucets while he lathered. He covered his face, his ears, his legs, his arms; every square inch of himself. His skin tingled pleasantly and his eyes glowed. Now for the rinse.

At this point, blessedly, with no commercial between scenes, we switch to the barns. It was five p.m. Forty thirsty cows filed in from the pasture and lined up at the drinking fountains. The fountains that had A-1 priority on the wells. Of this, Clarence was unaware. For him, all was serene. Humming happily, he turned the faucet marked "cold" and, out in the barns, the first line of cows was drinking deeply.

Humming less happily, Clarence turned the hand marked "hot" while, out in the barns, the second line of cows took the pressure down.

Buzzing like a hornet, Clarence turned both of the handles at once, while out in the milk house, Don turned the water into the cooler.

Clarence was licked. "Katie!" he yelled into the living room. "Bring me the alcohol."

Now Katie was not one to jump at her master's voice at the best of times, and just then she had her ear glued to the wall listening enthralled to the perfectly lovely quarrel going on next door. She was not about to be disturbed.

"I will not go to your mother's again this Sunday for dinner!" Katie heard through the partition. Breathlessly, she strained to pick up the reply. She was listening to Clarence with only half of her other ear and, besides, she didn't know what was going on with the water.

"I'm busy!" she yelled back, "and if you're mixing a drink, I'm thirsty, too!"

"The *rubbing* alcohol, you fish!" snapped Clarence. "The water's gone off and I'm all soapy! Hurry up, Katie!" he bellowed, as the soap began to dry. "It's starting to itch!"

"My, my, my," clucked Katie. "I thought they taught you better in the Army. I've got a little tube of that blue stuff hidden on the bottom shelf."

That did it! Clarence's Gallic temper exploded. All of Gaul was in three parts. He spoke to that shower in three languages and longed for a fourth one. I could hear him clear up in the attic, and almost fell down the stairs. I'd never heard such a variety of cuss words.

"What's up?" I asked, fearfully.

"Oh, nothing much," said Katie calmly. "Just a little water shortage. But then," she went on, raising her voice, "no one has ever been seriously inconvenienced by the lack of water in this house, have they?" There was the sound of a dish being smashed next door. Katie's ears perked up noticeably.

"Dear me," said Katie, loping back to her vantage point. "Carla and Eddie are really mad at each other. I don't want to miss a word of it! Sit down, Dear, and mix yourself a drink."

"I'd love to," I said.

Suddenly Katie was shocked to the roots of her hair. The acoustics were wonderful.

"Eddie!" we heard Carla say. "You know perfectly well that Katie is standing with her ear glued to that wall, drinking in every word we say!"

"I'll bet she's drinking, all right," said Eddie. "If that old battle axe . . ."

By the sound of the hassle, Carla had dragged him into their front room and slammed the door. Now some other tenant would pick up the quarrel.

"Oh dear," said Katie regretfully. "It's such a hot day, too."

"Katie," I said thoughtfully, now that we could hear Clarence again. "If Clarence bursts a blood vessel in there, Bill and I could be hanged for murder. There's not a jury in the world that would acquit us."

"Nonsense," said Katie cheerily. "They don't hang people for trifles. Just be sure to get me on the jury," she added. "I saw the best looking dress . . ."

With a roar like the breaking of the sound barrier, Clarence burst into the room. He was surrounded by a large Turkish towel marked "HERS", and he was mad. There was foam all over his chest.

"Clarence," said Katie pettishly, "stop dribbling lather on Pat's carpets and take off my towel! Get your own—you know where it is."

"With pleasure!" said Clarence, loosening his grip.

"Illegal!" I yipped. "Unarmed non-combatant present."

The Geneva Code worked and we blotted him into a chair, where he squirmed restlessly.

"Oh, my God! What I've been through! If I ever . . . . Pat, dear, so glad you dropped in. Have a drink . . . Again, try to keep clean in this . . . is this what the Chinese mean by the water torture? Katie! No soda! You know, honestly, it's the damnedest feeling. It's just positively frustrating! There just . . . How is Bill coming with his plowing? . . . is nothing like it. I'm at a loss for words."

"Funny," said Katie, dreamily, looking into the bottom of her glass, "how upset people get over trifles; like to build mountains out of . . ."

"Katherine!" said Clarence, choking, "one more ridiculous half-baked statement like that out of you, and I shall cancel my life insurance, or else make some redhead the beneficiary."

"In that case," said Katie cheerily, "I can't afford to let you strangle. At least you're worth something to me alive!"

And off she went to the kitchen, where she melted down a few ice cubes. Between that and a bottle of hair tonic, Clarence made do. We sandpapered a few of the toughest spots. He looked really natural when we got him dressed, except that he was a sort of fuchsia that clashed with his necktie. Normally Clarence likes to have his colors blend, but under the circumstances, he was lucky to be alive.

The next day Bill said to me: "Honey, I've been thinking. Don't you think we ought to have another well?"

I said "I guess so."

Lanz Brothers' peach branch found another spot just twenty feet from our original well, and they went down twenty-five feet, and it cost us $75. They got a stream that keeps fifty livestock and 240 acres of land as well as six families just swimming in water. We can't pump it dry!

"You know, I kinda miss priming those pumps," Bill said, with a sentimental note in his voice.

"You big oaf!" I replied.

CHAPTER 14

Country Livestock Auctions

Bill drove me over to Canandaigua to see the lake, and it was darn cold coming home. The heater was plugged up on my side for some reason, and I had a crack in the window. As usual, my hands were pale blue—always one of my favorite colors.

"Oh boy, I'd love to be in Florida right now!" I muttered, "In a sun suit."

Bill pulled down his long-sleeved underwear, which he wore under his winter shirt and fur-lined winter coat. I could see that he was wearing woolen socks and lamb's wool gloves; not that he needed them, as he had the working side of the car's heater.

"If you'd just stop dressing as though you were in Florida and put on some real clothes, you wouldn't want to be there so badly," he said. "You're a married woman now, Pat. You can afford to wear long-legged underwear."

"Yuck!" I said.

"Look at that tree!" Bill cried. "It's all sheeted with ice! By gol, that is pretty!"

"It would be twice as nice if it weren't so cold. Don't try to distract me, I'm cold. I can't unbend my fingers or straighten out my toes!" I answered.

"Poor little thing," replied Bill, unfeelingly, as he drove into a driveway. "Come on, I'll buy you a cup of coffee in here and you can get warmed up."

"Okay, Sport," I agreed.

We had arrived at a large barn sprawled over half an acre of land. Trucks were parked haphazardly in front of it and up and down both sides of the road. I saw a state trooper's car drive through.

"Livestock auction," said Bill. "We can get hot coffee upstairs."

He pulled open a small door and a hot, stinking clamorous din smacked me in the face. I should have been ready for it, but it was so unexpected that I pulled back.

"Don't stand in the doorway," Bill said. "Lets the cold air in!"

We climbed the steep wooden steps to the hayloft. I walked to the edge and peered over the rail. There was a semi-circle of tiers of wooden benches that faced a central ring and a high wooden desk behind which stood the auctioneer. The electric light bulbs screwed into the ceiling glared like the floodlight that beats down on an empty stage after rehearsals are over and the cast has gone home.

There was an air of a theater-in-the-round about the whole place. On the first two or three tiers sat men in business suits. They had pencils and notebooks, and the auctioneers called them differentially by their first names. They were fat and jowly and I got the impression they were sort of V.I.P.s. Above them, solidly packed in row up on row, almost to the ceiling, were the farmers. They wore blue jeans and blue frocks; they had broad heavy-muscled shoulders and weather-beaten faces. Their faces were deep-lined but direct looking. Farmers lock horns with nature, not with each other. Here they were all comrades.

The fumes from the oil heater were heavy, and the stench from the chickens was dreadful. A door to the left of the auctioneer opened and two men shoved and prodded a young steer that had just been weighed into the spotlight. The steer was stunned for a moment by the glare of the lights and the smell of men all around him. He tried to turn and make a break for it. The men in the front rows drew back a little, but the two men in the ring took over heading off the steer with canes that are the badge of cattle drivers. They tried to tucker him out a little.

"Now there's a fine steer," said the auctioneer, with practiced heartiness. "Who'll give me $75? $65? He's a nice one, boys, he's a nice one! Set your own price. $50? Thank you. "$60? Think I would, boys, he's a nice one. What do ya' say?"

The farmers leaned forward, looking down at the ring. Some of them were so intent, they leaned their elbows on their knees and sat with their faces propped on their hands so they could see better. Others almost toppled off of their benches. One of these men owned that steer. What would it sell for? The others knew that the price of this steer would set the price for their own stock.

"Let's go in back," said Bill. "I want to see what they have."

We walked out on a long narrow passageway, like an overhead catwalk, over the animal pens. Steers were crowded into pens so tightly together that they couldn't move. Good milk cows were treated little better. They were put in separate stanchions so that the veterinarian could examine them. We walked around examining the livestock. Pen after pen held piglets and calves. Sheep were bunched in together next to horrid old sows. A three-hundred-pound sow is a most repulsive creature!

While we stood there, a truck backed up to the platform and let down its tailgate. Squealing, terrified pigs were beaten on their snouts with small whips and shoved down the steep runway until they bottlenecked at the bottom. One stubborn old hog was half hauled/half kicked. The little pigs were picked up by one leg and held squealing while the auctioneer's assistant came up and clipped an identification tag in each one's ear. They would be on the auction block in no time at all.

"I thought they abolished the slave market," I muttered.

Bill gave me a dirty look. "I know, I know," I said. "I like steak as much as you do. Rare. And I'm fond of bacon and pork chops. Okay!"

The boy who handled the cows was having a hard time. He had to get the cows up to the door at just the second it opened and into the weighing room, so that the auction could move right along. Some of the cows were in heat and they would gang up and try to ride each other. The ensuing muddle had the lad at his wit's end.

"Come on, now, Girls," he would urge. "Stop giving me a hard time! Behave yourselves. Dammit! Come on now!"

The boy driving the pigs in was using his cane at a great rate. Even when the pigs were going in the right direction, he would beat them. I thought this especially vicious. I nabbed the veterinarian when he went by.

"Look," I said diffidently. "I know its business, but there's one boy with a cane . . ."

"Beating the hogs," he finished. "I know just who you mean. I'll fix that right now. And," he added over his shoulder, "it lowers the value of the hogs; it marks up the meat!"

I just stood there muttering. The squealing, mooing, bleating, and squawking was all mixed up with the yells of the cattle boys and the chant of the auctioneer. "Two and a quarter, two and a quarter, now a half. Two and a half. SOLD!"

And another live animal was shunted out of the ring to the slaughter. The door would open and another hapless creature would step into the spotlight.

I didn't know whether to write a new American folksong or to throw up my dinner. I find that being a farmer's wife has made me pretty hard-boiled about the theater-going tastes. When I hit Broadway, I head for a musical, just like those tired businessmen. By the third act of a "drammer", I begin to feel that the cardboard shows through. Farming is pretty, well, REAL.

"Nothing I want back here," Bill said. "Let's go have that coffee."

We went back to the hayloft. There was a wooden plank with a hot plate, an old-fashioned coffee urn; and a pleasant, plump woman wearing an old-fashioned apron, who was in charge. There was no nonsense about being seated comfortably while you ate. You stood up. The coffee was welcome after the cold, but my stomach was still a bit queasy from watching the auction.

"Sandwich?" asked Bill.

I sniffed the combined odors of manure and chickens.

"No thanks," I replied, warily.

"Well, now you know where it is," said Bill on the way home. "You can come over here and buy some pigs for me next week."

"Honestly? You'd really trust me to buy them all by myself?"

"Why not?" asked Bill. "We're partners, aren't we?"

"My, my, my," I said to myself. "You're in, Kid! You're in!"

I don't know how good of a bidder I would be, I thought, but I've always loved little pigs. They're one of the only things on a farm that I can look down on instead of up to. When they're really little and still have spotted skin, I want to take them in the house and put them on the mantel piece. All they need is a slot for the pennies to go into. It seems there is a little select coterie of people who feel that little pigs are darling.

We rented an apartment once to a man who said, "As long as you've got little pigs, I'll take it. My wife won't care what the house looks like as long as you've got little pigs around."

I could tell that he was a man after my own heart. Little pigs that are healthy are as round and plump as wedding rings. Their tails curl up and they talk with their ears. They are the most adorable little creatures, really. They are very choice about their ribs, and if you pick them up, they'll squeal like hell until you put them down again.

We once had four pigs whose mother died in childbirth. It was a highly scandalous affair and there was much gossip about it in pig circles. She was wooed and won by a stalwart boar and she started a family. Then she got flighty and forgot she was a settled matron, and off she went with a second boyfriend and got pregnant again! When the first batch was ready to be born, the second batch was on the way. By the time the second batch was born, the first were already dead, and pretty soon the mother was, too. Doc said he'd swear to it if I wanted to send it to "True Stories". I've been thinking about it, but I don't know if they accept animal stories.

We couldn't bear to lose the piglets of the second batch, so Bill made a cross bar with four holes in it and stuck four baby bottles with nipples on them through the holes. People came from all up and down the road to see those four piglets guzzling simultaneously. They *were* cute, at that.

We had a lot of little pig waifs. We had an orphaned pig that we raised in the house (thanks to washable tile flooring). He'd get hungry at two a.m., climb out of his box, and come trotting into the bedroom. Bill got so he could haul the baby bottle out from under his pillow and trail it on the floor without ever opening his eyes. One night Salami wriggled his way into the sleeve of a coat that had fallen on the floor. The more he shoved, the more he got entangled. It was like trying to drive through a tunnel in a nightmare. "Oink! Oink! Oink!" cried Salami, in a dreadful tremor. He was all at sea. Unfortunately, Salami didn't live long. When he found out what *he* was and what salami was made from, the shock killed him!

"Bring back a good bunch of shoats!" said Bill, as he started me off to the auction. (Shoats are small pigs, around seventy-five pounds.) I had a calf in the trunk all wrapped up in a burlap bag except for his head. There is something very defenseless-looking about a calf that's all wrapped up but his head—like a baby in a blanket. In fact, people often mistake it for just that.

The auction was crowded that day. I looked over the pens well as I was awfully anxious to knock Bill's eye out with my superlative cunning. I wanted him to respect my auction sense, so I was asking everybody's advice. I caught sight of Frank Dickson in the crowd and I pushed my way over to him.

"Hi, Frank," I said. "Any good shoats here today?"

"Yep," Frank replied. "A good bunch back in pen three."

I went back and looked into pen three.

"Gosh, Frank," I reported. "They don't look too hot to me. Don't you think I'd be better off bidding on these?"

Just then there was a change in barkers and Harold said into the microphone, "This is a nice lot, Mrs. Carr. Just look at these shoats! Better take 'em! Stand aside there so Mrs. Carr can see these shoats."

I was thrilled. It was much more exciting than being recognized by a head waiter! Besides, these pigs looked great. I nudged Frank.

"No," he said firmly. "Wait for the others."

They started at $12. Bill had told me to spend no more than $15.00.

"$13!" I bid.

"$14!" someone else yelled.

"$15!" from someone else.

"Frank," I whispered, "how high shall I go?"

"Stay in there," he replied. "Them are good pigs."

Frank used to work for Bill and Bill often said Frank was just like a brother. He certainly must know pigs by now, and he was a good farmer.

"$16!"

"$17!"

"Bill will be mad at me," I said.

"No, he won't," insisted Frank. "Them are good pigs. They'll weigh eighty pounds each."

"$17.50!"

"$18!"

"SOLD! To Mrs. William Carr for $18."

There were ten of them. Jimmy took the truck over after them the next day. They didn't look nearly so fat out of the ring, and they moved a little stiff-leggedly. I was a bit hesitant about calling Bill out to see them, but I finally got up the courage.

"My Gol!" Bill said. "I trusted you!"

"Well," I said, sniffling, "Frank Dickson picked them out. He said they'd probably weight eighty pounds."

"Sixty, if they weigh a pound!" Bill said. "Call Doc."

I was so deflated that both men worked hard to restore my confidence. Doc gave the pigs shots. Bill gave them antibiotics. I gave them pep talks and silently vowed never to trust Frank Dickson again.

Harold came around a few days later to see if we had anything to send to the auction.

"How did them pigs make out, Pat?" he asked.

"Don't mention it," I answered.

"Well, are these the ones? By Godfrey, they pulled out of that better than I ever thought they would."

"One died," said Bill, "but the others are coming along."

Harold shook his head. "You know when Frank Dickson brought those pigs in to be sold, he said . . ."

"When who what?!" Bill yelled, adjusting his hearing aid.

"Why, when Frank Dickson brought them pigs in to be sold, he said all they needed was a little care and . . . what's the matter, Bill?"

Bill was laughing until the tears were running down his cheeks.

"City slicker!" he said to me.

I guess I'd learned my lesson, or so thought Bill. My next buying commission was the same: more shoats. This time I asked the opinion of the stranger who stood next to me. I had drunk the bitter tea of General Yen and I was done with friends' advice.

"Nice shoats," I remarked, and I nodded to the auctioneer.

"Yep," the man replied. "Them are good thrifty shoats. Fatten up in a hurry."

The auctioneer looked at me and I nodded. My bid was in.

The man continued, "Won't have to spend much money gettin' them animals ready for the market. Thrifty, clean, purdy, too. Like a cross-breed myself, gain faster."

I nodded to the auctioneer.

"Never go wrong with a spotted pig; seen these when they come in."

"SOLD!" said Harold, "to Mrs. William Carr for $15!"

"Dammit!" my neighbor exploded. "I wanted to bid on them pigs myself!"

He spoke so loud everybody heard, and Harold laughed right into the microphone.

"So busy talking to Mrs. Carr he let her bid those pigs right out from under him," he said.

Everybody roared. I was mortified. Well, at least I wouldn't be thought of as a city slicker anymore!

By this time I was practically commuting back and forth to the auction and the men got used to seeing me there. At first I was the only woman bidding in the whole place, but now all of the women with eggs to sell go there, primarily to have the fun of watching them get sold. They'll probably put on my tombstone: "First Female to Bid at Livestock Auctions"!

Bill sent me over one day to buy a boar. Some of his pigs were getting big enough to breed, so he wanted a good, strong, healthy, aggressive male to breed with them. I figured before I asked anyone, I would have a good look for myself. I went around peering into the pens, but without much luck. I knew what I had to look for, all right, but the pigs were all lying down.

"Hey, Tony," I yelled over to a neighbor of ours. "Any young up and coming boars in today?"

I could hear Tony muttering to John, "Thought Bill sold off his pigs as fast as they growed. Told me he wasn't goin' to breed another sow."

I could catch John's reply, too. "She's sure been looking 'em over."

Pigs are the worst thing on the farm to keep at home. A pig can get the size of a full-grown collie dog and will go through a hole in a fence the size of a teacup. God only knows how the rascals do it, especially if your neighbor doesn't think too highly of your fences. The Martins live just to the north of us and they played host to our wandering pigs once too often. Then they decided that they'd had enough.

"Godam it!" roared Jack Martin over the phone. "If you don't come over and get 'em tonight, I'll take 'em to Buffalo myself in the morning for slaughter. I've bed them all summer, so I might as well deliver them and collect the check!"

He hung up in my ear. "Darned old blow hard," I said to Bill. "I'm so embarrassed. You'd think we'd planned to board them out."

Later that afternoon Bill was dynamiting. He wanted to blow some tree stumps out so he'd gotten a permit and bought ten sticks of dynamite, which he stored in the work shed. I got six gray hairs every time I passed the place for fear that some child would get to them.

A neighbor told me "I keep mine in the oven to keep the moisture off of them. Don't worry, they won't go off. My wife sure gave me hell, though, when she opened up the oven door and found out she didn't have room for her pies. You know, Bill," he went on, "those sticks might sweat a little at that in this hot weather. Maybe you could use a hand. C'mon down and I'll help you set them off."

I went along to watch. The roar almost knocked me on my ear. "Very satisfactory show," I told Bill, who was watching the proceedings distractedly.

While we stood there waiting for the dust to settle, Jack Martin came loping over the hill madder than a wet hen.

"Oh, Dear," I sighed to Bill. "What's wrong now? It can't be the pigs again. None of them have gotten loose lately."

Jack ran up to Bill. "Did you set that stuff off?" he demanded.

"Why, yes," said Bill.

"You got a license to use it?"

"Sure," said Bill, digging into his pocket and fishing out the permit. "Why? What's wrong?"

"What's wrong?" roared Jack. "What's wrong he asks. I'll tell you what's wrong. Here I am, setting in my own kitchen, minding my own business, with a can of beer just nicely up to my lips, and you set off that godam dynamite! I jumped so that godam beer went all over the place! Everywhere but in my mouth, that is. Whaddya mean shooting me out from under my beer?"

As the country auction idea caught on, every large barn in the county ran an auction night. Pretty soon we could go to used car auctions, used machinery auctions, and several of us were waiting for a used husbands auction. Among the other advertised auctions was a horse auction, with each and every animal there to be sold. Bill still owned a western saddle horse that nobody every rode. She was a nice little mare that he had paid $400 for.

"Send her over to that auction," I told Bill.

"I've been offered $150 for her," he objected.

"Well, that's no problem," I replied. "Set that value on her."

"Guess I'll take mine, too," said our neighbor Don.

No matter what we do, it seems as though there is always someone who says "Me, too!"

"How much do you think she's worth?" I asked.

Don scratched his head. "Lucky if I get sixty bucks for her."

The auction is a messy affair. No system. While Don's horse was in the ring, I crawled through the door behind the auctioneer. I wanted to have a ringside seat, for one thing.

"The next horse is bid at $150," I hissed.

The auctioneer immediately bellowed, "I'm bid $150 on this horse. Best one at the auction!"

"No! No!" I yelped. "The *next* one!" But I was lost in the din. The fanciers ran it up to $200. Don was delighted.

Bill's horse came in. He was probably expecting at least $400 by now.

"What am I bid?" asked the auctioneer limply. "Name your own price." She went for $100! Don looked at his check and Bill looked at his.

"Just goes to show you," Bill said. "The hen that crows the loudest lays the fewest eggs."

CHAPTER 15

Tomato Season

After weeks of poring over blueprints and mortgage rates and conferring with real estate salesmen, Carla and Eddie and their new baby, Jenny, moved into a home of their own. We parted with firm commitments to keep in touch.

"Now remember," I said sternly, "I shall expect a letter from little Jenny when she's three!"

"Oh, my gol," Bill said, shaking his head.

"Girls are smart!" I informed him. "Now, if she had been a boy . . . ."

Without the baby to drool over, I had more spare time and I was hell-bent to know the farm at gut level, so when Bill remarked one morning at breakfast (our usual frugal repast consisted of a pitcher of freshly squeezed orange juice, oatmeal cooked in a double boiler, bacon, eggs, toast, fried cakes—not doughnuts—a pitcher of fresh cream, warm milk from the morning's milking, and a hunk of last night's mincemeat pie), "Honey, I'd figgered to transplant the tomatoes today and I'm short of help. Think you could ride the transplanter?"

"Well . . . ," I started to answer dubiously, "I've never done it before."

"Easy!" Bill said flatly. "Child of four could do it."

According to Bill, a "child of four" could do just about anything but run for President of the United States, and I expect any day now there will be a write-in "Youth Ticket". Darned Whiz Kids!

"Well, OK," I said, biting the bullet, and we rode down the lane.

179

I had never seen a transplanter, let alone ride one. Bill drove me to the edge of the field, remarked that Willie would show me what to do, mumbled that he had a field to plow, and left me stranded—the louse! I surveyed the terrain. The transplanter, or setter, was bolted onto the back of the tractor. Built like a lawn chair with the legs cut off short, it was mounted on small rubber wheels about six inches off of the ground. It was made from a solid piece of tin. I was supposed to sit on this thing and ride with my legs stretched out in front of me over the stones and the potholes in the field. Talk about medieval torture tools! Obviously, it had been designed by a chiropractor or a liniment manufacturer with an eye to the "Main Chance". There was a footrest (a bar at the end of the longest part) to use as a brace when going over a bump, but it must have been designed for a giant as I couldn't touch it with my toes. I longed for a cushion, but this luxury was frowned upon by the pros. "Two candles," I promised St. Cecelia, "if I get out of this one alive!"

Bolted to the side of my seat and less than an arm's length away was another seat and on it sat the Other Woman, my working partner. She was middle-aged and grim-faced, and hell-bent on doing her job.

Willie put a heavy box on my lap full of freshly pulled plants with clumps of dirt sticking to their roots. "See them little plows?" he asked, pointing to a set of plows scaled down to doll's house size and fastened alongside of my seat. "Them plows digs a trench. Y'all grabs a plant wif yo lef' han', gives it to yo right han' wif the stem down, an' when yuh hears a 'click' an' the hose squirts water in the trench [there was a water tank strapped onto the tractor], yuh sets the plant up straight in the groun' an' yuh lets go quick or the packin' wheels that firms up the dirt aroun' the plant'll go righ' ovuh yo han' an' squeeze yo fingers off."

All this in the space of thirty seconds.

"Pretend it's a dance routine," I said to myself. "Grab with the left, hand to the right, set, release, kick!" Now, if I could just pick up the beat!

Willie started the tractor and away we lurched. I grabbed a plant, spattered dirt in my face, jerked up my knees and WHUMP! The box of plants tipped over and landed bottom-side up on the ground with the plants going every which way.

"Whoa!" I yelled.

Willie jumped off of the tractor, picked up the plants, and reassembled me. The Other Woman never opened her mouth, but her thoughts sizzled in the air.

"Ready now?" Willie called.

"Ready!" I yelled, with fingers crossed.

Grab with the left, hand to the right, set, release, kick!

"Click!" went the water while I was still in midair.

"Click!" I missed the beat. Frantically I tried to catch up.

"Click! Click! Click!"

I threw my hands up and screamed. And that damned Other Woman reached over and set both rows: hers with her right hand and mine with her left hand. There is no justice! When we got to the end of the row, she remarked acidly: "Must be nice to be the boss's wife and have other people do your work for you."

Wow! I had never been so thoroughly cut down to size in my life. Not even in show business, when I was accused of having two left feet! Leaving me in shreds, she flounced off to get a drink of water.

"Ne'er min'," Willie consoled me. "She so mean, she cain't stand her own self! Duz you miss one, fergit it."

"If I could just brace myself against that bar," I wailed. "I flop all over the place!"

Willie broke up an old crate and made a new footrest custom-sized for me, and it helped. A little. Off we went on the return trip. This time I missed only half of the "clicks" and the Other Woman sniffed only half as loud. Finally (Thank you, St. Cecelia!), I caught the beat. One, two . . . PLANT! One, two . . . PLANT! Easy—once you knew how. By the time Bill came to pick me up, my rows were standing up as straight and proud as the Other Woman's, and she even smiled when she said "Good night."

"See?" Bill said smugly. "Told you it was easy. Why a . . . ."

I finished for him: "Child of four could do it. Darling, you have no idea how it bolsters my ego to know that I can meet a fout-year-old on an equal footing."

I uncranked my spine an inch at a time. I would probably be a hunchback for life! I tried to remember which liniment I had used when I was working at acrobatics dancing. I wobbled when I went to the truck, but I had worked. And I had shut up that Other Woman permanently.

Bill put me on the "Weed Detail" next, but that was a lost cause. No matter how carefully I swiped at a "weed", it was always a "plant" that I chopped out; and the name of the game was "Keep the Plant".

"Well," Bill suggested delicately, "you're such a good con artist, I'll put you to work to rustle up some more hired hands."

Getting help on the farm when you needed it was like trying to win the Irish Sweepstakes, and for the same reason: a lot of people are gunning for the same thing. There are long arid spells between the time that the last cultivation is finished and the last hoe is laid down, and that long awaiting time is when the tomatoes ripen and you need help to pick them when they're ready. During this in-between time, carloads of men drive up and the crew leader knocks on the door and begs for work for his men. All you can say is: "When we start to pick . . . ." But, almost without warning, the days grow warm and the sun shines and Presto! There are the tomatoes in all of their luscious ruby red glory! Then where are the pickers? Why, they're working for someone else by now because when our tomatoes turn red, every other field turns red and all of the farmers are screaming for help to pick them. Farmers who are Elders in the church and upright citizens will steal help without a quiver. I would have a crew lined up to start early the next morning, I would think, but then no one would show up. I'd start down the road hunting down my crew and they would be waving gaily from the field of the neighboring farmer, who had offered them a penny more a basket than I was paying. Good old supply and demand. The crunch was on.

I scoured back lanes and I followed every lead. I found one man living in a chicken coop; literally. The walls had been whitewashed and the outside covered with tar paper, but there was no question as to who (or what) the previous occupants had been. The man carried water from the house and went behind the barn when nature called, but he was healthy and he wanted to work.

Then there was the "Fresh Meat Market" in the city. On a corner, near the employment office in the city, men gathered each day hoping for farm jobs. These were men who wanted a day's work for food, rent, a drink, or even just a chance to spend a day in the country, some of them being on vacation from their office jobs.

But the supply of help was unpredictable. If it turned cold or looked like rain, the men just didn't show up. I saw a neighboring farmer on our road one morning driving a passenger bus. "Hey! What gives?" I called out.

"I expected to pick up forty men at the 'Meat Market' this morning. I rented this bus, got up at four a.m., got to the city by five a.m. and only four men showed up! Four men! And I promised to load a tractor trailer with a hundred hampers of picked tomatoes by tonight! What in hell do I do now?"

"Beats me!" I said cheerily, and drove on. Tomorrow we might be in the same fix! I was headed for the dilapidated old house on the corner in back of us where someone told me a "crew" was shacked up for the summer. I knocked on the door. No answer. I knocked again. Still no answer, but I could hear all sorts of thumpings and squawkings inside. Finally I opened the door and a little old grandmammy came shuffling towards me. She was waving her apron and shooing a gaggle of children of all ages and sizes from toddlers to ten-year-olds. After age ten, children worked in the fields. She almost shooed me out with a swipe of her apron!

"All the mens and wimmens are workin' on the farms and ev'ry chile in the camp is here wi' me," she told me.

I soon discovered that she was blind!

"Ah duz declare!" she said. "Thuh chilluns drives me plumb 'stracted!"

I had nightmares over that one. Dear God! What if the oil stove exploded while she was there alone, or one of the kids got ahold of a kitchen knife, or . . . ? Several nights later, a fire alarm blew. Bill and I raced to the window and peered out. Flames were lighting the sky on the road in back of us.

"Bill!" I screamed. "It's the house I told you about! The one packed with children! The children!"

We got there before the volunteer fire truck, and the neighbors formed a chain and we got all of the children out. Kicking and screaming, they were tossed from one hand to another, but we got them all out safely. The house was a tinder box! The wood was so old and dried out, it flared up like a bonfire. By the time the firemen got there, it had burned to the ground. We divided the kids up among us, bedded the men down in hay mows, and tried to comfort the women. The next day, the Red Cross swung into action and everyone was fed and given clothing.

Bill always put in two separate fields of tomatoes. One was contracted to the factory at a set price and the other was on the open market with the price determined by supply and demand. In a good year, with over-bountiful yields, the contract price was apt to be lower. In a bad, year with tomatoes in short supply, the open market price soared. Bill told me once that according to price, he made sure to take more tomatoes off the field at the higher price; and him a Deacon in the church!

It was a good growing season that year. The sun stayed out, as it was supposed to do; the nights were cool, but not too cold; and the vines were bursting with blossoms. The first picking is always light and expensive. The tomatoes are so scattered that the men will work only by the hour for wages, and, while the very first tomatoes in market baskets at the Farmers' Market bring as much as five dollars for a fifteen-pound hamper, the price drops drastically as the supplies come in. By the end of the week, the retail market has collapsed. No jealous wife ever inspected her husband's shirt collar for traces of strange lipstick more zealously than I inspected that field to see how soon we could pick. (Tomorrow? I would beg St. Cecelia.) And then, at long last, Bill would come into the kitchen with his cap cocked over one ear bellowing the tune: "Oh! The boy stood on the burning deck!" in raucous profundo. This was a sure sign that all was well.

Once, when he was in this mood, I said generously, "Sweetheart, if you ever feel like a quick roll in the hay with some fresh talent, I won't mind, as long as it's me you came home to." He got very angry!

"Oh, you would, too!" He said, scandalized. "You would, too!"

"Well," I said, "how do you know I'm not playing around?"

"I know you aren't," he replied.

"But how do you know?" I persisted.

"Oh, somebody would tell me." He said, confidently. Obviously another local custom.

"So, what put you in such a good mood?" I asked.

"Tomato buyers are in town." He replied. "Price is real good. Get dressed up and we'll go into town to Marty's (our token supper club) and mingle with our betters."

Well! I had worked in the fields all day and I was tired. My best dress was at the cleaner's. My hair needed a shampooing and my feet hurt.

"Early to bed . . ." had been my motto for the evening, but Mom had always said: "Go when they ask you, or, after a while, they won't bother to ask you anymore." So, I washed my face, put on my best red lipstick, and off we went.

It was Saturday night, and, in our town, Saturday night is shopping night. The women clerks were rushing to get through work as their beaux were lined up outside of the doors of the stores. Neighbors yelled to each other across the street and the kids jaywalked in all directions. Police Chief Macguire personally directed traffic, waving his arms and bawling out all and sundry for double parking, but as fast as he got one side of the street unplugged, the other side filled up and traffic was snarled clean up to the library! The babies all squalled at the top of their lungs; the cars backfired; and the bus driver had to lean on his horn the whole length of Main Street. Talk about "Opening Nights"! Times Square couldn't hold a candle to downtown Albion on a Saturday night!

In the parking lot of Marty's, jalopies jostled with Cadillacs; and, inside at the bar, dinner jackets and blue jeans toasted each other. Everybody toasted everybody else. The tomato buyers were in town! The tomato buyers for the open market are the last of the "True Americans". They are buccaneers and pirates; they are sharpies; and when the prices are high, they are the farmers' "White Hope". They are as swashbuckling as Errol Flynn. Every farmer's wife was on her most gracious behavior.

All winter, the farmers plan for the tomato season (the tomato buyers pay cash on delivery), and so do the stores, the hash joints, the posh eateries, and the people who own any kind of dilapidated old house that can be pressed into service as a "camp".

The migrant workers pour in by plane from Jamaica; the "wetbacks" swim the Rio Grande from Mexico illegally; and we drain the southern states. The "elite" workers, who can earn "executive" type wages at piece work, drive here in the newest model cars. Others come in trucks, crudely enclosed and fitted with wooden benches. Babies have been born en route on those benches. Some of the more unscrupulous crew leaders, hungry for men, go into saloons and drag out men who are drunk. They are "impressed" into work like the early nineteenth century sailors who were slugged and woke up at sea, too far from shore to make a break for it. The "shanghaied" field hands were in somewhat the same boat (sorry about that!). By the time they sobered up, they were in a strange state and the crew leader withheld so much of their wages for transportation, food, and lodging, that they never drew enough wages to go back home. Frequently they had almost nothing to show for their summer's work, although all of them have the hope of striking it rich!

The large registered camps are rigidly supervised by the state as to sanitation, cubic-feet-per-occupant, etc., but the men complain that they have nothing to do after hours and the result is a lot of drinking of alcohol. The smaller "bootleg" camps are the "ghettoes". It was one of these smaller camps that I was headed to one day when we were desperate for help.

I drove down an overgrown cow path into a small clearing. Some old barns had been cleaned out and the men were living in these. I stopped the car and called out: "Anyone want to work today?" and the men crowded around.

"How you pay, Missus?" they asked.

"Every night, as soon as you're finished. In cash." I said.

"I'll go!" "Me!" "Me, too!" they chorused; but a burly man came out and strode up to me.

"You don't understand," he said angrily. "You'll have to see The Man to get hired help."

He took me to a space that had been a stall for horses. A young black man was lying on the floor on a worn-out blanket. There was no chair, no table, nothing else in the stall.

"Missus," he drawled. "All my men is wukkin'." (And all of those men standing idle in the yard!) "But Ah'll send you to anutha camp."

He sent a man with me, and we rode and rode. The other camp was always just around the next curve or over the next hill, but it never seemed to appear. Finally we ended up back at the original camp. All of the men who had been so eager to work had disappeared and the only one in sight was the first man I had spoken to, nursing a bruised eye. (Why did I fall for this again? Didn't I learn my lesson last time?)

"Don't you want to come work for me?" I asked.

"No'm," he answered.

I was shocked, puzzled, and guilt-stricken. That man sure didn't have a bruised eye when I had driven in. When I told Bill about it, he looked stern.

"Pat," he said, "you have to face facts the way they are. You should have dealt with the crew leader first. He collects the wages for the men. The search for the 'other camp' was to get you out of the way so they could force their men to not go with you. Without question, that man was beaten up as a warning to the others."

In my roaming around the countryside for help, I often rode for miles with a carload of "young bucks", as the locals referred to the young black field hands, and the other farmers' wives would shudder when they saw me.

"Aren't you afraid?" they would ask me.

"Of course not!" I said. "I've never had any reason to be."

I told Bill once that it wasn't very flattering that he never worried about me, but he just grinned. "You're a big girl," he informed me.

Since I had worked in night clubs, I had been propositioned in six different languages, including the involuntary; but the most delightful proposition came when I picked up a man who had worked for us and offered to give him a lift in the pickup as he was trudging down the road. It wasn't until he got into the truck that I realized that he had been drinking. After we had gone a couple of miles, he turned to me and said solemnly, "Miz Pat. Would you be 'fended if I axed you to . . . ." That one I was tempted to frame!

All I could say was: "Oh dear! I just remembered that I promised to pick up some fertilizer for Mr. Carr. I'll have to turn around and go back. I'm sorry!" Now, that should get me a job with the diplomatic corps!

Twice, to my chagrin, I met my comeuppance as a con artist. The first time was with "Uncle Red", a Native American of great age and dignity. He had come out of nowhere, walked up to one of my workers who was doing her grocery shopping and said: "Ma'am, can I come home with you?" Of course she said "Yes". It is the poor who will share with the poor.

"But aren't you afraid to leave him with your children?" I asked.

"Why no'm," she replied. "He's a nice old man an' the chilluns is old enough ta scream." Shades of our over-protected, middle-class progeny.

Uncle Red had a small pension, but he longed for that extra can of beer, or that extra pinch of snuff, so he teased and cajoled and twisted my arm to give him a job picking ripe tomatoes.

"Be sure they are RED," I cautioned him. Uncle Red was color blind.

In spite of all the extra pressure, the weather, the help, and the delivery appointments at the canning factories, harvest time was a happy time on the farm. I loved to walk through the fields when the field hands were working. The women wore full swinging skirts over tight overalls. They bound their hair with brilliant bandanas and straw hats with brims that rolled up to the crown on the top. They swung their bodies free from the hip and they kept up a soft, velvety murmur of words or laughed in deep throaty tones. I had learned to stop softly and move lightly coming down the lane so that I could hear them sing. The expert piece workers, of course, earn much more than they would earn in a factory, but I think they would still work in the fields even if the pay was less. It's the feel of the sun in your bones and a light breeze on your sweaty back, and the glowing red of the tomatoes all around you.

Just once, I was badly frightened. I had picked up a new crew fifteen miles from home on a lonely road. It was all right by daylight when I picked them up, but I had three shifts to take home and I had left them until last (mistake number one.)

As usual, we were to pay them off in cash when we took them home. While the total wasn't much as payrolls go, nevertheless I had to have a plentiful supply of tens, fives, ones, and silver in dimes and quarters so that I could leave the correct amount with the crew leader for each man, and the bulk looked large. Plus, I carried it loose, in a paper bag (mistake number two).

At harvest time, everything moves with such speed (a whole year's receipts are crowded into six weeks), that I had fallen into the booby trap of doing things the easiest way. I had cashed a large check just before quitting time, and, when I paid off the first two crews, I just reached into the bag and came up with a fistful of paper money and change, in full view of everyone in the field (mistake number three).

Our arrangement with the new crew was that I paid off the crew leader in the camp when I took them home. (I had learned that lesson.) It was dark by the time that I got to the camp and unloaded the men. I asked where the "office" was, but the men had disappeared and I had to find my own way. I walked to the rickety old steps onto the sagging porch of the old house and stepped into what should have been the "office". It wasn't. It had at one time been a kitchen, but it was now the completely enclosed "drinking room" for the whole camp! The room was crowded and there were empty bottles strewn on the floor. There were bottles in the men's hands and tilted to their mouths, and there wasn't a sober face in the whole bunch. A gaudy juke box flashing red and green lights was blaring at the highest possible pitch, and some of the men who were still able to stand up were shuffling across the floor. In one corner was a curtained cubicle—the office? All I could think of was that time in New York City when I had wandered into an East Indian restaurant that was a front for an opium den. The stage manager told me afterwards that I had been lucky to get out of there alive! There was no door to this room except for the entrance, and the curtained cubicle had to be the office. I pushed the curtain aside and came face to face with a black woman who was obscenely fat. Her breasts hung below her waist and her arms were as big as my thighs. She could have strangled me with her thumb and one finger.

The cubicle was a blind corner about the size of a trap. It probably was a trap! "My bill?" I asked bluntly. (I wanted to get out of there as quickly as possible.) She stalled and stalled about figuring it up. I didn't know if she had trouble adding or whether it was to give the men enough time to grab my money. Finally she came up with the total. It was much higher than I had figured it should be, but I grabbed a fistful of bills out of the bag hoping it would be close enough to the right amount so that I wouldn't have to open the bag up again (mistake number four). Again she stalled, but apparently no one had the guts to tackle me while I was still inside the camp. I walked to the curtain, swept it aside, and streaked to the porch. Then I remembered! The gas tank had been almost empty when I left home. I had intended to stop at a station, but there weren't any along the way (mistake number five).

I noticed a small gas tank at the end of the porch. "Mister," I said to one of the men, "I'm almost out of gas and I don't want to get stuck on a back road. Could you sell me enough gasoline to make it home?" How could I have been so stupid?

"Well, now, Missus. I cain't spare none. Muh own gas man didn' come this mawnin'."

But another man nudged him and winked. "Mebbe I cud spare a gallon like," he conceded.

As I paid for the gas, he called out, "Lady in the office figgers she made a mistake an' yuh owes her five moah dollahs."

Of course I did not, but I pulled out a five dollar bill in a hurry. Anything to get away from there! I shot out into the road.

At night, all country roads look strange to me and since I had been over this road only once before, I had no landmarks to guide me. The speedometer on the truck was broken and I had no way to judge how far I had come. I began to get frightened about the gas. I came to one house that was lighted up and I was tempted to pull into the driveway and call Bill, but he had worked hard all day, so I decided to take a chance and kept going.

A little farther down the road, there was another house all lighted up with a car in the driveway, and by that time I was ready to admit I was chicken. I stopped and knocked on the door, but no one answered, although I could hear someone moving about inside. This might well have been the last house on the road, so I decided to turn back and try the first house I had seen. A short way back, I noticed an old jalopy pulled off the road under a tree. I had noticed a jalopy like it in the yard at the camp.

"You idiot!" I stormed at myself. "You prize IDIOT! You showed them a paper bag full of money, you let them take you for five bucks, and then you told them your gas tank was nearly empty! You idiot!"

When I got to the first house, I was shaking. I pounded on the door. The porch light snapped on and a man's voice called out, "Who's there?"

"I'm Bill Carr's wife," I said, praying that these people knew The Judge. Almost everyone knew Bill.

"Sure, I know Bill," the man said, undoing the bolt. "Come in. What's the trouble?"

"Well . . ." I stammered. "I'm not sure, but . . ." I explained my predicament.

"You're probably right," he said when I had finished. "That's a new camp and it's got a bad reputation. Been quite a spot of trouble this year; the men who drive the labor buses are all carrying guns. I'll get out my car and I'll follow you to the junction. There's a store that sells gas and you can get on the main highway from there."

Halfway to the junction, a jalopy slipped from a side road and started to follow me, but when my escort closed in, the jalopy fell back.

"Where have you been?" Bill demanded when I got home. "I was beginning to worry about you!"

"Oh," I retorted, "for once you were going to worry about me!"

"I had a right to," he said shortly. "You should have taken those new men home first. That camp is too rough for a woman after dark."

And he was right. The late news broadcast that night reported a murder at that camp an hour after I had left it.

On a farm, everybody does everything, especially during tomato season. The truck broke down one morning and Big John had to load twenty-five or so baskets across his shoulders and scatter them on the roadway for the pickers.

"Wal-l," he announced beaming, "Ah mought jes' as well git goin'. Ah ain't nothin' but a truck this mawnin. Das all Ah is; jes a truck."

The basket situation is intense. They're much scarcer than you might think. If duels were still fought, they would be fought over baskets. New baskets cost twenty-five cents (the tomatoes in the baskets are worth around forty cents—planted, hoed, fertilized, picked and delivered), and when you hand the filled baskets over to the trucker, he hands you back whatever empties the factory has handed him. Of course, you have no idea in advance what you'll get; the factory claims that they hand out what you have handed them and the circle is complete; but, somehow, it never seems that way.

Tomato prices go up and tomato prices go down—the market is unpredictable. But, no matter what the state of our tax returns, our conversation piece is: "Well, we didn't do much *this* year, but *next* year, we'll give 'em hell!"

CHAPTER 16

That's Our Patrick!

The long hot summer days came on. My city friends began to talk casually of vacationing in the country. I was in the country alright, but I wasn't vacationing. In fact, I was probably working harder than they were. I was eating three hurried meals and sleeping a harassed seven hours. When the farm quieted down for a day or two, I'd get an empty apartment. That would be time enough; at this point, I had a standard advertisement which hadn't deviated much from our original one: "Ideal for baby! The Pillars colonial farm estate, reconverted into six apartments." At dusk, a gleaming new car drove up. A short, plump, shinily-groomed man in his early thirties got out. One look at his face and I knew his name—he was beaming at everything in sight. "Patrick," I said to myself, "or Ryan, or Murphy, or McGinnis; maybe, but it's sure to be a Patrick."

His wife followed. Agnes was fat, but mostly it was where it ought to be. She was very blonde. "Waitress," I said to myself, "and I bet you sling a mean hash and a pretty fair comeback!"

He was beaming, and so was she. "Beautiful place here, just beautiful," he said. "I sez to Agnes here, I sez, 'Agnes, this can't be. Why this is a mansion!' I sez. 'These people wouldn't take in strangers. Are you sure you're not kiddin' us now?' But, this is it, alright. This is wonderful! We been sleeping in a trailer camp. Can we sleep here tonight?"

"The ad says 'Ideal for Baby'," said Agnes.

Her husband interrupted her. "We sure want one, but she's had three misses, and the army doctor says she can't try for a while. Honolulu my

191

last one was, wasn't it, Honey? Yeah, I'm just out of the army," beamed Patrick. "Got a wonderful job, had it a month. Get $125 a week and my car. Traveling salesman. Wonderful firm. Really going places. And, now . . ." said Patrick beaming even brighter, "I've got this wonderful home! Gee, it sure is nice."

"So, I thought," said Agnes, "since we don't have a baby, you wouldn't mind if we brought our baby, Suki. Here, Suki, baby!" A 150-pound red-brown Alaskan Husky leaped out of the car. I gurgled. If this is a "baby", then I need my head examined!

"Oh, gosh, this is wonderful!" said Patrick. "Know what I'm gonna go? I'm gonna bring my rocker right out here on this little porch and I'm gonna rock and rock. That'll be just the thing for me. It's wonderful."

"Bring the suitcases, Hon," said Agnes, trailing through the door. "We'll just chain Suki fast to the radiator while we go downtown."

"And hope he doesn't tear it from the wall," I thought. "Poor Katie," I sighed to myself; for Agnes and Patrick would share Katie's kitchen. I relented to the extent that I hitched the new couple on to our bathroom, but within a few days, Katie and Agnes discovered that they had quite a few things in common; among them, Patrick's beer.

The next night Patrick and Agnes invited us all to the movies. Bill was enthusiastic, so we agreed to go.

"We'll drive," I suggested.

"Wouldn't hear of it," Patrick said. "Take my car; company pays all the bills. Tell you what; we'll take both cars and fill 'em up—on me."

"Bill," I said when we got to the box office, "you go in there and carry our share of the white man's burden. I know the signs."

"Aw, let Patrick pay it," said Agnes, shrugging. "He's got a good job."

Bright and early at nine a.m. Monday morning, Patrick took off on his job. He was excited as a kid on the first day of school. He worked until five. He and Agnes drove down to the lake and left Suki tied to the radiator. She howled like a werewolf. I thought she was lonesome, so I went in to keep her company. When she saw me, she got so mad she bit a chunk right out of the solid hand-carved American walnut door! I decided she was an introvert and wanted to be left alone.

Tuesday morning, Patrick started out bright and early to his job at ten a.m. He was back home at four-thirty. "Ah, this is the life," he beamed as he rocked in his rocker with his bottle of beer and his slippered feet. He looked like a king surveying his kingdom.

"I feel so good here," said Agnes. "Better than I did since I was in California. That's when I had my second miss and my appendix out at the same time. That's when I started to get fat. Maybe I'll get knocked up out here. Patrick just stared ahead.

By the end of the week, Patrick's spit and polish wasn't quite so spick and span. He was enjoying his home, make no mistake about it. "I'm gonna throw a big party," he announced, "for everybody. Got a good job, expense account, never had a home before—always been in the army. Big party, yessir, and you're all invited! Yes, this is the life."

"Bill," I said, "I know the signs. I'm afraid . . . ."

"Wouldn't wonder," said Bill.

The party was a smasheroo. We had cold ham and beer, cold tongue and beer, and cold sliced chicken and beer. Patrick was a marvelous host. "He's just like a little boy," Agnes told me. "He's just like the baby I've never had." Patrick just beamed.

"Our little boy" was entitled to two weeks' vacation a year and, since he had been working for the company for a whole month, he felt that it would be a good time to take his vacation. "I'm gonna enjoy my home," he beamed, smiling at everyone in sight. He let his cheeks get stubbly and stopped polishing his shoes. He didn't feel it was necessary to notify his firm that he was on leave. He figured they'd know that much when he stopped sending in his reports. He was just the soul of optimism.

By the middle of the week there was a letter marked in the upper left-hand corner: "The Housewives' Friend Co.". It was addressed to Patrick. "Bill," I said that night after we had gone to bed, "there was a letter for Patrick today from his firm."

"Uh-huh," replied Bill, "what else is new, Honey?"

By the end of the week, there was another letter. "Bill," I said, "there's another letter."

"Uh-huh," replied Bill.

I tried to rush in—delicately—where no angel had trod. I decided to approach Patrick's missus. "Agnes," I said, "do you think that, well, do you think it's business-like for Patrick not to contact his firm?"

Agnes laughed, "Oh, Patrick's alright. He's just a little boy. Ain't it awful how fat I got since my second miss? Wonder why Patrick loves me so much."

The beginning of the next week brought another letter. I was really getting worried. "Bill," I said, "there's another . . ."

". . . letter from The Housewives' Friend Co." finished Bill. "Won't be long now."

By noon, Patrick had a phone call. By night the car was gone. "Took it to the garage for an overhaul," explained Patrick. He acted like nothing had happened.

"Hell, Honey! Stop lying!" cried Agnes. "Tell them that you lost your job."

Patrick just shrugged. "So, I lost my job; I'll find another one."

But it wasn't so easy. Leslie, who lived upstairs in the back, owned a tractor trailer truck. He was always broke. One day, he and Patrick got to talking and he painted a glowing picture of life as a knight on the rolling road. "I'll be a truck driver," declared Patrick, "earn a hundred and a quarter a week. I'm going to go with Leslie on a trip and learn the ropes."

Once again, he was all enthused. He was really going to go with Leslie as an unpaid helper, but that was between him and Leslie. The trip was uneventful, except that Patrick fell asleep at the wheel and Leslie grabbed it just in time. Patrick was now a seasoned, experienced truck driver. Since he now stood to be paid, Leslie found he couldn't use him. In fact, he couldn't wait to get rid of him.

But, there must be hundreds of truck owners panting for good men. The only hitch was that Patrick didn't know any of them. I went down to Lunch Room (the "Free Information Bureau") and came back with the news that Harry Kurt was hankering for a driver.

"All I know is that it's two runs a week to Canada and back. Something 'hot', whatever that is. Has to be got there in a hurry and right back again for the other one. Go see him."

It wasn't exactly the greatest, but it could tide him over till he found something else.

"Drive me down?" asked Patrick. It was about a mile down the road.

"I'm awfully busy," I hedged.

"That's alright," said Patrick, "you don't have to wait for me. I'll call you to come after me when I'm ready."

"Uh-huh," said Bill, when I told him. Well, he was getting very laconic in his old age!

At four o'clock, I had to leave Bill to bring the cows in alone while I went to get Patrick. "Nothing to it!" he beamed to Agnes. "Got all upset over nothing didn't you, Hon?" He sat down heavily in his favorite rocker.

"I hope so," said Agnes, trailing into the kitchen in a bathrobe, with her hair up in curlers. Clarence always greets hair curlers with an icy stare.

Harry Kurt's outfit was one of those eight-wheel jobs, not too hard to manage. He called up about noon. "Now, about that man that's been driving for you," he began, but I stopped him straight off.

"What man has been driving where for us?" I asked.

"Well," he answered, "jeez, after you brought him down here and came after him, and all; and he said he'd driven for you for a long time and that you'd vouch for him. I only hired him because I figured I could depend on anybody that you would send."

I didn't quite know what to say, so decided on the truth. "Harry," I said weakly, "he came out from New York City about a month ago and I really know very little about him."

"Well, I was in a spot, anyway," said Harry, "but I'll fix him. City slicker, huh? I'll find out if he can take it."

Once more I had rung the bell, only it was the wrong door. Twenty-four hours later, Harry called me back. "Your man, Friday, has quit," he said. "Come and get him."

When I got there, I saw that Patrick really looked beat. He had a five-o'clock shadow, and dragged his feet. There was eighteen tons of cement on that truck in one-hundred-pound bags. He'd had a hell of a time along the road, then, when he got to Canada, he unloaded on a long runway. There was no helper, no dock hands, no one to help him. Patrick had carried 36,000 pounds of cement off that truck all by himself and almost died. Then he had driven back and Harry told him to load up again right away so he could make the trip back again.

"Hell, Pat, I just wanted to see if he could take it," he told me later. "I wasn't really going to make him do it!" He was apologetic, but I could tell he was a bit amused, too.

"OK, OK," I said wanly.

"I love you both, but Suki will eat. She will have her horse meat, even if I have to give up my beer. And you have to give up your rent," Patrick declared.

"That's what I thought," said Bill.

Patrick was bent on getting a job. He shaved the next morning and started out on his own. By now he knew his way around a little, so he went down to the Lunch Room and got his own job. He was to drive Freddie Gage's tractor trailer with a load of cabbage to Rome, New York. "But this time," said Our Little Boy, "there's to be no unloading. I know my rights. I've looked 'em up. I am a driver. I don't unload. I know my place."

About noon, Freddie called me. Freddie is an old friend of ours. "Now, about that man that's worked for you . . ."

I threw in the towel. Why bother with the truth? "If this keeps up," I said to Bill, "you and I aren't going to have a friend left in this town."

"I know," I answered myself, "but Agnes has followed that man from one army camp to another ever since they were married. She wasn't always fat. She probably wasn't always blonde, either. She loves the guy terribly and I know how she feels about having a baby. She wants so much to take root."

"Uh-huh," said Bill.

Patrick drove the tractor trailer truck out to the house to show it off to Agnes. "Watch me back it up, Honey," he said, and polished off our fifth mailbox. He was a little tyke with a new toy.

"He's just a little boy," said Agnes.

Bill yanked at my elbow. "Don't look now," he said, "but there's a long deep dent in the roof of Our Little Boy's trailer. See?"

I saw. "How the hell did he do that?" I asked. "What can you hit with a roof?"

Patrick took the load of cabbage to Rome. He took four hours to get there instead of three and the day crew had gone off duty and there was no night crew to replace them. "Load of cabbage," he announced importantly.

"Yeah?" said the night watchman.

"Where's the helpers? Where's the loading crew?" asked Patrick.

"Ain't none," replied the night watchman.

"Well, what'll I do?" asked Patrick.

"Dunno. Up to you."

"Well, I can't unload it myself."

"You could."

Patrick unloaded. Suki must eat. He reported back to Freddie and Freddie took one look at the roof of his brand-new-only-made-the-down-payment-in-it-truck and blew his top. "Guy tried to tell me that he stopped under a tree in Syracuse and the tree blew over on him. Did he expect anyone outside the loony bin to believe that? What's he think I am, a nut? What he probably did was try to back up and backed into a telephone pole, and the pole busted off at the bottom and fell right across the roof of the trailer."

"Probably," said Bill.

"Mamma Mia!" Freddie cried as he smote his forehead melodramatically. "Probably already there is a bill coming to me from the phone company!" And, so there was.

Into the breach leaped Agnes. Somebody had to buy Suki's horse meat. She went down to the Lunch Room and, in five minutes, she had a job behind the counter. So, she was to be the breadwinner. She had a white nylon uniform and combed her hair down slick. She bounced the wisecracks back before they got started. She was darned efficient. This time I beamed. Patrick kept looking for a job and wrote to the Reform School for a job as social director. He would have made a good one, too.

"Maybe it'll turn out alright," I said to Bill. I was hoping for the best, but Bill was not so optimistic.

"Maybe," replied Bill.

The hot drowsy summer came on. I was too busy to worry. Suki minded the heat, but she didn't chew on anyone, for which I was at least grateful. I began to sleep nights.

Patrick saw the *Penny Saver* in the mailbox and came bounding in. "I got it! He cried. "I got it! 'Wanted: Plumber's apprentice. Will train under G.I. Bill.' I got it! Those plumbers make $125 a week! Drive me downtown, Pat!"

So, off we went again. I was starting to feel like his private chauffer!

The plumber was Mike McGinnis and Patrick's brogue got thicker. "Monday morning, you can start. I'll send you out with my brother on a rush job—very important."

"Yes, sir!" said Patrick.

On Monday, we called Mike's office. "Patrick's in Brockport on a job," said Mike. "Sent him out right away. My brother's with him. The two of them left this morning. I've going over myself later."

At two o'clock, Mike drove over to the job. No plumber's truck. No boss plumber. No plumber's helper. They hadn't even been there. With the instinct of a rat terrier, Mike made for the nearest saloon. The truck was outside. "Mike McGinnis Plumbing" it said on the sides. Mike strode in. There was Patrick and Mike's brother, Jerry, arm in arm, voices raised in Irish songs. They were toasting each other with their Irish brogues and American beer. Mike, who is Irish, too, smashed the mugs on the bar and spun the men around. "Get out!" he yelled to his brother. And, to Patrick, "You're fired!"

"Jeez, what could I do?" Patrick asked me later. "Being it was his brother and all. He suggests we hoist a few. Jeez, I wouldn't have gone, but it was his brother!"

Tuesday morning, Patrick came into our apartment looking worried. "I have to call the Lunch Room," he explained. "Agnes is sick."

I jumped out of bed (usually we just pull the covers up when people need to use the telephone), and went in to Agnes. I didn't like her expression. "What's the matter, Kid?" I asked.

She looked white and there were dark circles under her eyes. She wobbled to the john and threw up. Patrick was understandably concerned and took her to the doctor's. When they came back, Agnes was glowing. "It's a baby!" she said.

Patrick looked like the happiest guy on Earth.

"Doc gave me a shot and says if we start right away, we can save this one. He says to go to bed for a week, and to come back so he's sure. Oh, Pat, I'll go to bed for a year if I can have this baby!"

Patrick and I got a couple of cake tins to use as cymbals and banged our way through the halls, much to the amusement of the other tenants. "The Town Criers have an Announcement!" we yelled.

The girls sure rallied around us. They made Agnes's bed up fresh. They fluffed her pillows. They brushed her hair.

"Now, when I had the twins . . . ," said Dottie.

"Be sure to stay in bed," said Mary Lou.

"I'll get your breakfast every morning," offered Katie.

"Let me make your lunch!" said Judy.

"A spot of tea at four," I said.

We hovered around her like mother hens.

I told Bill that night, after we were in bed, "Who said so?" he asked.

"Dr. Joe," I answered. Dr. Joe had very recently been untied from his chief's apron strings and he sometimes overshot the mark a little.

"Uh-huh," said Bill, rolling his eyes. He wasn't impressed; he had seen babies before.

The situation called for drastic measures. "See that field?" I asked Patrick. "We've run out of friends, but we haven't run out of tomatoes. Start picking! Fifteen cents a basket for ripe ones. Agnes and Junior have to eat."

"Don't forget Suki," he said, donning his sun hat.

"Soon as there's a baby in the wind," Bill said, "all the old hens get together and cluck!"

Agnes glowed. She stopped bleaching her hair. The girls even invited her to go to the movies, just a small crowd. She called the doctor. "Do you want that baby?" he asked.

"More than anything in the world!" she answered.

"Then, go back to bed," he told her.

Patrick did alright for two days, and then on the third day, the weather got god-awful hot and the picking slowed down. I could tell that he wished he were in a tavern. Bill came into the house to get me and his lips were set in a thin line. "I can't have it, Pat!" he said. "My own reputation—our whole business—is at stake. If the inspector sees Our Little Boy's baskets, the whole load will be turned down. They're absolutely horrible! You did tell him 'ripe', didn't you?"

"Bill, you can't fire him now!" I pleaded. I went out to the field. The baskets were bright red on top, but just by glancing along the cracks in the side, you could see the bottom was filled with green tomatoes. "Stacking" it's called in the trade. Now *I* was a bit hot under the collar. I called Patrick to one side. I tried to explain.

"But it's good for you," he argued. "They buyers will think they're all red and you'll get rid of your green ones."

"Look," I said, "it's this way. Buying tomatoes is those hot rods' racket. They know all the angles, see?"

"Roger," said Patrick. Then he added, in a discriminate tone, "Pat, I gotta make money for Agnes."

That night Agnes went back to the doctor's. When she came home, she went to the bathroom and poured a bottle of bleach onto her hair. "Well?" I asked breathlessly.

"Well what?" she asked flatly.

"Well, well?" I asked again.

"Well," she intimated, "I'm going to work in the morning. The doctor says it was a psychological phenomenon or maybe indigestion. Pat, you know, I should have believed that doctor in Honolulu. I may as well forget about it."

But Agnes's job was gone. A cute little slim trick had walked right into it. Agnes has common sense. And she knew Our Little Boy. "Pat," she said to me, "so, I wanted a home and a baby. So, I tried. Patrick will get another job, but he'll quit or he'll get fired. We'll be back to the army. Patrick will retire young and I'll handle the paycheck."

I drove him down to the recruiting station. Patrick enlisted that afternoon and they left a few days later.

Three years had gone by when a strange man came to the door. "Mrs. Carr?" he asked. I nodded. "FBI," he said, and showed his credentials. "Do you know a Patrick Ryan?" I nodded again.

"What has he done now?" I wondered to myself.

"Know anything about him?" the agent inquired.

"In what way?" I hedged.

"His loyalty. Just a routine check. He's being considered for a very confidential mission."

I almost fell over. I told Bill about it that night after we had gone to bed.

"Uh-huh?" said Bill.

CHAPTER 17

Holy Cows, Cows!

After lunch one day, Bill jumped into Jezebel and leaned on the horn. "Coming?" he yelled. "If you are, hurry up! I can't wait all day, you know!"

"Alright, alright, I'm coming," I called. "Where to?"

"Calf hunting," he said. "Riverdale Dutch and her baby are somewhere in the woods."

"Oooh," I said, "you mean I'm going to get right up close to a cow again?"

"Why not?" said Bill, "I keep telling you, there is nothing to be afraid of!"

Since I am a woman who screams and runs at the sight of an ounce-and-a-half mouse, the prospect of practically shaking hands with three-quarters-of-a-ton of hide and hair was slightly disconcerting. I had, of course, acquired a nodding acquaintance with our cows, and I even remembered some of their names. I knew they came complete with horns and a built-in kicking system; and I hoped that some day, some bright young man would find a way to add air freshener; they smelled of milk, hay, and manure. But my closest contact with the dairy industry before I married was a song with the line: "A dairy maid am I, what ho" that I sang in a fetching peasant costume with hip-length nylons.

I often thought about it when I blundered into those soft booby traps in the barnyard at night when I sure didn't feel like a dairy maid, what ho? Obviously, my relations with our cow population could not be termed as "intimate", but having married a Holstein-Freisian dairyman, it was time I married his cows (which always seem to be getting loose) so, I went calf-hunting—again.

201

When we have our model dairy, all our pregnant cows will repose in white-washed maternity pens and we'll hoofprint each calf; but my spouse's idea is our present state of rugged American ingenuity: just turn all the cows out to pasture together and, if a cow that is "close-up" doesn't come up the lane to the barnyard at night, we know she's "come in". If she hasn't, it's just too bad.

Bill and I jounced along the lane to the backwoods following Riverdale Dutch's tracks. Such a marvelous place to have a baby! I tickled Bill's ear. "Behave, now!" Bill said firmly. "We're down here to find Riverdale Dutch and for no other reason. Got that, Woman?"

"Aye, aye, Sir!" I said. "Minds on our business."

It was so beautiful out here in the wilderness. The woods smelled of pine cones and green leaves. It shut out the rest of the world; there was just us two. "Can't stop now," said Bill. "Got to get that calf up to the barn."

"Spoil sport!" I snarled.

A few days later, my hubby said to me, "Well, now that you can handle a calf, why don't you try milking a cow?"

"Oooh, glory Hallelujah!" I said. "I'd rather not."

But, I made an attempt, although a somewhat unorthodox one. I hooked up the radio and drove Bill distracted. He couldn't hear whether the milking machines were working right or not. "Here's the feeding chart," he said. "Follow it."

"Bambi, four pounds," I read. "Oh, Bill, that darling little thing that looks like a fawn only gets one scoopful? That's not fair! Let's give her an extra helping." I said.

"That's all she earns," said Bill.

"But, she's so pretty!" I said, sneaking her another scoopful.

"Stop that!" yelled Bill. "Grain costs money. You'll be sorry when the feed bill comes in."

Daisy was next. She was a low producer, too. I gave her one scoopful.

"Don't wash her hind quarter," said Bill. "She's got mastitis and we can't sell the milk, so there's no point in it. And don't get too close—she's blind in one eye and she's liable to kick."

She did, too, but she knew who dished out the grain and so she kicked sort of gently and remonstratively. Cows are not stupid!

"You ought to see the way she kicks Doc when he treats that bad quarter!" said Bill. "She's got Doc so buffaloed that he just bypassed her when he did the physicals for the herd. He wouldn't go within six feet of her! She kicked me once, too," he added, "but I fixed her. I kicked back!"

Every time Bill passed the stall, Daisy would reach her head through the bar and nudge him. "Sugar Daddy," I could almost hear her thinking. Bill sneaked the scoop into the grain box. "Oh no you don't!" I said, "not for that little hussy! Grain costs money! It seems we ought to sell Daisy; all that extra grain and one bad eye and mastitis in one quarter and all. Don't you think we ought to sell her?"

"By gol, no," said Bill, as that little gold-digger reached out and licked his coat. "There's times when I'd rather sell you! Much rather!"

Cornation Mable Pietie had the best racket in the barn. She had a moo like a banshee with a Russian background. She got fed first every time. That moo was god-awful, so it was mostly so that she would shut up.

Our barns are just a big roofed-over area floored with straw. "It sure don't look like the fancy dairy barns you see in the movies," I told Bill.

"Well," Bill replied reasonably enough, "You don't look like Betty Grable, either. But the thing that counts is this: in both cases, it works."

"What's that long coop thing along the wall?" I asked.

"Dinner table," replied Bill. "That's the milking parlor and all the rest of it . . ."

It's a "bathroom" by the looks of it to me! Where are the little men in white with brooms?

"Uh oh, these cows'll kill each other," I said, as two cows collided with a deafening (to me) crunch.

"No they won't," said Bill. "They're just trying to find out who is Boss Cow and goes first in line. Social standing means a lot to cows. There's an awful lot of human nature loose around the barns. We could learn a lot by watching! Half of our cows are pure-bred and half are grade, but it's every man for himself and only in America could a cow without a lineage walk in to dinner ahead of a cow that's got one."

When Bill got so he grunted every time he bent over to tie his shoelaces, he decided that instead of his crawling in under the cows to put the milkers on, he had the idea of raising the cows up to his level. I thought he had in mind something like the hoist that the mechanic uses when he looks at the tie rods on the car and I always forget to get out and end up in the air with the car and sit there and holler like crazy because I'm scared. The mechanic won't let the car down till he's through working on it, so I've spent some of the loneliest moments of my life up on that damned thing!

But no; Bill just dug a trench three-feet deep and lined the cows up on the edge of it. He would never make a good director. He makes the most complicated things look so easy. Now, why hadn't I thought of this?

It's my job to let the cows in from the stable one by one into the milking parlor. Most of them weave in like Gypsy Rose Lee on a runway, but we have one cow, Old #7, who got so frustrated when she was pregnant and couldn't be milked that she simply refused to come in; however, she wouldn't stay out, either. Instead, she just stood there and butted all comers.

As they come into the barn, Bill, who stands way at the other end, will call out "That's Tiny—extra scoop. That's #3, scoop and a half."

I asked, "How do you do it? How can you tell them apart from so far away?"

"Oh," Bill answered with a wink, "I know my teats!"

Occasionally, all is not serene in the barn area. Sometimes we get awoken in the middle of the night by the anguished bellows of a mama cow whose bull calf we have just sold to the butcher for $15. When the calves are heifers, we raise them.

One of the things that I had done was to overcome my fear of the cows. Mother always explained it by saying that I drank so much milk when I was a child that I probably was ashamed to look a cow in the face. However, now that I sign the check for the monthly feed bill for the dairy, I feel that the situation is reversed: the shoe is on the other foot.

Bill never lets them bother him; he knows how to handle them. "Don't let them boss you," Bill was always telling me. "If a cow gets in your way, slap her. Tell her to move on."

I tried it. Rag Apple Dunloggin stood in my way. I slapped her. "Git!" I said. She got, and I was so thrilled, I began to wonder if I had sadistic tendencies. Bill came up a moment later.

"Lookit," he said, "just don't get too smart for your own britches, Little Girl. That was MISTER Rag Apple Dunloggin you just smacked!"

Well, it wasn't my fault—I didn't have a scorecard!

One of the reasons that Bill likes our system of stabling is that there is a lot more straw and we can save much more manure. To the city slicker, there is something faintly disgusting about the stuff. One of the remarks around town when we were first married was, "My dear, Mrs. Carr helps clean out the barns! Who were her folks?" I'm not quite sure what this means.

I do clean out, but not the barns—I'm not that good! I clean the milking parlor. The walls are old and windswept, the doors are open and the windows down. I've smelled many a diaper that was richer, and even a day-old calf raises its tail and is careful not to muss itself, unless, of course, it has the scours. So, I turn on the radio and work. Tchaikovsky never had it so good!

When the kids and I go walking down the lane, somebody always giggles and looks around to make sure nobody is there but me, and then he screws up his face and sniggers "Look, there's cow shit!" And they all giggle. Well, to a farmer, "cow shit" is fertilizer and the richest, best, most evenly balanced food there is for a hungry soil. Don't turn up your nose either, because your richest vitamins, your most necessary minerals, even your prime roast beef and reddest apples, are the more delectable because of manure!

After this lovely little homily, I'll let you in on a little secret: When my husband is completely frustrated; when his cows jump fences, his fruit rots, his bank is snotty, or he pounds his thumb with a hammer, he comes out with one good, strong, four-letter word that he keeps for just such occasions: "Oh, shit!" he bellows; and thereby adds one more important contribution to the American way of life.

The pen stables take a lot of work from Bill's shoulders, and a lot of worry off his mind, but we never seem to suffer from a lack of either. There's always enough to get to us, if we let it. Bill took me back to New York City to a hospital, and for the first time since we were married, we were away from the farm and cows for two weeks. Two whole solid consecutive weeks. We phoned home for John and Isabelle (hired help on the farm and lived in one of our apartments) to meet us at the station in Rochester. They couldn't wait to see us and we were anxious to get back.

"Howdy, Mistuh Bill," said John, grinning from ear to ear. "Ever'thin's fine; just fine."

"Jes' fine," added Isabelle.

"Well, that's good," said Bill.

I kept still; I was still a little shaky. We got into the car and, after we had driven about two blocks, Bill inquired, "John, sure was nice of you to bring your own car to meet us, but I thought Jerry would have our Mercury done by now."

"Reckon," answered John, edging up to a red light, "Jerry 'lowed that Mercury ain't nuthin' but junk no how. Says you bettuh haul it righ' off to the junk yahd 'cause it ain't wuth fixin' no how. He say tha' blankety-blank . . ."

"That's alright, John," said my husband, "I don't need any quotes, I've heard Jerry swear before."

"But don't fret none," said Isabelle. "Ever'thin's jes' fine."

We passed a car that was doing fifty in a thirty-mile-an-hour zone. "Too bad we didn't know where you was in New York so we coulda called you. Mebbe us coulda done sumpin' about them hawgs. Willie an' me, we called the doctah, an' he gib 'em all a shot an' says he hopes they all live, but this mawnin' all twelb o' 'em hawgs tuhned up der toes an' died. Mebbe I coulda sold 'em somewhere iffen I coulda called y'all an' y'all say so."

"Oh," said Bill, beginning to regret our time away.

"Now, doan you git all upset. Right aftah you dun got op'rated on," said Isabelle, "cuz ever'thin's jes' fine."

"Don't hardly think I'd pass that car, John," said Bill, as a word to the wise. "That's a state trooper!"

John slowed down. "'Pears mighty funny to me," he said. "You know dem dere folks in dat 'partment? Wahl, is dat your'n furniture?"

"Yes," I answered, thinking of my lovely antiques. In the back of my mind I knew something bad must've taken place there, too.

"Now, dat's what I tole Isabelle," said John, triumphantly. "Ah sez yesteddy, y'all is comin' home today an' this mawnin' in all dat rain, dey dun move out an' it taken two trucks to move dem. Seem mighty strange to me."

His wife turned to me kindly and said, "You looks peaked, Honey. Didn' feed you none too good, mos' likely. When Ah had my 'pendix out . . ." And she launched into a long story.

We rode for a few miles in silence. "Us dun git da watah fixt dis mawnin'," said John. "Me and Willie, us was two days huntin' fo' da leak. Us kep' da watah turned off in da house an' Miss Dottie, she so mad, she gonna move, but us foun' da leak this mawnin'. So ever'thin's fine. Jes' fine."

"Jes fine," repeated Isabelle.

We rode along. "Mistah Bill," said John, skidding around a turn, narrowly missing a tractor trailer truck, "Ya' know dat white cow you so fonda? She got da bigges' lump on her bag. Reckon you hafta call Doc; but don' worry cuz . . ."

"Ever'thin's jes' fine," said he and Isabelle together. "Jes' fine!"

"John," asked Bill, "let's save something for tomorrow. Everything sounds just a little TOO fine!"

CHAPTER 18

Joan of Arc Lives Here

It was fall; a log hissed on the fireplace; I sprawled on the floor; Bill had his feet propped up on a footstool; Herta and Clarence sat with their ankles crossed; Dottie clutched Little Mike's shirt tail (we had coaxed his parents to let him visit); and Katie buzzed round with the cocktail shaker.

"Wouldn't it be nice," I mused as we gazed into the flames, "if we could get some nice normal tenants for a change?" (Patrick, his wife, Agnes, and Suki, their 100-pound-plus Husky dog that chewed hunks out of our doors, had just moved out.) "Just imagine," I continued, "an interval of peace and quiet!"

"Amen," they all agreed solemnly, except Herta, who observed tartly, "What this house really needs is a resident psychiatrist!"

"Oh, my gol', NO!" Bill protested, "we'd drive the poor guy nuts!"

"I'll do my best to please all of you," I promised, and I chose Eric and his wife, Tisha, and their three-year-old-going-on-four son, Timmy. They were Canadian English (Canadian English are more English than the English!), and everybody was pleased. Herta beamed over Eric's formal manners; Katie noted that Tisha had an "air"; and Little Mike glowed at the prospect of a new playmate in Timmy. Little Mike had been moaning ever since Suki left—it seemed that none of the rest of us would let him poke us in the eye or pinch us in unlikely spots. All of us liked Eric, and he was good-looking, but he reminded me irresistibly of a cow. His face was long and narrow with his forehead and chin completing the rectangle. If Eric had stood beside a cow and the cow looked up and Eric looked down . . . I

207

expected him at any moment to answer our questions with a mild "Moo-oo". And, when he gazed over the tops of his glasses while he pondered a point, I was tempted to ask him if he was chewing his cud.

"My husband is a musician," Tisha told me, when I asked her what Eric did.

"Oh, dear," I said, dismally, mentally fixing to tell her that there had been some mistake and that the apartment was already rented. (I was still smarting from Patrick's "gee-tar", Jimmy's "gee-tar", and Judy's accordion, and the groupies that visited Dottie.) "What instrument does he play?" I asked.

"Oh, he isn't that kind of musician," she said, with a superior air, "he's a composer."

And, apparently, he was a good composer. "Might be a comer," his boss later told me. "We've commissioned him to do the background music for our national display. Quite an opportunity for a young man."

But, his bosses were smart enough to give him a "package deal". Eric was to pay the musicians and pay for the rehearsals, as well as doing the composing. Eric got so enthused over the project that he decided to make it a production. He hired extra musicians and scheduled extra rehearsals until he had just the effect that he was striving for. The result was impressive and his bosses were delighted; but Eric wound up on the wrong side of the ledger: he lost money.

"Now, Bill," I said, when my husband began to fret about the overdue rent. "I know just how he feels. He's got to make a good impression. I worked for a producer once who would have been tops if he hadn't been so penny-pinching. He rented our costumes and he rented the scenery; no extravaganzas for him! So the critics always second-rated him."

"All well and good," Bill muttered, "but Eric has got to come to grips with money somewhere along the line."

"Now you're making a noise like a landlord," I scolded. "Don't you remember the time that Willie told us about his girlfriend's landlord, who told her to 'pay or get out' and how indignant Willie was because he (the landlord) didn't even ask her if there was something important she wanted to do with the money?"

Bill laughed—crisis averted.

Tisha and I had gotten off to a rather bad start. Eric's office was in the city, and, since he didn't have a car, I offered to drive him to the railroad station. "No bother at all," I assured him, when he protested.

"Oh, no?" Bill muttered under his breath, "who furnishes the gas?"

So, I dropped Eric off in the morning and lined up with all the wives who were waiting to pick up the family wage-earners in the evening. The commuters' special consisted of a coach and a baggage car, and an O'Brien's Express (a hand cart) was there to unload. All of us got out of our cars and waved as the train pulled in. Quite suburban! Eric stood on the steps of the coach and waved his briefcase. "Tisha gave me a shopping list for you," I said, as he got into the car. "Coffee, bacon, and milk—skim."

"Let's see if I have any money," he said, feeling in his pockets, "yup, that's OK."

"And be sure to get the trading stamps," I added. He came out lugging a huge Dale's Super Market bag. ("Never send a man to do the grocery shopping if you're on a budget," a friend of mine warned me. "Men go hog wild over food!")

"Saw some steaks that were a real bargain," he explained, as I glanced at the bag.

"Wise guy," I commented. There was a pause. What on Earth would we talk about? "Your Timmy said the cutest thing today," I said, to fill the silence. "He said 'Auntie Pa-at' just as plain as could be."

"Hmm," muttered Eric.

"And, how did your day go?" I inquired.

"Oh, I finished the symphony I was working on," he said.

It was my turn to say "Hmm."

That night after dinner, Bill and I were sitting on the lawn with a glass of iced tea in our hands and a rare moment of peace in our hearts. Tisha's windows were open and voices carry in the country. "Did you remember to get the trading stamps?" she called in to Eric in the next room.

"They're on top of the refrigerator," he called back. "Pat told me to be sure and get them." There was a silence. Then we heard Eric come into the kitchen. "Did you have a good day?" he asked.

"Darling, the most exciting thing happened," Tisha said, with a quiver in her voice; "Little Timmy said . . ."

"Auntie Pat," Eric finished for her. "Pat told me on the way home."

There was a pause for station identification . . . "Humph!" Tisha exploded. "That woman!"

Bill grinned and poked me in the ribs. "That'll learn you!" he remarked.

"Aw, quit it," I said crossly, "you're spilling my tea."

The following night when I picked Eric up, I decided to play it cool; casual; impersonal. "Have you seen today's Times?" I inquired. "What do you think of the editorial on the international situation?"

When we pulled up in front of our house, Tisha was standing on the porch in a trimly starched dress and a new becoming hairdo. "Darling," I heard her say to Eric, "you must be tired of hearing me talk about Timmy and my problems every night. What do you think of the international policy as outlined in the Times today?"

Well, as my mother used to say, you can't win them all!

Eric's company continued to be enthused about his work, but they held him to a drawing account that never seemed to be enough. Rent days came and went but by now Bill was getting involved. When we lingered after church one Sunday, his friends would say, "Hear young Eric is out there with you. Heard one of his songs on TV the other night. Pretty good, isn't he?" And Bill would bask in the reflected glory.

But as for money, it reminded me of an older woman who worked for me occasionally. "Miz Pat," she would say, "y'all lend me sum money?"

"Can't," I would reply, "short myself just now. You just got your welfare check." I would point out.

"All gone," she would tell me; "y'all cain' give me none, reckon I'll jes' hev tuh tell dem welfare ladies they jes' hev tuh give me jes' a little bit mo'!"

Having locked horns with our local welfare on several occasions, I just gawked.

And then Eric got the idea that it would nice if he had a studio of his own and could do his composing at home. Over my raised eyebrow, Bill knocked through a wall and put in a door to an extra room. "The man has to have a place to work in," he explained. The "studio" had wood paneling that I cherished. Eric promptly painted the woodwork blue: it went better with his "vibes". The final touch was a private phone in the studio with an extension in the living room. Poor Eric! He would have made a delightful mantelpiece for a well-to-do widow who was interested in the Arts; but he had fallen in love with Tisha, they had begotten Timmy, and then the bills started rolling in. Eric solved every crisis by putting another tier on his ivory tower.

In the meantime, Tisha and I had been getting better acquainted. The morning after they had moved in she called to me: "Mrs. Carr, please come here. I want to show you something."

"Oh, dear, what now?" I mumbled, as I climbed the stairs for the umpteenth time that day and opened her door. A horrid sight met my eyes.

"Five," said Tisha, "six, seven, eight . . ." and she laid the eighth little dead mouse tail by tail with its brethren. "I opened the vegetable bin in the refrigerator to put in my potatoes and there they were. Really, Mrs. Carr, what kind of people live here?"

"That's a very good question," I said, and fled.

Young Doc (our vet) was waiting in the kitchen to pick up a check, and I told him my tale of woe. "I feel so . . . so mortified!" I said; "like we had small pox or leprosy or something!"

"You're just tired out," he consoled me. (Bill had scolded me for wrestling fifty-pound sacks of feed off the truck when the men were all busy.) "And you're making a mountain out of a molehill. Why, when we moved into that old house on Lee Road, we found rats! Rats, mind you! Caught three in one night! My wife howled like a banshee!" And he chuckled at the thought.

"Not funny," I reproved him sternly. "In fact, it's sick!" But, of course, I giggled, too.

Later in the day, when I saw Tisha hanging out clothes, I called over: "Feeling better?"

"Oh, yes," she answered, "much better. I took four aspirin and they're working."

"Four?" I asked, "What happened?"

"Well, I was cleaning the venetian blinds, and the valance fell down and hit me on the head."

Some days you just can't make a nickel—not even with inflation. Hopefully, the rest of the day would be calm, cool, and collected. Hah! In the middle of the afternoon, I made some iced tea steeped with real lemon and took a pitcher in to Tisha with my apologies. While we were chatting, I heard an ominous drip . . . drip . . . drip. Faucet running? No. Drip . . . drip . . . drip. Busted pipe? Nothing showed. "Well, something's wrong," I said, with a fine display of logic. Suddenly Tisha pointed.

"Look!" she yipped.

An inch of water was oozing out from under the door to her clothes closet. Her clothes closet! And it was steaming hot! We yanked open the door; water poured from the ceiling and cascaded down the walls. While we watched, a glob of plaster peeled off and landed, PLUNK!

"Oh, my God!" I said, and grabbed an armful of clothes off the hangers. "Mop! Pail! Rags!" I snapped.

Dottie heard the commotion and ran in from the yard. "Yikes!" she gasped, "It's my sink! Sorry!" and she tore upstairs.

Katie came in lugging her cocktail shaker.

"Put that damn thing down and help!" I snarled.

We mopped and we sopped, and we huffed and we puffed, and we finally stemmed the tide. Then we all pitched in and hung Tisha's clothes out to dry. I sneaked a worried glance at her. She was beaming! "Aren't you mad?" I asked incredulously.

"Gadzooks, no!" she answered giggling, "All that excitement? All that lovely destruction? I just loved it!"

After we went to bed that night, I told Bill about it. "She said she loved it!" I reported, "she said 'all that lovely destruction'!"

Bill rolled over and stared at the ceiling. "Honey," he said, after a long pause, "I'm beginning to wonder: With all the shenanigans that go on in this house, do you suppose . . . is insanity catching?"

Since I could never have any children of my own, I drooled over any child within reach. Naturally, I drooled over Little Timmy, who Eric and Tisha had decided would be an only child ("One is enough," they both told me.) Timmy was a charming child, physically. With Tisha's pale gold hair and milky skin and Eric's grey eyes flecked with brown, he could have adorned any Christmas card or served as a shepherd in a child's nativity scene. But, along with Eric's eyes, Timmy had inherited Eric's ivory tower. Not for Timmy were the lightning changes of mood that enlivened Little Mike's day; Timmy was placid. Little Mike leaped from crag to canyon; Timmy lived on a plateau. Little Mike was thunderheads and sunshine; Timmy was a misty afternoon. Timmy trailed around the house all day humming little tunes and patting the walls in a rhythm all his own.

"He's a musician," Tisha told me, proudly; "At his age, imagine! Maybe he'll be a genius."

Maybe, maybe, but I began to read books on child psychology and then, one day when I went into their place to visit, I thought I detected a slight odor. Always uneasy about our nip-and-tuck self-installed sewage system with its septic tank, its distribution box, and its hundreds of feet of underground soil pipe (sanitary facilities in the country are a little more complicated than just pushing the lever on the john), I inquired anxiously, "Do I just imagine it, or is there . . . ?" and I sniffed the air delicately.

"Oh," Eric said casually, "it's probably Timmy. He refuses to be housebroken."

"Oh, my gosh," I said, giggling, "so does my puppy. What do you do about it?"

"Well, frankly," he answered, "we keep him outdoors as much as possible," and we both smiled. Puppies and little boys! But, that night I tried to talk to Bill about it.

"Timmy is almost four," I pointed out.

"Stop worrying," Bill advised me; "Honey, every child is different. Timmy just figures that when you gotta go, you gotta go! And he's right. Come on, now; let's listen to the news."

If the way to a man's heart is through his stomach, the way to a mother's heart is through showing an interest in her offspring. Tisha began to turn to me for advice (which she then threw out the window), and sympathy (which she lapped up). In return for this "Older Sister" status, she became hell-bent on "helping" me. Everything she did, she did with such a purple passion and such single-minded dedication, that Bill starting calling her "Joan of Arc".

"So, what has Joan of Arc done today?" he would inquire as he washed up for dinner. And I would tell him. But, one day she outdid herself. I was in the barn scrubbing the milk dishes. I had just gotten an impassioned call from the milk inspector.

"For God's sake, get cleaned up out there," he had begged; "my boss is coming out with me."

So I was scrubbing like crazy. Bill was nearby loading the truck to go to the mill and Willie was in the field gunning for woodchucks (horrid little creatures that chewed up our crops). In the midst of all this industry, Tisha came tearing down the lane.

"P-P-Pat!" she stuttered, "There's a cow in the road! In the road!"

"Well, get it out of there," I said brusquely, "I'm busy right now!"

"Who, me?" Tisha quavered.

"Yes, you!" I retorted. "Just get in back of her and wave your arms and yell 'Co, Boss' and she'll move. Here, take Petie with you." Petie was our farm dog whose roots are so mixed up, when I asked Doc what kind of dog he is, he grinned and answered "Confusing".

Tisha and Petie took off, and five minutes later there was a squeal of brakes and a horrendous shriek. "HELP!" It was Tisha.

I dropped the dishes and ran. Bill zipped up the lane with the old truck, blowing steam like a calliope. Willie threw the tractor into free-wheeling with his rifle at the ready.

"C-c-cow!" wailed Tisha.

"What cow? Where?" we demanded.

Tisha pointed behind her at the fence. There was no cow.

"Well, well . . ." she stammered.

A car had come speeding up the road. Tisha had run in back of the cow flapping her arms and shouting, "Boo! Scat! Git!" Petie had nipped at the cow's heels. The cow had kicked Petie and he had sunk his teeth into the cow's leg: Boing! The cow lunged forward, stuck her head through the fence rails, got her shoulders stuck, and hung there bawling. And, believe you me, cows can bawl!

At this point, Tisha shrieked and ran for help. As soon as Tisha and Petie fled, the cow, like any sensible cow would do, backed up, pulled her head free, found a hole in the fence, and was now peacefully grazing in the field. Tisha turned red from her ears to her toes and back up to her ears. "Well, it was there," she said lamely. There was a pause.

"Gotta get back to the dishes," I said.

"Gotta get to the mill," said Bill.

"Them woodchucks is a-hustlin'," remarked Willie.

Trailing her armor, Joan of Arc clanked into the house.

October changed into November; November gave way to December; and December brought Christmas: that time of peace on Earth, good will towards all. For once, everyone seemed satisfied. Katie gave Clarence Irish whiskey and Clarence gave Katie Irish linen tea towels. Herta gave General MacArthur (her cat) a brand-new collar and a can of imported tuna. Little Mike gave Dottie an extra-sloppy kiss. But Tisha came into my kitchen with a doleful expression. "Pat," she said, "what do you suppose Eric gave me for Christmas?"

"No idea," I answered. "What did Eric give you?"

"Well, with all the bills that we owe and all the things we need . . . He gave me a silver teapot." Then she burst into tears.

"There, there," I said, consolingly, patting her on the shoulder. "Join the club. One year, Bill gave me a mop. A mop, mind you! I bawled all day. It was even worse than the time that he forgot my birthday and I carried on so he went downtown and came back with an expensive string of pearls with a diamond clasp."

Tisha sniffed, then smiled. Since I kept the books, I knew the exact state of our finances, or the lack of them. I never teased for luxuries we couldn't afford, like a brand-new bright red pickup truck; but, at Christmas, I yearned to have Bill go into the bank and emerge dripping with mortgages and mink. When I finally got the message across, he just grunted. No mortgages. No mink.

After the holidays, Tisha decided that, like Patrick's wife, it was up to her to keep the home fires burning. So, like Agnes, she got a job as a waitress. The boss was pleased; she would "class up" the joint. But it didn't work out all that well. With her fairy-tale-princess gold and white coloring

214

and her air of aloofness, the customers were somewhat turned off: they couldn't bitch at royalty if she slopped the soup. The boss began to cool, and Tisha asked me what she could do to hang onto her job.

"Well," I said, thoughtfully, "aside from letting him drive you home late at night alone . . ."

"Yuck!" cried Tisha.

Then I had a brainstorm. "Tell him to put on a smorgasbord. This town has never seen a smorgasbord."

"Beautiful!" Tisha agreed; but, as a matter of fact, that blew it. The boss was outraged.

"What's the matter?" he snarled, "Ain't my food good enough for you? You're fired!"

So, Tisha started to draw get-well cards for a living; Bill pointed out what happened when I got involved in other people's problems; and Eric went on writing music and tearing up his bills.

One day I was in the kitchen struggling with a lemon pie (hand-squeezed lemons—no artificial flavoring for Bill!) with a crust rolled to a delicate flakiness with an old-fashioned rolling pin; it was an act of love for me to bake a pie, and I was all floured up when Katie and Clarence barged in with the mail. All of our mail was put in the roadside mailbox and whoever was expecting a letter watched the road and jumped up and down, yelling "The mail has run! The mail has run!" when the mailman drove up. Then the whole schmeer was brought to me to distribute.

"Pat," Clarence said, as they came in, "we want to talk to you." He slammed the door behind him.

"Alone," added Katie, who tiptoed over to the window and pulled down the shade.

"Oh, come on now," I protested. "I'm in the middle of a pie! What's all this cloak-and-dagger stuff?"

"This is serious," Clarence declared solemnly.

"It's about Eric," Katie added. "He's got another letter postmarked 'Russia'."

To Katie, civilization stopped short with Paris, France.

"So what?" I demanded, "he studied in Russia."

"It's the third one this week," Katie said, looking down her nose and talking out of the side of her mouth.

"And, you know," Clarence cut in, "there's that top-secret missile base not too far from here. And I heard at the Veteran's Club that there's an FBI man in town, and I think . . ."

"And, so do I," Katie said firmly.

". . . he's an infiltrator," Clarence finished.

"We think he's a spy!" they chorused and rested their case.

I bit my lips to keep from giggling. Mild, inoffensive Eric? A spy? Then I reviewed their arguments. Yes, Eric did get a lot of foreign mail. Yes, there was a top-secret missile base with its barbed wire and sentries and warnings to "KEEP OUT". And, when I thought of the bemused expression in Eric's eyes as he gazed over the top of his glasses into the far, far distant horizons . . .

"Wow!" I said, and ran to find Bill.

"Nonsense!" Bill snorted when I told him. "Honey, Eric is a musician!"

"But that's just his cover!" I gasped breathlessly. (I have a whole bookshelf full of "Super Sleuths".)

"Pat, Dear, I hate to ruin your day," Bill said, "but you know this town. If there was any top-secret hanky-panky going on, the mailman would know it, the Ladies' Aiders would know it, and the waitress at the coffee shop would have told me long ago. Be a good girl and go in and start dinner—I'm hungry."

As I trailed off, he called over his shoulder, "With your imagination, maybe you should write a book!" A happy thought.

In February, the farm work started to slacken off, and I coaxed Bill to take me shopping. "I haven't got a pair of pantyhose to my name," I said, "and my slacks are so old, they're about to fall off me."

"Can't let that happen!" Bill agreed, "come on, let's go."

It was heavenly to shop in a real store again, instead of the village "general merchandise".

"Dinner?" I suggested hopefully, after I had bought some clothes. "Lobster, maybe?" (Bill loved lobster.)

"Don't mind if I do," he answered. So, we had dinner at a restaurant with a four-page menu, and after dinner I bought a newspaper. In the "Theater News", I saw that a leading man that I used to work with was appearing locally.

"Please! Please, can we go?" I implored.

So, we went to an honest-to-goodness theater with footlights and applause, and afterwards, the leading man and I brought each other's lives up to date. It was a full evening, but it wasn't over yet. Not quite yet.

When we came out of the theater, the parking lot was covered with snow. Big fluffy flakes that showed no sign of stopping were falling. The rearview mirror was plastered with ice a half-inch thick. So was the rear window and the ice scraper wouldn't begin to touch it. I had to open my door and lean out into the weather to guide Bill from the parking lot into the street.

"It's a bad one," Bill said, and turned on the CB radio.

"Warning!" a voice blared, "All highways are closed! All highways are closed!"

"Guess that does it," Bill decided. "We'll pull into a hotel."

It was such a safe feeling to stand at the hotel window and see other people hemmed into doorways or scurrying to get to their homes. And the hotel was warm. Warm?!

"Oh, my gosh, Bill!" I exclaimed, "I forgot to put water in the furnace before we left! What if the fire goes out? What if the house gets cold? Everybody will be mad!"

"Forget it," Bill said, "if those guys get cold, they'll just crawl under the blankets further. This is the first night I've had off in months, and I intend to enjoy it."

But, I was worried, of course, and called home on Eric's phone. Joan of Arc answered.

"Tisha," I said, "will you go in the cellar and turn the little knob on the boiler that lets water into the furnace? When the glass shows full, turn it off. Be sure to turn it off, or the furnace might explode!"

"Will do," Tisha promised; "don't worry about a thing."

I went to the window and stared at the street lights. Oh, the street lights! There was only one light on our whole road at home, and that was the one Bill had installed at the entrance to our driveway.

At midnight the phone rang in our hotel room. Trouble!

"Pat, Dear, I'm so sorry," Tisha wailed, "I turned the water on and then Timmy fell out of bed and I tended to him, and now there's water all over the cellar floor, and . . ."

"Tisha!" I yelled; "go turn off the main switch at once! Do you hear me? Tisha?" The line was dead.

I jerked the blankets off of Bill and kicked him in the shins. "Get up!" I snapped. "Tisha is planning to blow the house up!"

Bill grunted and opened one eye. "Huh?" he said, drowsily. "Tell her to hold off a while, it'll take us an hour to get there."

"I'm serious!" I said. "She's let the furnace run over, and, if the wires get wet, it'll explode!"

Bill reached for the phone. "I'll get a hold of Clarence; must be one sane person in that madhouse."

He tried to dial, but the operator cut in. "Sorry, sir," she said sweetly, "all wires are down in that area."

"What'll we do?" I asked.

"Pray!" Bill answered.

I walked from the window to the door, back to the window.

"Sit down!" Bill snapped, "you're making me nervous! Here, read a book!"

He handed me a book off the night table. It was a copy of Gideon's Bible.

We both sat up all night, but no word came through. At the crack of dawn, we started home. The snow had stopped, the sky was clear, and everything was sparkling. A good omen? When we were several miles from home, traffic started to pick up.

"Lots of cars for so early in the morning," I observed.

"Farmers going to market," Bill said casually; but I noticed that he speeded up a little.

Farther down the road, we came across more cars—parked—on both sides of the road. And, when we hit the top of the hill, we saw the fire truck in our driveway.

"My God!" Bill mumbled, and jammed the gas pedal flat to the floor.

But, when we turned in the driveway, the Fire Chief flagged us down.

"Didn't want you to get upset," he explained as he leaned through the window. "Everything's fine except for a couple of charred beams in the barn."

"In the barn?" Bill and I exclaimed together.

"Yup," the Chief said. "One of your hired men ran his car in there to clean the spark plugs and he had a basin of gasoline and was a mite careless. You know how that is. And one of his tires caught fire and . . . . Say! You've sure got a smart bunch of women out there! They rolled that car out into the field and grabbed the fire extinguishers and made a bucket brigade. All out before we got here. Sure got a smart bunch of women!"

"Think so myself," Bill agreed smugly. I swatted him.

"Been thinking about you lately," the Chief went on. "Do you remember the first grade that teacher we had? The one with the red hair?"

Just then the "All Clear" sounded and we went into the house. The furnace was on, the house was warm, and everything was normal.

"How did you manage?" I asked Tisha.

"Oh, I woke up Clarence and he fixed it. Clarence knows all about those funny wheels you turn."

"Glad to do it," beamed Clarence. "Thought it was a shame if you and Bill couldn't have one night of peace and quiet. By the way, Pat, did Bill ever tell you that he and I went to school . . ."

"Spare me," I begged, "it's been a long day's night."

At long last, Eric's bills caught up with him. Letter after letter came from lawyers' offices or credit bureaus. Even Bill tossed in the towel.

"It's been a bad year on the farm," he admitted, "and subsidizing Eric is a luxury we can't afford."

"I'll speak to Tisha," I promised. I knocked on her door, but there was no answer, although I knew she was in. I tried the back door; no one came. I had promised Bill, so I plodded through the cellar and came in through her kitchen.

"My," she said scathingly, "the strangest things crawl out of the woodwork!"

They left during the night with no forwarding address.

"Pity," his boss told me, "Eric had a lot on the ball as far as talent went."

We all felt glum and I worried about Timmy. "If you just wouldn't get so involved," Bill scolded me. But, he watched the mail as anxiously as I did. Finally a letter came postmarked Canada.

"Maybe it's good news," Bill said. He waited while I opened it.

"Dear Pat," I read, "How I miss you. How I long to see you, if only for a few minutes. I need you so much. I took Timmy to a specialist last week. He talked to Timmy for a long time and then he called me into his office and told me to sit down. He said . . ."

"How dreadful," I said to Bill. "Poor Tisha!"

"Why? What happened?" Bill asked.

"Timmy is in a home for mentally retarded children now."

CHAPTER 19

Cherry-Picking, Oh No!

My friend, Angie, has the nicest way of asking my opinion, as if she thought it was worth something, and then doing the exact opposite. "I don't know," I started to say, and then the horrid impact of the word "we" struck me, and I sat straight up. "Oh, no you don't!" I said, "I'm not going to go out and pick cherries!"

"Well, let's ask Mr. Carr," said Angie, "poor Mr. Carr. Works awful hard, deserves a heap, don't he? Poor devil. Mr. Carr, come up and get a cup of coffee," she called. She handed him a cup of coffee—black.

"Cream and sugar, please," said Bill, having none of her nonsense.

"You've put on a little weight, haven't you Mr. Carr?" Angie asked. "What do you think about us picking cherries?"

"Just say the words 'us picking' to him," I was thinking.

Bill cleared his throat. "Why, Angie, it's pretty good. You can make $15, $20, or $25 a day. It's piece-work, you know; depends on the cherries, you know."

"Think of that," answered Angie, "$25 a day. It just goes to show you, don't it, Mr. Carr? I work for a dollar an hour, and you work for a lot of debts, and those cherry pickers get $25 a day."

"Not everyone can do it," Bill said, "you have to be good, of course, to get that much."

"Oh sure, sure," Angie replied, "you got to be good; but, we're good, ain't we, Pat?" And she gave me a nudge. "Have another piece of cake. Aw, c'mon, I like to see folks eat. Won't hurt you a bit."

"Thanks," I said.

She blinked her eyes and looked at Bill, then launched her attack. "Mr. Carr," she said earnestly, "can you get us a job?"

"Just pass the cake, Angie," said Bill, "and I'll get you any job you want. Pat's got me on a diet." All the cherry men were screaming for help, but Bill played the scene straight. "Give Dave Naston a call and say I told you to. He'll make good use of you."

"You do it, Pat," said Angie, "you'll do it better than I will."

"Poor Pat," I groaned, but no one encouraged me.

"You know, Honey," said Bill, "all my kids used to go cherry-picking every year when they were young. Nothing wrong with it, you know. They had a lot of fun."

"Those darn Whiz Kids again!" I muttered.

Angie got me up at six so that we could take Bob to work first. "Poor Pat," I said, but nobody noticed me. We parked the Cadillac that poor, underpaid Angie was driving, right in with the jalopies. In a trade that paid $25 a day, I had expected to find much more chrome. Well, I had Bill to thank for this predicament.

"Dave's in the east orchard," said Mrs. Naston, so we went over there. The east orchard had nice little baby trees that just came up to my eyebrows and which I could walk around.

"Sorry, girls," said the foreman, "got all the help we need here. Better go someplace else. Try the old orchard across the lane."

We ambled over the lane and found Dave. The old orchard had had a booster shot in its pituitary gland and could have been a stand-in for the beanstalk in Jack and the Beanstalk. "Poor Pat," I moaned. Angie strode ahead and flipped her cigarette back at me.

"Hi, girls," said Dave. "Get your ladders. Here; take this row. You'll get paid tonight. You know what to do. Any questions?"

"Yes," I replied, "why did I ever come here?"

Angie and I walked over to the pile of ladders. They were fifteen feet long—honest to Pete they were! And me, who gets seasick when I climb up on the table! These were not stepladders, mind you, but ladders: two poles with rungs in between.

"Well, don't just stand there moaning," said Angie, "we gotta get going if we're gonna earn $25. Come on, Pat, let me show you what to do." She grabbed the tail end of a ladder, swung it around and smacked her fanny. "Damn!" she cried.

"This calls for thought," I said, "brain work. Let's cooperate. Both of us take hold of that ladder."

"Some little thinker, ain't you," replied Angie, "well, I allus say you ain't got nothin' to lose if you don' try. C'mon! Let's lick this orchard, Old Gal!"

We could reach the bottom branches of the trees easily, and we could pick fast. Bill had strapped belts around our waists and hooked a gadget to our pails so that we could pick with both hands. We were well-equipped, alright. We were very practical-looking, although not exactly chic. But, this was just a come-on. Bottom branches are called "bottom branches" because there are branches above them. These are known in the trade as "upper branches". Pretty complex, huh? I used my brains on this problem, too, but the tree was still sixteen feet high.

"Poor Pat, poor Pat," I groaned.

"If I had a cracker, I'd give it to you," said Angie, "you sound like a parrot! Gimme a hand with this ladder."

"Maybe," I said, "if we took the ladder by the top end and sort of edged it up the tree?" It couldn't be "edged". I grabbed it by the middle and it buckled fore and aft. Angie laughed. She was obviously tickled by the whole damn project. Then she lifted it by the rear and she was so far away from the tree, she couldn't see the trunk.

"Let's have a cigarette," suggested Angie. Fortified by the cigarette, I edged and Angie reared, and we worked the ladder up into the branches. "Now," said Angie, "we're making real progress, Pat! We'll put my ladder up in that tree over there, and we'll be all set."

"That's what you think," I said to myself. I wasn't even this scared in the Empire State Building. Bill was going to be downright pained that he didn't have any insurance on me; but I was going to be more pained if I let those Whiz Kids get ahead of me. Why did I always have to compete with them? I climbed up the ladder.

"Angie," I hollered, "can you reach your cherries?"

There was a disgusted snort. "No, I can't!" she hollered back. "They're just out of reach."

Angie and I peered at each other through the branches. "Well," I said, "I guess cherries are where you find them."

Down we climbed. We grabbed the ladder in the middle and backed it up. We looked around. We sighted carefully and drew a bead at some thick clusters and ascended.

"Angie! Look out!" I yelled. She swung way out to reach some cherries and her ladder swung smack against a limb, almost breaking completely in half. I heard a gawd-awful swear word, and Angie climbed down.

"My God!" she said; "look at all those other people picking cherries. Mr. Carr will never let us hear the end of this."

"Especially the Whiz Kids," I muttered, "carry on."

Fired with the stuff which takes people from rags to riches and a few broken bones, we reset our sights and picked some more cherries. This time we did it. Success! We ate them. It was a hot day.

"If you'd just cooperate a little more," I said.

"Who're you talking to?" asked Angie, belligerently.

"The ladders," I answered,

"Look, Kid," she said, "I'll take the high rung, and you take the low rung . . ."

"And I'll be in the Cadillac afore ye!" I finished. This was ridiculous; neither of us were even Scottish!

Angie climbed out on a limb and the limb cracked. That made Mr. Naston mad—cherry growers take good care of their trees. All around us, Whiz Kids were filling their pails up. Some man came over and offered to place our ladders, but Angie drove him off and remarked loudly, "Well, I got to get home soon and fix my husband's dinner," and he slunk off. I wasn't so ethical, but apparently I wasn't so attractive, either.

The sun got hotter, and we began to perspire freely. We wiped our sweaty hands on our dirty jeans and then pushed our hair back out of our eyes. Then we got to giggling.

"You know," said Angie, "I don't think it's fair to Bob not to have a pie ready for him when he comes home tonight. Here it's my vacation and I don't even have a pie baked. That's the least I could do for the poor lug."

"Angie," I said severely, "not even a nice cherry pie? It's our duty to go! C'mon!"

We backed the Cadillac from among the jalopies and went home. "Such fun!" we said, wiping our noses. "And we made a lot of money, too."

"Oh?" said Bill, picking my weight slip up off the floor, where it had fallen. "You did?" He read it out loud: "Mrs. Wm. Carr, wages $3.42. That's marvelous, Dear! My kids all loved to go cherry-picking! It was fun!"

I rubbed liniment on my lame muscles that night. "Honey," I said meekly, "is there anyone who would like to hear me sing?"

I had no offers on that, either. Poor Pat!

CHAPTER 20

Cows . . . Again!

"**J**eepers, I'm pooped!" I said, as I flopped on the davenport in Roxanne's apartment. "I've been clipping cows all afternoon!"

Roxanne and Gerald, our newest tenants, sat up and piped in unison, "Why do you clip the cows?"

I could see the term was puzzling, so I launched into an explanation. "Well," I started, "in my case, it's positively Freudian, but it's supposed to be good for them. It's like getting a haircut all over. It gets rid of the manure and body lice, and the black and white Holstein skin does look so fresh."

They do pink up, though, in the frost, and, if one of them should get pneumonia, I can just hear Bill saying to himself but loud enough for me to hear, "How did I ever run this farm without you?"

In other words, it was like taking out insurance pre-Bill. By this time I was beginning to think of myself as an Old Cow Hand. I knew all the cows by name and they would come when I called, if I was careful to hold the grain dish right out in plain sight. I could do almost all the things that Bill's kids could do when they were four years old. So, I was ripe for the axe. I would show those Whiz Kids!

I went out to the barns to feed the calves, and Bill looked up impatiently and said, "Go bring in Betty."

"Betty who?" I asked. After all, there were the dogs, the lambs, the tenant's children, and assorted neighborhood kids.

224

"Betty Betty!" Bill answered disgustingly, without taking his eyes of his work. "You know . . . Betty. She's out in the side pasture, and she ought to be milked out tonight. Her calf hasn't taken enough."

This wasn't quite down my alley. Betty is our biggest cow, but the Master had spoken, so the slave acted. Out I went. There is an accepted technique for getting bovine mamas into the barn: You bring the calf in and mama tails it. This idea, like price supports and international protocols, looks good in theory, but I had to practice it. "Co boss, co boss," I said, and Betty responded with an earth-shaking bellow. "Co boss, co boss." Another bellow from Betty, plus a shake of the head.

Clearly, she was saying to her son, "Have nothing to do with this creature. Go underground. Will write." Pretty sound advice, if you asked me.

"Co boss," I said and started for the calf. Betty picked up her front hoof, pawed the ground, and snorted. To me, her flaring nostrils looked like Milton Berle making love. "Co boss," I repeated, for the last time, as Betty pawed her hind feet and made for me.

Though tempted to run, I stood my ground. I flagged both arms up and down and squawked. I hollered that I wouldn't even look at her baby. On she came, eyes afire. I tried to quell her with the human eye, but when she poked her horns on my bosom, I fled. I am no lesbian! What would I tell my spouse? Oh well, I'd have to face him.

Inside the barn, Bill looked up in an innocent—very innocent—fashion. "I forgot to tell you," said he, "she's apt to be a wee mite troublesome. Aw, c'mere, Baby," he added, as my lip quivered. "You're a farmer's wife now." And he'd hug me later.

At the dinner table that night, Bill looked worried. "'S matter?" I asked when he ate silently with a preoccupied frown.

"Oh, nothing much," he answered with his usual understatement. When Bill hears Gabriel's horn, I am convinced he will turn over and say mildly, "Pat, dear, someone's blowing something." So, I knew if he admitted it was "nothing much" that it was probably a situation where I would have called out the state militia.

"You might as well tell me," I said.

"Well," he admitted, "Old Number One acts like she's trying to have her calf. I think she's started, but she's not getting anywhere. In fact, she's getting nowhere. Guess I'd better go down and watch her."

If a cow doesn't have her calf within two to four hours, it is a pretty good indicator that she's in trouble. By ten o'clock, Old Number One was down and groaning, but there was no calf. "Call Doc," said Bill.

It's always been my job to call people because Bill doesn't hear too well; and sometimes I get buffaloed on both sides.

"Can't you pull it out?" asked Doc. Doc is over sixty, and he's a little tired out from a lifetime of tearing around the countryside with a black satchel and some rubber gloves. When you think about it, you'd probably be tired out, too.

Quite often farmers can do their own obstetrics. They tie a rope around a hoof of the unborn calf and then run the rope over a pulley so that, if a man pulls with all his strength, he can pull out the calf. It always surprises me that both mother and child usually survive this primitive delivery. It may sound unbelievably crude, but it works.

This time, however, Bill sensed a tougher problem. "Nope," he said, "tell Doc he'd better come."

Doc sighed. He knew Bill wouldn't call him needlessly. I could hear his grandchildren playing and his television was on, but he said he'd come. It was pitch dark in the part of the barn in which Old Number One had chosen to have her calf. Bill allowed that I could stay in the house if I wanted to, but somebody had to hold the flashlight, so there was Old Pat doing it.

Doc knew immediately that the calf was dead. He told Bill that it was a fine big one; in fact, that was why it was dead. It was much too big for Old Number One to handle. There was nothing he could do, so he hauled out a little wire saw—a flexible thin wire with saw teeth on it held taut between two tiny handles. He was able to get his hand in around the calf, and by pulling the wire back and forth, he sawed through the calf's body, then through each of the severed halves. This made each quarter small enough so he could slip a rope around them and pull them out in chunks. It was most disturbing; I had to turn away. Nobody offered to give Old Number One—or me—even an aspirin, although the men did keep up a running comment of "Co boss. Stand still, girl. There, there. Whoa! Alright, alright, girl."

The electric lantern threw a harsh concentrated glare. Bill and Doc looked a little like ghouls. Doc dusted Old Number One with an antiseptic and came into the milk room to wash up. He looked at me a little oddly. "Kind of a long ways from the bright lights of Broadway, aren't you?" he asked me, matter-of-factly.

Doc always had the impression that he feels he's missed something by being a vet in a small town. I looked down at my blue jeans and my manure—and blood-spattered shoes and I felt a little sickish.

"Yeah," I agreed, brandishing my flashlight. "But look how useful I am up here!"

"That's so?" said Doc, "Five dollars, please." Then he got back into his car and went back to his grandchildren and TV.

On the other side of the picture was something that happened a long time ago, just after I came. Looking back, I am appalled at my own bad taste, and my only apology is that, at the time, animals, to me, certainly weren't people. I must've been totally unsure then of their sensibilities. One of the horses had gone down in a mudhole and couldn't get up. Bill told me that he was going down to shoot him. We had just started renting apartments, and I was floundering around in a frenzy of worry as to how young newlyweds used to the distractions of the five and dime and beauty parlors and the movies, would adjust to the monotony of country life. I was up to here trying to think of distractions. So I went up to the house and told Katie and Dottie that a horse was down in a mudhole and Bill would have to shoot it and did they want to go down and watch? Of course they did; they didn't go to fires or stop to look at accidents.

Bill courteously explained that he preferred to go alone, and he was furious with me. "What," he said, when we were alone, looking at me with distaste, "do you think this is? A picnic?"

I went down the lane with him and he went up to Ned and said, right in his ear, "Sorry, old man," before he shot him. Bill and Ned had worked together for a good many years and were close friends.

Bill and I did a lot of chores together, and it's a wonder that we didn't kill each other over some issue or other because we were together practically twenty-four hours a day and differed on all major points and a few minor ones, as well. Usually love won out, but the law of averages was still working. It was "one of those days" (you know, the kind that give you numerous sleepless nights) and the evening's milking had started completely squee-jawed. I had chased the cows out of the cornfield and caught my boot toe in the husks and fell flat three times. Petie had aggravated them by barking at their heels until they kicked up their heels and ran. Our general financial condition depended on the milk check, with the result that we hovered over each cow taking temperatures at the slightest sniffle. My husband was really concerned about this normally, but he forgot the time and appeared late. (This is unforgivable as cows work on a strict schedule.) He was tired, I was tired; the cows were flighty; the young ones were plain silly; the milking machines went "squawk-squish-squawk" instead of "chug-chug-chug". Like I said, it was just one of those days.

There was an air leak we couldn't find. We took off the air tube, the teat cups, the pulsator, no luck; there was no trace of air at all. The air leak turned the gentle suction on the teats into a spastic jerk and turned the cows into hellions. Don't tell me machinery doesn't have a soul! It has a fiendish soul that delights in torturing amateur mechanics. If nothing else, I learned that one thing that day.

At this point, Number Five, a heavy producer, got out of her stall. In the general confusion, she didn't get her extra grain. This was calamitous—so many pounds of grain equals so many pounds of milk. I cried for help. "Bill," I yipped, "Number Five got out! Head her back in and feed her."

"Aw, the hell with it!" muttered Bill.

This involved one of our most delicate points: the fact that there are some things that Bill feels just aren't worth the trouble, or else he doesn't give a damn about it at the moment.

"Well, gee whiz," I sputtered, "here I work in this damned old barn and do without things and wash up the milk dishes and haven't a new dress to my name, and I try to do what I can to help and you don't even care enough to go feed a little old cow that's hungry! That's a fine thing! Aren't you ashamed of yourself? If my mother knew some of the things I do . . ."

"Alright, alright!" Bill cried, and went to turn three-quarters of a ton of hoof and hide clean around and back in a space twenty-four inches wide. Since bossy Number Five didn't know there was dinner at the end of it, she didn't co-operate. I heard her bellow. There was a horrendous scuffle, then a thud. Bill stalked back into the milking alley. He stuck his head in the feed box and remarked very clearly and distinctly to the back wall, "Goddamned old bitch! Damn near broke my goddamned leg! Why, you godamed . . . yakety, yakety, yak."

"William!" I gasped, while the stalls went round and round. "William Carr!"

"I meant the cow, the cow!" he remarked hastily. Nobody can out-think that guy in the clinches!

We each stepped forward one pace and saluted, while the cows took sides; but before we got in one thrust, we paused there on the threshold—the absolute absurdity of the whole thing struck us both at the same time, and we howled in laughter! When we were done howling, we had a good comfortable home-style buss, right there in front of the cows, and they didn't seem to mind the intrusion any. As Willie would say, "Love done come down on the old folks in the cornfield. Oh, Glory Hallelujah!" The milk pails were full.

We breed most of our cows by artificial insemination, and I always feel sorry for the cows. It seems to me that a certain amount of dash and romance has been snatched out of their lives. I mean, what if we humans had to do that? Ugh! The cows prance around and get dewy-eyed and then I call the inseminator, and that's the end of it. Things must be pretty dull when the Machine Age takes over courtship. The young heifers turn up their noses at the whole idea; they're not stupid, anyway! That's why we keep a bull.

I keep the breeding records, but when I insisted on going to a breeding meeting, Bill was in a tizzy. I drove with him as far as the barns where the meeting was being held, and then he delivered an ultimatum. "You stay in the car," he decreed, "I will not be disgraced!" So, I sat in the car and froze, and Bill's name went undisgraced.

Young Doc is the one who can really tell the stories. If you can believe everything you hear, Young Doc must lead quite a life, at least to hear his version. ". . . and there that dang cow stood" . . . one tiller of the soil will tell another . . . "never said a word, you know, 'til Doc got right up close to hear, and then wham! She damn near kicked the side of the barn in!" Doc's had some hair-raising adventures. Once in a while, Doc would make a pass at a fractious cow. "Doc," I chided him on one such occasion, "every cow in this barn is a lady!"

"Maybe so," he answered, "but some of them are darned uncouth!"

Like every other Big Business, the dairy industry has its pet phrases. Cows, believe it or not, have what is known as the Dairy Temperament. Don't laugh—they're people, too! Nice people! When you pay a good round sum, which is more than you can afford, for a first calf heifer with a family tree that goes back to the Ark (just where did the cow come from, by the way?), and she "comes in" and doesn't cover the bottom of the milk pail, you just sigh and say, "Well, she doesn't have the Dairy Temperament." That is, if you're feeling charitable, you say that. And, when a little old scrub that has ribs you can hang your hat on and that you don't kill because she wouldn't bring anything for beef shows up with two brimming pails, you say, "Well, she's got the Dairy Temperament!" It's all a questions of temperament, simple as that.

I have gotten myself something of a local reputation as having, for a woman, some slight judgment as to the excellence of cows, at least among the other women. My method is simple: I go to the auctions. I hunt up an auctioneer's assistant. I put on my flattering "My, but you're such an authority, aren't you?" expression. I say "Which cow would you buy?" And he gives. In fact, he's pleased as punch to do so: reasons, prices, pedigrees. Then I saunter over to one of the more canny buyers and I say, "Well, now, what do you think of Number 13?" And I cite all of the auctioneer's assistant's stream of data. Of course, he immediately trots me over to another stall, giving me the lowdown on this cow and sings her merits. I listen absorbedly, and then, at the end of the oration, I crease my brow; lean my chin on my hand; look the cattle over carefully; and say, in a measured tone, "Now, of course, I know that you know, but, tell me honestly, do you think she has the Dairy Temperament?" This always gets a raised eyebrow or two! I hear that there is a somewhat erroneous local opinion that Mrs. Carr is a pretty smart girl! And that's how I get by with cows.

Bill is always afraid I'll open my mouth and come out with a really dumb remark, so when my step-son-in-law, the one who runs a model dairy, stopped by, I showed him the barns and we chatted for an hour. Bill acted like a perturbed mama. "I hope you had sense enough to keep quiet and let him do all the talking!" he said. "What did you talk about, anyway?" he wanted to know.

"Oh," I answered airily, "I just showed him the cows that had the Dairy Temperament."

"By gol," said Bill respectfully, "Honey, I'm proud of you! My kids couldn't have done better, not even at four years old!"

CHAPTER 21

Cabbage At $4 A Ton Stinks!

Bill wiped his mouth with his napkin and gave a satisfied grunt. "Darn good meal, Honey," he observed, "you're improving!"

I'd just served his favorite dish: standing loin rib roast of pork circled with tender new potatoes that had been basted in the pan drippings. "Now, how about helping me with the dishes?" I hinted.

While we were clearing the table, he said "Pat, no more new tenants, especially the ones that don't pay any rent. Right now I need you on the farm."

Bill had been surprised and pleased at the way I handled the role of personnel manager. I had made one or two mistakes when I first started, like the time he sent me down to check on a crew that was hoeing, and I came back wailing: "They won't mind me!" (My baby sister, Mary, who was a teacher, had the same complaint.) But, after a while, I caught on. If I were working with a crew of young men (boys, really), I would say: "If I take my long skinny nose out of here, will the work be done when I come back?" The boys would snicker—they would show me! And the field would be in tip-top shape when I returned.

I always said, "This is the way we've been doing it. If you come up with any easier way, hop to it." Usually the easiest way was the best way. It went faster and the boys had to prove their point.

Bill bragged about me so much downtown that I began to get puffed up. "Pride goeth before a fall," Mom had always cautioned me, and I sure took one helluva tumble with Pancho. Pancho was a Mexican "wetback" (he swam the Rio Grande River at night and eluded the border guards) along with a dash of Hawaiian Chinese and American Indian. He had served in the Navy and he had somehow acquired the most meticulous diction I had ever heard. A voice coach for a Hollywood starlet could have taken lessons from him. And he had a touch of the exotic in his looks, so all the women in the house got together and decided to "uplift Pancho". Everybody was enthused except Pancho.

He liked his wiry hair sprouting out like a porcupine; he liked his lop-sided diet of beans and hot peppers; and he loved his daily gallon jug of cheap wine. Pancho never got drunk, he just got happy. If I overtook him on the road coming back from town in the morning with his jug, I would "liberate" the jug until after work, and Pancho would just chuckle. He had no idea about hygiene, and, on a dare from the men in the field, he pushed back the scum on a stagnant pool, lay on his belly, and drank deep of the stinking liquid. "You'll die!" the men warned him. Pancho just shook his head and grinned.

One exceptionally hot Monday (a real scorcher), I was working in the field running the transplanter with a crew of five. When the men took a break in the shade, I trotted to another field to check on the men pulling plants. Pancho came to work too late to join either crew, so I put him off by himself pulling weeds. I left a jug of fresh water in the shade to keep cool and went back to juggling the other two fields. Half an hour later, up stalked Pancho in a foul mood. He had been drunk all weekend and was fresh out of money and vino. "Ice!" he demanded. "Water's too warm."

To get ice, I would have had to hold up five men while I drove two miles to the house. "We'll take a break soon," I replied. "I'll get it then."

"NOW!" Pancho ordered.

Between the heat and the pressure and the frustration, I blew. "You're fired!" I yelled, "get out! I'll pay you this afternoon."

Off he trotted towards the house. Half an hour later, he came trudging back. "Hey, you guys," I said to the men, "turn your pockets inside out and see if we can dig up enough to pay Pancho off." He had only worked two hours.

With quarters, dimes, and dollar bills, we made up the total and I walked over to him. "Here," I said, holding out my hand.

Quicker than lightning, Pancho snaked his hand out of his pocket and pulled out a piece of the cutting bar from the mowing machine and struck as hard as he could at my temple. My glasses flew off and I staggered against the wheel of the tractor. It had happened so quickly, the men were stunned.

I put my hand up to my face and blood dripped through my fingers. It was as though I had touched a block of wood and there was no sensation. "He's sliced off part of my face!" I thought.

He came towards me again, but the men jumped into action. There were five of them and they soon has Pancho pinned. Willie rushed me to the emergency room, and one of the others called the state troopers. By the time the troopers got there, Pancho was crying because he had hurt me.

As usual, the doctor on call in the emergency room was nowhere to be found, and, when the nurse asked me to sign a release for permission to perform any necessary surgery, I signed myself out and went to the next town. The force of the blow had burst an artery, and my eyebrow was split open.

The doctor in the Medina ER sewed me up and, on the way home, I saw particles of fire—like fireworks exploding in the air. At first, it was like a drizzle; then a downpour; and, after a while, a gushing waterfall. It was interesting, but not reassuring. The retina in my eye had been disturbed, and it would be six months before it would either heal or detach.

"St. Cecelia," I promised solemnly, "next time I won't fool with a guy who has a hangover."

"Bill around?" asked Vic, a neighboring farmer, "I'd kinda like to see him."

"Will I do?" I asked.

"Well," said Vic, "there are times . . . But this is business."

I started the car and went after Bill. He was down the lane. "Vic's at the house," I called, driving up to him so he could get in.

"For Pete's sake," said Bill, glowering, "do you have to drive over my cabbage bed?"

I looked all over the field. I couldn't see a thing. "Right here!" said Bill, pointing out a chunk that looked just like the rest of the field, as far as I could tell.

"I guess I'm just dumb," I confessed. "But, you can't complain, Dear, you picked me out!"

That stopped him. "I like to sow my own seed," said Bill as we drove back to the house. "Nobody else gets my rows straight." Bill is gimlet-eyed and iron-jawed about getting his rows straight.

"Hello, Vic," said Bill, "how's cabbage going to do?"

"Forgot my crystal ball today," Vic answered. "Let's hope it's a good year."

Bill had told me when we were first married that putting in cabbage was like buying stocks on margin: you made a killing or you got wiped out. I was all set for a good show. We had been all over Hell's half-acre to get the particular kind of seed that Bill wanted. "You're like a ballplayer with a 'lucky' bat," I said, when we drove miles to find the last two pounds of Bacon strain.

"I like my cabbage heads a little large," said Bill, "then, if it's a bad year, I can sell them to the kraut factories. If your heads are small, 'The Market' wants them big. If your heads are big, 'The Market' wants them small."

"Well, how can you tell which to put in then?" I asked.

"That's my little Whiz Kid," Bill said tenderly.

"Well, gosh," I said, "I used to live with a girl who was in Vaudeville and read Tarot cards."

"Call her up!" said Bill.

I had had quite a workout on this cabbage deal the day before. Bill dips the seed in calomel and gum arabic. The calomel is to kill off the maggots that eat the roots of the young cabbage plants, and the gum arabic is to make the calomel stick on; the same purpose in reverse as the orange juice making the castor oil go down.

"You're the fifth person in here today to want that stuff," said Mr. Taylor in the local drug store. "I'm all out. Get some for you by Thursday."

"But, Bill needs it today," I said.

"Next Thursday," repeated Mr. Taylor.

"Today!" I said, again.

There we were, stuck like a broken jukebox record.

"Next Thursday," said Mr. Taylor firmly.

"Dammit! Why didn't you lay in a supply?" I asked, even more firmly.

Mr. Taylor went to the phone and located some in Rochester, but the set of his back said plainly that, in a small town, ladies don't say "Dammit".

Bill hung over his cabbage plants like a mother hen. They have to grow straight," he said. "No crooked stems, or the transplanters can't set them. They can't have 'clubfoot'; 'yellows'; or 'carry' bugs."

"Oh?" I said.

"And they must be just the right size to transplant by the Fourth of July."

"Can you order the sun and rain, and the heat and cold, just the way you need them?" I asked.

"Nope," replied Bill, "but I can worry."

He did, too. He got so involved about the whole thing that he went in there and sprayed them with liquid nitrate to pep them up, and the sun burned them black. Bill gets downright emotional about his cabbage.

Like bread and jam, cabbage plants and transplanting time never come out even. The plants are too small or too big. The fields are too wet or too dry. If everything else is right, the tractor blows a gasket or the hired man falls sick or walks off in a tizzy.

"Corn knee-high, hay in the barn, and cabbage all set by the Fourth of July," is the rule. Obviously, we don't celebrate the Fourth of July by setting off pinwheels at the crack of dawn or relaxing on the lawn with martinis in the drowsy summer twilight, while the crickets chirp and the birdies tweet. Not us! No, we're out "riding the cabbage setter"! This is a good meaty phrase that I was to store in my mind along with "Remember the Alamo!" and "Hold 'em Yale!".

Bill's old setter had laid down and died. The Army still had materials tied up, so all we could do was to shop for a used one. I haunted the "For Sale" columns, and, when I saw one advertised, I called up the man and asked him to hold it for us.

"How much do you think I should offer him for it?" Bill asked on the way over. Bill admires my ability to haggle.

"Well, how much are new ones worth?" I asked.

"Five-hundred dollars," said Bill.

"Offer him $250, that ought to be fair," I suggested.

When we get to Bailey's Machine Shop, we asked a man standing there if he was Mr. Bailey. "No," he replied, "I'm waiting for Mr. Bailey; I want to buy his setter."

"Oh," said Bill.

We stood there. A little before one o'clock, a youngish man came up to Bill. "About that cabbage setter, Mr. Bailey," he said.

"I'm not Mr. Bailey," Bill told him.

"Excuse me," said the man.

Mr. Bailey came in a few minutes later.

"How much do you want for that setter?" asked Bill.

Mr. Bailey counted up the house. "Four-hundred dollars," he replied.

I kicked Bill. Bill took out his check book. "How," he started shaking out his fountain pen, "how do you spell your name?"

We took it home with us on the truck.

"Bill," I said that night as I stood there admiring its $400 worth, "can I help set the cabbage? Can I? Please?"

"Might," said Bill.

But the next day he sent me down to pull cabbage plants. I got on my hands and knees and pulled cabbage plants with both hands. In a spasm of tidiness, I shook the dirt off the roots until they shone silver-gray.

"NO!" cried Bill, "all those little roots are feeder roots and they'll stand the hot weather better if you leave some of their own dirt on them."

"Aye, aye, Sir," I said, and pulled them with the dirt on.

Then I packed them tight in a bushel basket.

"The stems are crooked!" cried Bill.

So, I turned the baskets on their sides and laid the stems straight.

"My gosh," I said, "by the time it gets cut up into cole slaw, who's going to know what the roots looked like?"

"You found out when you learned to transplant the tomatoes," replied Bill. "Are you sure you'd like to ride the cabbage setter tomorrow?"

After the cabbage is all transplanted, we must have rain within seventy-two hours or the plants die. If it's ten acres, then it's ten acres. If it's fifty acres, then it's fifty acres. Or five-hundred. They all die. And you have to dig up the land and start all over again—*if* you can find more cabbage plants, that is.

"What's so darn mystical about the seventy-two hours?" I asked Bill.

"You'll see," he replied. He plunges into depths of a no-rain life. He's sure it won't rain. I've never dared to tell him it will be "damn dry if it don't". He'd probably strangle me on the spot.

A cloud blew right up to the edge of the field the afternoon of the third day. "Please, God," I prayed, "please!" The cloud blew off down the road and rained all over Laura's cabbage. It wasn't fair. She's no more Christian than I am!

Apparently, the weatherman was unconcerned about religion as the cloud blew back again during the night, and it rained. The field had been stretched out flat the night before, every stem and leaf, dragged on the earth. Now the stems looped a little, and only the leaves were dragging. By the next day, the plants had started to grow.

A field of cabbage is as wonderful as a rose garden! The rows are so straight and evenly spaced, and the color of the heads is such a delicate nuance of blue to blue-green to bluish-green. The leaves are swirled, and the head is in the center, like a bud. Cabbage fields carry an echo of hoes and picnic lunches in the shade and babies playing. Cabbage fields are alive.

We sprayed the cabbage every ten days for bugs, for wilt, for all of the ills that cabbage is prone to. The spray tank is a round monster that trails a crossbar with holes in it and the poison spurts out through the faucets. Insects must hate us. The tank is filled with water from our own pond. Anyone who fills the tank at five-thirty in the evening does so at their own risk because Bill and I go swimming in the pond.

In the fall, cabbage needs wet, cold, nasty weather to harden the heads and make them grow. "Oh," I'd groan with my coat bunched around my ears and my hands hurting from the cold.

"Good cabbage weather," Bill would say.

The first year that I helped plant the cabbage, we had a wonderful crop. So did everyone else. We went for a ride through the back country.

"Dear me," I'd say to Bill in a lofty tone as we rode along, "there's a man who doesn't have his wheat in yet. We do, don't we Bill?" Bill grinned.

"Look at the fields of cabbage," he said.

We went down the Ridge Road, up by Lake Ontario, in around Carlton, back to the north, inland to the south. "I don't know, Honey," Bill said. "We'd be taking quite a chance to harvest it. It won't be worth much. We'd better let it rot."

I was horrified. "Bill!" I cried, "all that cabbage I helped to pull, set, and spray! Oh, no, you can't just let it rot!"

John and Isabelle wanted to go back South that winter because they needed work. So they tried to persuade Bill to harvest the cabbage, too. "Jes' seem lak da cabbage got to go up, Bill," said John.

"Well, we'll see," replied Bill.

August came, then September and October, and D-day approached for the harvesting of our cabbage. It had been a good growing season and our crops had done fairly well. But the money from the sale of the cash crops had gone into the harvesting of the late-maturing crops, and, by the end of the season, we stood to make or break on the last crop: cabbage.

Bill believed in "diversified" farming. The staples, like grain, oats, hay, and straw to be stored through the winter to keep the dairy going; the cash crops, like apples, cherries, cucumbers, and cauliflower, to keep up the cash flow during the summer; and the "gamble" crop, like cabbage, for which the price fluctuated wildly, depending on supply and demand.

Any banker will tell you that the farmer is a compulsive gambler. He gambles on the weather, the labor supply, the trucking facilities, and the market. Diversified farming is a way of hedging the farmer's bets. If one thing goes sour, the farmer tightens his belt, increases his mortgage, lies about his assets, and vows "We'll give 'em hell next year!"

In the rare year when he makes a killing, he pays off his notes, trades in his car, buys a new tractor, gets the little woman the wristwatch she has been longing for, and goes broke the following year again.

It was show business all over again. Opening and closing, opening and closing. And, of all the temperamental, prima donna-ish, unpredictable things to gamble on, cabbage is the queen.

A small acreage is contracted to the sauerkraut factories; this is the cabbage grown for large heads, nothing is too big. The heads are lopped off at the root, the outer leaves are left on, and the heads are pitch forked onto a truck and carted to the factory. It is not too expensive of a process, but, oh my goodness, the loss of face! It's like the difference between mutts and purebreds.

The cabbage for market is handled with much more care. The government and the chain stores would like all of the heads to be two pounds in size, but there ain't no way to do it: cabbage heads, like their human counterparts, are all oddballs.

In the fall, the farmers who want to get off the nut sell (if the price is good) out of the field and bank their checks. Those who like long shots go for broke, store their cabbage in their barns or in cabbage storages, and say their prayers. The only time that the price of storage cabbage soars like a rocket is when the south, around Orlando, Florida, or the Rio Grande Valley in Texas, has a freeze. For them both to freeze at the same time requires an Act of God. There is just one wind that blows straight down from Alaska that can do it.

That particular autumn, the price of cabbage dropped clean through the cellar. We had had just enough rain. If we had had a dry spell, the cabbage heads actually shrink instead of growing. Too much rain and the leaves grow too fast and spread too loose so that the head is "punky" and won't store well. Bill and I used to ride around the country looking at the fields. Bill would get out of the car and walk through another farmer's field to check on his cabbage. I was scandalized. To me it was snooping, but Bill assured me it was the proper thing to do. Everybody's fields were yielding way above average, and, because of the glut, the price was $4 per ton when they started cutting.

"Guess I'll leave ours in the field to rot," Bill decided. "Can't even pay for the cutting at that price."

I had a vested interest in that field. I had helped to transpose it: Grab a plant, wait for the "click", stick the plant in between the rollers, and snatch your hand away before it got mangled. It was while we were working in the cabbage field that Pancho had clobbered me. And now Bill wanted to leave the cabbage to rot in the field. No way!

John, our second in command, wanted to earn enough money to go back South, so we ganged up on Bill.

"Well, if I should cut that field . . ." Bill said. I knew he was licked. If Bill had made up his mind not to do something, he wouldn't even discuss it. He knew I could outtalk him any day of the week. ". . . where would we get the help?"

This was a good question. The Jamaicans were booking the airlines. The people from Florida were collecting their crews for the trek south. That left the local help. The weather was drizzly and cold, and cutting cabbage often meant slogging through muddy fields. Not a very inviting prospect.

"Oh, Miss Anne's crew will come," I said, confidently. Miss Anne's crew had picked tomatoes for us, and they had earned a good wage. She and I got along well. Her job was to fill the baskets and mine was to rustle up the money for the payroll; to pack lunch for them as they had forgotten to bring any; and to make innumerable trips to town for soda, snuff, and cigarettes, which were conveniently forgotten on payday. Miss Anne and I each knew our places and so we got along very well.

"Hmm," Bill mused. "OK, we'll start Monday."

Bill told me that you couldn't start cabbage while there was any danger of a warm spell. The heat would start the cabbage rotting in the barn. We had an excellent natural storage. It had been the basement of the barn (the barns were even larger than the house). The walls were built of stone two feet thick, and there were two entrance doors, one on the east end and one on the west end, to let the wind swoop through the building and carry off the heat from the cabbage. Cabbage is stored in bins made of two-by-fours with eight—to ten-inch spaces between to serve as vents. The whole idea was like putting food in the refrigerator at once when you get home from the grocery store.

I tore up to see Miss Anne, quivering with excitement. "Will you?" I begged.

Miss Anne smiled, "Us'll be there," she promised.

Sunday night, I read most of the night. Who could sleep with cabbage-picking starting in the morning? Monday dawned. No Miss Anne. Well, of course, it was laundry day. Tuesday came. No Miss Anne. It was November and Bill had told me: "From the first to the seventh, you can count on the weather. From the seventh to the fifteenth, it's risky. After Thanksgiving, only God knows. Come a sneak freeze and, unless the field has an insulating blanket of snow, you might as well forget it."

Wednesday I took the bull by the horns and went to see Miss Anne.

"You promised," I wailed.

"Us chilluns got tuh go tuh school," she said, reproachfully. "Us cain' neglec' thuh chilluns." And she shut the door in my face—just like in tomato season.

My frantic searching was of no use. Every warm body had left town or was working from someone else already. As usual, time marched on.

Bill had been having trouble with his help all summer. Ol' Sam would come to him and say, "Mistah Bill, dem black boys put dried snakes in my bread. Hexed me right up! Cain't live with dem boys, nohow."

Ol' Sam was a good worker, so Bill fired the first boy. The second time, he fired the other boy, but with a few misgivings. The third man came to Bill and said, "Ah gurts, Ol' Sam, he got some white powdah he put in my tea an' make me sick, and dat boy keep his razah sharp."

"I've been wondering," said Bill. He gave Ol' Sam a good talking to. Everything was quiet for a day or two. Then Ol' Sam cornered Bill in the garage.

"Mistah Bill," he said, taking some loose change out of his pants and a few bills out of his jacket. "You are da smahtes' man Ah know an' the mos' reliable, an' Ah wants you to keep mah money from me."

About five minutes later, Ol' Sam told Bill, "Ah specs mebbe de Sheriff be up aftah me."

Ol' Sam was right. Sheriff Mack came up and with him was Sam's roommate. He had been carved pretty. There was a long gash under one eye and a black-and-blue cheek. Ol' Sam went quietly enough. Bill called up the local judge. "I need him for work, John," Bill explained.

"Thought maybe you did," John answered, "so I only gave him three days. Had it on my mind to fine that black man but Howard turned him upside down and shook him, and not a cent fell out."

"You don't say," said Bill.

We took Ol' Sam back into the fold, but his drunks kept getting more and more frequent. Bill could handle him but, when we were away from home on a trip, he got out his knife again and, when the Sheriff came for him, he hid in our cellar and scared the daylights out of everyone in the house by taking a swipe at the Sheriff. Reluctantly, Bill had to let Ol' Sam go. We lost another worker too when a jealous girlfriend took a hunk out of him with a knife. The labor camps are so crowded and the life so primitive that it's no wonder the drinking bouts are continuous. Bill is the only man I have ever seen who will walk into a labor camp at midnight completely unafraid.

With cabbage at $4 a ton, Bill felt a little reluctant to take over the headaches of a harvest. It would cost him $7 or $8 a ton to cut and store it, but, with John twisting both his arms, he agreed to think it over. "I'll see!" was all we could get out of him.

Bill came back from town one day beaming from ear to ear. "Honey," he said, "guess I got you fixed up."

By now, the cabbage was referred to as "Pat's project".

"I bumped into a crew leader that used to work for me. He's promised to come as soon as they finish up in Bergen. Be here next week."

Bill was sort of smug about the way he had solved the problem, but what did it matter, as long as we got the help? For another week I chewed my fingernails up to my shoulder blades. (What did it matter? There wasn't a manicurist within miles.)

Again, Monday dawned, and again there was no crew. The crew leader stopped by. "Sorry I let you down," he said. My people are anxious to get back home. I heard of another crew that's stranded. The farmer didn't settle up and they don't have enough money for the trip home. I'll send them over."

The days dragged on. I stayed glued to the TV weather reports. The temperatures stayed reasonably cold, but it drizzled a lot and the fields turned into repulsive mud. I finally gave up hope. "My" cabbage was slated to rot in the field and be "turned under".

One noon I looked up from lunch totally uninspired, to see car after car drive into our driveway and stop. The cars were mostly jalopies, battered and rusty, with a sprinkling of beat-up trucks. People poured out of them, and a man came to the door and knocked.

"Bill!" I shrieked. "They're here! They've come! But, where will we put them? There's at least twenty of them plus the babies! What will we do?"

"Now, don't panic," Bill said sternly. "Willie and John can sleep in our attic for a week, and that gives us one house. Run across the road and ask Tony if he'll lend us his tenant house. I know it's vacant. Then take the truck and get Lazzie (Second-Hand Furniture, Antiques and Junk) to give you ten double and ten single mattresses and some old quilts. Get all of the pots and pans he has and a bottled gas cook stove. Tell Lazzie I sent you."

Tony opened his door when he saw me coming. "Know what you want," he said. "Saw 'em drive in. Glad to let you use the house. Bill has done a lot of favors for me. Only thing is, there's no water—well's dry. And the electric's turned off."

"They can haul their water from my kitchen," I replied. "And go to bed early."

On target for number one, I raced to Lazzie's at a speed that should have landed me in jail. "Not a mattress in the place," Lazzie said, regretfully.

"You lie through your teeth," I informed him. "I saw a big stack in the loft when I was trying to find that grandfather clock you hid from me."

"Those are promised to someone," Lazzie said blandly, falling back on his second line of defense.

"We need them worse than they do," I said. "Bill said to tell you . . ."

At once Lazzie switched teams. "If it's for Bill . . . why Bill and I . . ."

"Oh, shut up and get me loaded," I said rudely. "I gotta get back."

I raced back home with twenty mattresses on the truck, pots and pans stacked on top, and a cooking stove riding grandly in the air. Before dark, everybody was fed; water had been hauled to Tony's tenant house; and the gas company would come the next day. That night, for the first time since l'affaire de cabbage got under way, I snuggled contentedly in Bill's arms. We would attack at dawn.

The alarm went off promptly at five a.m., and I rushed to the window all bright-eyed and bushy-tailed, ready to begin work. When I looked out of the window, I let out a yell. "Bill!" I squawked, "it's snowing!"

"Yup," he said, "so it is."

It not only was snowing, it had snowed all night, and it kept on snowing, dropping those fluffy white flakes that poets label "beautiful". By noon it had cleared and the air was crisp and fresh, but the fields were blanketed. The cabbage was a series of bumps.

"St. Cecelia," I wailed, and called a summit conference. There had to be something that we could do. Mom had firmly believed that when one door closes, another one opens, but how could you cut cabbage in the snow? We looked at each other. Finally Leroy, the crew leader, spoke up.

"Us has got to git money to git home," he started slowly. "Mah peoples ain't got no boots, none uv 'em got ovuhcoats, an' them canvas gloves ain't no good no how. Iff'n yuh could . . ."

Where in hell, I thought desperately, could I get twenty rubber coats, twenty pair of rubber boots, and twenty pair of rubber gloves in a village the size of a postage stamp on a Saturday afternoon?

Willie spoke up next: "Tomato factory's gittin' ready to close down," he said. "I seen thuh men hosin' thuh catwalks yistiddy, an' they wuz wearin' them firemen's rigs."

"Well, Pat," Bill said, "guess it's up to you."

Jeepers! Would any of the big brass be in on a Saturday? Could I con them into lending us that much equipment? "Tune in tomorrow, same time, same station," I thought, and dashed to get dressed. "Always look your best when doing business with a man," Mom had cautioned me. "They have their baser instincts." So, I hauled out my pony skin and suede pant suit that had come from Lord & Taylor; my form-fitting, custom-made brassier:, my pointed-toe boots; and the last of my hoard of special-tint lipstick. I grabbed Leroy as backup and off we sped.

The factory gates were open; point one in our favor. I stopped a minute to figure out my role. It had been so long since I had been professionally charming. Not for me the brisk young executive, I decided. I would be the "shy diffident wife" striving to be a helpmate to her husband. It was true, too; somehow the whole thing had turned into my project!

"You're in luck," the yard man told me. "They're having some sort of final conference. All the big shots are in the conference room. First office down the hall to the right."

I knocked on the door. "Go for broke," I told myself, and walked in. There they sat: engineering, maintenance, accounting, all of the V.I.P.s from the main office. They had just come back from a long lunch, and they were in an expansive mood.

"I'm sure," I said in conclusion, "that you gentlemen can appreciate the importance to a farmer of getting his crops in."

"How many outfits would you need?" the chairman asked.

I turned to Leroy. "Twenty," he answered.

"Got a hundred hanging in the stockroom," the maintenance man said.

"If a security deposit . . ." I began, hesitantly.

"Not necessary," the local superintendent said, in a tone equivalent to a pat on my head. "I've known Mr. Carr for years. Why Bill and I . . ."

"Yes, I know" I said.

We drove home triumphantly with a truck load of goodies. Twenty rubber slickers, twenty pairs of boots and gloves, even twenty hard hats. Holy cow!

"Miz Pat," Leroy said, as we unloaded, "uh, mebbe a little bonfiah to warm us hands?"

"Burn up the apple crates," Bill said recklessly. "Won't need them any more this season."

"An', uh," Leroy suggested, delicately.

I got the message and trotted in to Katie. "I know you've got a couple of bottles hidden under the kitchen sink," I informed her brutally. "If you don't kick in, I'll tell Bill!" Katie kicked in.

"Now," Leroy promised, "us'll cut."

And cut they did. They had to brush the snow off of the tops of the cabbage, but every basket they filled took them one step nearer home, and

I was one step nearer filling the barn. At first, the work went smoothly, but, as the weather thawed, potholes became a booby trap for the truck. As the baskets were ready, the men dragged them over to a roadway, where the spray tanks had gone through early in the summer. The baskets were loaded onto the truck to be hauled to the barn. Bill told me to take the big tractor to the field and, when the truck got stuck, he would jump out; attach a log chain to the tractor; and, between the two of them, get the truck out. I was quite perky about being trusted with the big tractor, but Bill made me take the truck when it got stuck.

"Now remember," he said sternly, "you've got to let the gear in real easily. Too fast, and you'll start with a jerk that could snap the chain. Too slow, and you get too much slack."

He got on the tractor and yelled at me: "GO!"

Tensed for the big deal, I shifted gears. The truck surged to the lip of the hole and fell back.

"Again!" Bill yelled.

Again, the truck climbed to the lip and fell back. Bill began to lose his cool. We were holding up the workers (a Cardinal sin). Suddenly, Bill glanced up and saw Leroy doubled up laughing.

"What's so funny?" Bill demanded. "Let's share the joke!"

Leroy said, "Big boss pull forward, little boss pull backward!"

"Pat!" Bill roared. It was true. That damnable, treacherous, sneaky truck had six gears. There wasn't room enough on the stick for all six, so you shifted from neutral into low, and by pulling down a tiny lever, you shifted in the same spot for reverse. In my nervousness, I had shifted into reverse. Bill started to laugh, and then the whole crew was laughing. I could have died from the embarrassment, but then I hit the same wavelength and I started to laugh, too. After that, whenever things got sticky, someone would mutter: "Big boss pull forward, little boss pull back," and good humor would be restored.

The weather remained spotty, and occasionally there were squalls, but the crew stuck to it. Once, as I drove along the lines, I said to a gray-haired woman: "Willa Mae, your baskets look lovely!"

"Thank you, ma'am," she said, pleased.

Then I did a double take. Here I was snug in the cab of the truck and there she was, cutting cabbage in the snow, and I had dared to compliment her. I could have kicked myself for my smugness.

After a week of good hard work, the field was finished, and the barn was full. Leroy and his crew were paid off and we parted with a feeling of satisfaction on both sides: mission accomplished. Now all we had to do was to keep our fingers crossed and hope for a change in the market. It had crept up to $15 a ton, but at that price, there was no way we could break even.

Thanksgiving was over, and Christmas was in the offing. Clarence came to Bill with a marvelous scheme for making money. Clarence had a dozen brilliant ideas for making money if someone else could dig up the "up-front" cash.

"Good year for Christmas trees," he confided. (Christmas trees are even more temperamental than cabbage!) "I know where I can buy some in Canada. You can truck them down to New York State. I know where there's a red hot place to sell them in Buffalo. OK?"

Bill thought about it. "OK," he said.

So, Bill, Clarence, and I found ourselves selling to the retail trade. Bill was an excellent salesman (surprise!). He had bought so many trees himself, he knew all the points that were important. One day, I was showing some trees to a young woman. She looked very worried and not at all in the festive mood. She wavered from one tree to another and finally said: "How much is this one?"

I looked at the tag. "Five dollars" I informed her.

"Oh, dear," she said, and burst into tears. "My husband just died, but the kids have got to have a tree. I shouldn't spend that much, though."

Bill had heard her and walked over. "You want a tree with a good straight trunk," he told her. "And the branches should be even so that you can stand it anywhere. The tree you have picked out will trim nicely. Let me look at that price tag. Pat!" he said, glaring at me, "you've got the price tags mixed up. This tree is only one dollar." He turned to the woman. "Should I put it in your car? And, try to remember, the children must have a good Christmas."

"I'll do my best," she promised, and then she smiled. "Thank you."

That night, when I curled up in Bill's arms, I whispered: "Honey, there are times when I really love you!"

"My, my," replied my husband.

The Christmas trees sold well, and we showed a sizeable profit. At least we could eat until the cabbage sold. I discovered that, although the cabbage was under cover, it was by no means safe. The temperature had to be kept as close to freezing as possible. This meant climbing up on the roof and opening the vents in the storage area, and it meant going to the barn at two a.m. to make sure that the portable gas heaters had clicked on if the temperature chilled suddenly. The heaters were supposed to be automatic, but there was too much at stake to take a chance. If the cabbage froze, it would look bright green and fresh on top but, as the frost melted, the heart of the cabbage would heat and you got "red heart". Woe betides the farmer who shipped cabbage with red heart! He was blackballed forever more. Even if a load got by the inspector at the barn, by the time it got to its destination, the whole schmeer would stink. The buyer would refuse it and the farmer would be stuck for the cartage to and from. So, we checked the storage area every morning at two a.m. From two a.m. to six a.m. is the coldest portion of a twenty-four hour span.

One night, when Bill's asthma was especially bad, I insisted that he let me go. It was kind of scary down the lane at night with all of the houses dark, but the stars were brilliant and I felt very brave. I opened the door a tiny crack and checked the heaters and the thermometer. Thirty degrees, perfect! Now to get back to the house and my warm bed. It had thawed a little the day before and the surface snow was still hard, but here and there . . . Whoops! My right leg crunched into a hole, the soft snow packed around my boot top and I couldn't pull my foot out. I screamed for help, but who could hear me? A brisk wind carried my voice into space. I sat down and tugged, but it was no use. The snow was very cold. I could hear my mother saying: "If you'll stop being panicky and use your head . . ." So I did. I wriggled my foot out of the boot—the hell with the boot—and I crawled back to the house. Bill was giving himself a shot of adrenalin.

"Is everything all right?" he asked.

"Fine," I replied, and collapsed into bed.

Still nothing happened on the market. It didn't budge. It was really "go for broke" now because the outer cabbage leaves were shriveling and would have to be trimmed off. This meant more labor, more expense, and of course, more loss in weight. Jeepers!

The house (thank God) was peaceful for once. Even Katie was behaving. All we could do was wait and hope.

We were just finishing dinner one evening when the phone rang. Bill answered.

"It's for you, Dear," he said, "long distance."

"Maybe its Mom," I said. "It's about time for her to call."

It was my baby sister, Mary, instead. "Pat, dear, Mom is sort of sickish. Nothing much, maybe it's just indigestion, but the doctor wants her in the hospital for a few tests. Thought you'd like to know."

"By all means," I said. "Call me tomorrow night. I'll be waiting."

The next day, Mary sounded a little more concerned. "They're going to do exploratory surgery. Can't seem to pinpoint the problem. Probably it's minor, but they want to make sure."

"Shall I come down?" I asked.

"It's your busy season, isn't it? Why don't you wait until she's convalescing and you can enjoy your visit. The doctor doesn't seem alarmed, and I'll keep in touch."

I slept very little that night. What if something should happen to Mom?

The third phone call was more urgent. "Come at once if you want to see her alive. It's terminal cancer."

Bill drove me to the airport, but he couldn't go with me; the farm work must go on. "I'll be standing by," he told me, as I boarded the plane. "If I don't answer the phone, the Sheriff will come out and find me."

I had vowed once never to ride in a plane. I have a phobia about heights and I had this vivid picture of the jet bursting into flames a mile up in the air and of me plummeting through the air with my mouth open screaming every inch of the way down. I must have looked as scared as I felt because the stewardess, ever on the alert for jittery passengers, came back and talked to me.

"Look at that red light," I said, pointing out of the window. "Is that a warning beacon on a mountain top? Will we crash?"

The stewardess smiled. "Is this your first flight, Honey?" I nodded. "That red beacon is one of our own lights."

I was humiliated, relieved, and mad at myself, all at the same time.

When we got in the holding pattern at LaGuardia and circled around and around, I figured that that was the way things were done. It wasn't until we were unloading and the passenger in front of me said to the stewardess: "We thought the gremlins were after us," that I realized that I could have legitimately been afraid.

When I came into the hospital room, Mom rallied for the first time since she had come out of surgery. We chatted about this and that as though it were an ordinary visit.

"You know," Mom mused, "it really was a dreadful thing for me to let you go to New York City alone when you were so young. But you always seemed so grown up and, of course, your baby sister, Mary, needed me."

"Oh, come on now," I answered. "I landed on my feet all right, and I got Bill!"

"Yes, and he handles you very well," she replied.

Once more I was taken aback by Mom's practical common sense. I had never dreamed that Bill "handled" me at all and that Mom had been on the sidelines watching.

"It's a good marriage," she said. "There's only one thing. I wish that . . ." I knew what she was thinking. Mom had longed for another grandchild as intensely as I had longed to give her one. She had grieved when my baby had been lost. I made up my mind to lie to her; she would not live long enough to find out the truth.

"Mom," I said. "I've got something wonderful to tell you. I'm pregnant!"

Her face lit up. "Oh, Darling," she said. "How I wish that it was here now so that I could see it!" Then she lapsed into a coma and never regained consciousness. I never regretted that lie; it was the last gift I could ever give to her.

"Primary carcinoma of the liver," the doctor told us. "It's rare to find cancer starting in the liver. Usually it starts somewhere else and then spreads to the liver."

Out of the past, a childhood memory flashed into my mind. Like every well-groomed matron of her era, Mom wore a "boned" corset. The whale bones were very light, but they ran lengthwise from under her breast to the middle of her thighs. There was always one bone that worked its way through the edging on the top and gouged into her flesh. "Drat that thing," I used to hear her mutter as she rubbed the sore spot. Perhaps . . . but who knows why or where or how cancer strikes?

"Terminal," the doctor said. "She may live a week, a month, or six months, but she will live in agony."

"St. Cecelia," I begged, "let her go quickly if there is no hope."

Twice the Sheriff's car sped us to the hospital, but each time she lived. For days after, she could no longer eat. Her hand kept brushing at her mouth. She craved water.

Ten days later I went home. Bill was waiting for me at the airport and I climbed into the car. "Mom is dead," I said.

CHAPTER 22

Cabbage Of $150 A Ton Stinks Downright Purdy!

After Mom died, my "baby sister", Mary, changed overnight into my "sister", Mary. With no sibling rivalry between us, we discovered that we liked each other, at least most of the time. Bill missed Mom as much as I did. There had always been a strong bond between them.

"We both know how ornery you can be," Mom explained.

Whenever Bill and I failed to see eye to eye, Mom would always line up on his side! "Now remember," she would say, as she dredged up advice from her own married life, "don't expect expensive gifts after you're married. When your father was courting me, he gave me a sterling silver bureau set for Christmas. It was so extravagant that he didn't want his mother to see it, and he sort of smuggled it out of the house. The first Christmas after we were married, he gave me a pair of bedroom slippers!"

I know just how she felt when Bill gave me a new mop for my birthday. A mop! Warning or no, I squalled all day. But, whenever I'd get into too much of a snit, I could hear Mom saying: "Now, remember . . . ."

January came in with a record-breaking frost (check the barn every morning at two a.m.). This was followed by a January Thaw (make sure the vents in the barn roof are opened). Every day, more of the outside leaves of the cabbage shriveled up and would have to be trimmed off by hand when we sold it to the market. That would mean less weight.

Nasty comments floated behind my back, such as: "That city girl that Bill married'll drive him plumb into bankruptcy." Or "Mr. Carr is too smart of a man to have to haul his rotten cabbage out in the spring." Damn! It was like the that time I got my first job in the chorus and everyone snubbed me.

The bank was far from cordial when it came to renew our notes. Banks are as changeable as the weather. Early in the summer, when we were harvesting tomatoes, Bill had loaded the truck to take some pigs to the livestock auction. Just as he was turning out of the driveway, there was a horrendous TH-WUMP and the truck stopped dead. Bill came into the house and phoned the bank.

"Luther," he said (they were on the Ag Board of Directors together), "I started out for the auction with a load of pigs, and the truck quit. I passed out a few checks today because I expected to come back with a check of my own."

"How much?" Luther asked. Bill told him. "How long before you get the truck fixed?"

"Wal-l," Bill said, "if it's what I think it is, might be a week before we can get the parts."

"We'll cover the checks," Luther assured him. "Stop in next time you're in town and sign a note."

But, that was in the summer, when the tomato money was rolling in. Right now, we were the mavericks who were holding onto our cabbage. "Banks," as someone remarked, "are glad to furnish an umbrella when the sun is shining."

The market moved; $20 a ton. At that price, we were still way to hell and gone behind the eight ball. We would have to trim every head by hand (500 to 1,000 heads per ton), weigh it into fifty-pound sacks, sew the sack leaving a loop on each end for the loaders to grab when they transferred it on to a truck, and clean out the barn afterwards.

One night, while he was reading the newspaper, Bill sat bolt upright. "My gol!" he exclaimed. "Look at this!"

It was a short item tucked in the back page that there had been a record frost in Florida.

"Wow!" I said.

But, after that, there was no more news. The Florida Chamber of Commerce is not fond of pictures of bathing beauties with mink coats over their bikinis.

Still, the market lagged. I was practically eating aspirin. Finally, I called a friend of ours, a produce man with branch offices in Florida.

"Yes," he said, "Florida cabbage was hurt, but the dealers still have an over supply in the terminals and some of the fields were saved. Take three weeks for the buyers to feel the crunch. Hang on!"

In the meantime, I suffered. Really suffered! One night, Katie's husband, Clarence, gave me a change of trouble. He came back at dusk looking white around the gills.

"Good Lord!" I gasped. "What happened to you?"

"Well," he replied, "I was taking a walk, and I guess someone took a shot at me."

He held up his hat for me to see and indeed there was a hole through the crown.

"How awful!" I exclaimed, "call the Sheriff, or I'll call the Sheriff!"

"No, no, probably an accident," Clarence protested.

Accident? Then the truth came out. From time to time, all of us had wondered how Clarence made his money. He had no office, he mailed no letters, he didn't even have a telephone. Now we know. Clarence was an off-track bettor's man. He collected money from his clients and then "forgot" to go to the track in the nearby town, betting with himself that none of the long shots that his customers favored would come in. On the night of the "accident", one of the long shots had come in, and poor Clarence didn't have the money to pay off his customer. His customer didn't like it, which was understandable. Think of the damage to Katie's social status and Clarence's friendship with The Judge if the truth leaked out.

This wasn't the first time our quiet little hamlet had known violence. Twice, dead bodies had been found in alleyways. "Couldn't they find out who did it?" I asked Bill.

"Wal-l," Bill said slowly, "the question is: did anybody want to find out?"

Long before I had come to Western New York State, there had been a local legend about one of the local citizens who had been caught in a raid.

"You know," Bill told me, "it was a right smart shindig. Everybody knew what was going on, but most of us were rootin' that the guy would make it. He rented an old boarded-up factory, and he made gin (this was during prohibition). But, when he placed an extra big order for sugar and smoke began to pour out of the chimney of that old factory, someone turned him in. Seemed like sort of a pity, after he'd gone to all that trouble." This from my husband! As Mom said, "No wife really knows her spouse."

Before this citizen got raided, he made enough money to get his son into Yale by way of a generous contribution to the college. Unfortunately, Junior inherited the old man's instincts. When it became known that he was brewing bathtub gin in the sacred tubs of Eli, he was requested to depart. He came back to our little closed circuit society and went into politics. Wow!

"Bill," I said solemnly, "if cabbage is a bust, could we make gin?"

"There's no market now," Bill said, grinning.

Monday, the market was still slow, but Monday is inventory day, when any produce left over from Saturday is reduced in price to make room for the new stocks that were shipped in on Sunday night or arrived at dawn on Monday morning.

Tuesday . . . Wednesday . . . would the damn price ever go up?

"Please, St. Cecelia," I cajoled.

"I don't approve of gambling," I heard her answer in my head.

Thursday the price jumped to $55 a ton, and the weak sisters sold out.

"I was offered $55 a ton," one of our friends said, "but I told them I wanted $60. My wife was so mad, she won't speak to me!"

The next day he got his $60 a ton. And, that afternoon, three cabbage buyers knocked at our door.

"Just driving by and thought we'd stop in and say 'hello'," they said. "Still hanging on to your cabbage?"

"In a pig's eye, they were 'just driving by'," Bill snorted. "They're sniffing out where the cabbage is."

I talked about, dreamed of, and even served cabbage. "Oh, my gol," Bill moaned when he saw it on the table, but he ate it.

The price climbed, and the real war of nerves was on. $75 a ton. $80 a ton. "What do you think, Honey," Bill asked.

"I think," I said firmly, "that I'd like to go see Aunt Allie and get out of the line of fire for a day or two."

When we got halfway to Binghamton and Aunt Allie's, Bill stopped in at a wholesalers that he knew. "How's cabbage?" he asked.

"So-so," the man answered. "Guess a few loads changed hands at $50 a ton."

"Zat so?" Bill said. "Up our way, it was $80 a ton this morning."

The man gave Bill one of those looks that said plainly: "You're a liar!" But he was too polite to say anything out loud. "Excuse me a minute," he said and went back into his office. A few minutes later he came out and he was absolutely pale. "Go right back home," he said, "and sell every damned head of cabbage you've got. She's pegged at $90 a ton!"

Bill turned to me. "Well?"

"Well," I said, "Aunt Allie is expecting us, and she'll be awfully disappointed if we don't show up. Lead on McDuff!"

At $100 a ton, everybody with any common sense unloaded. Everybody but us and one other die-hard. "$125 a ton . . . by this time, there was a rumor that Holland Cabbage was on the high seas, and Holland Cabbage is to the cabbage market what Black Friday was to the stock market. Once it hit New York City, the price would plummet. But, I had a vague idea in the back of my head. It mushroomed like the image of a TV camera panning in on a close-up. VROOM! The bomb exploded, and the late news reported: "For the first time in history, New York State cabbage is quoted at $150 a ton!"

"Oh . . . My . . . Gol . . ." Bill said. We had it made!

I slept the sleep of the just and the exhausted until midnight, and then my subconscious nudged me awake. In my one-track pursuit of the magic figure, I had overlooked the obvious. I began to do some plain arithmetic in my head. Two hundred tons at $150 a ton came to . . .

"Bill!" I shrieked, and poked him in the ribs.

"Umph?" Bill grunted.

"Bill! Wake up! Do you know how much money we've got in the barn? The bank will kill us if Holland Cabbage docks before we can sell! Do something! Call somebody! Right away! NOW!"

"In the middle of the night?" Bill asked placidly. "Go back to sleep." He rolled over and started to snore.

Twenty cups of coffee later, dawn finally dawned. Eight o'clock. No buyers pounding on the door. Even the "Big Boys" were cautious about buying until they had a market lined up. Nine o'clock. I guzzled aspirin like candy. Ten o'clock.

"Someone will run with the bait," Bill said staunchly. While he was speaking, a car drove up to the barn. The buyer inspected the bins carefully as there was a tidy sum of money involved, then he turned to Bill with a big smile. "Nice bit of property you've got here. Cabbage looks good. Two hundred tons? I'll take it all. Expect you'd like a binder?"

"Could use a little money," Bill admitted grinning.

And the deal was made.

Our friends were slightly awed. Again the rumors flew, but this time it was to the effect: "That girl Bill married has got a right smart head on her shoulders." Jeepers! It was like the time that I went on stage as an understudy and the critics had said I was an "interesting new personality".

Bill had always said that at $40 a ton, it was a damn smelly job to trim our cabbage."

But, at $150 a ton, it was sheer heaven! We paid top wages, we promised a bonus, we put on extra help, and everybody smiled at everybody else. Just once we had a spot of trouble: our old friend, "The Bottle".

I searched in all of the usual hidey holes with no luck. There were certain Marquis of Queensbury rules about "The Bottle". Digging a hole in the cabbage was out of bounds; all hands agreed that if I thrust my arm in a hole and came up with a rat dangling from my little finger, I would depart in a straightjacket. I was really uptight. There was a lot at stake. To a man, the workers looked me in the eye and swore that they were working just as hard. However, with cabbage at that price, I had to be extra careful.

Finally a fink (thank God!) whispered in my ear. Of course! Why hadn't I thought of it before? The men figured no lady would go into the outhouse marked "Men".

"Well, I ain't no lady!" I announced, "and if you men don't get your kidneys under control, I'm going to go out there and sit!"

We had no more trouble.

Three days after we shipped the last of our cabbage and our barns were empty, the long-heralded Holland ship steamed into New York City harbor with its cargo of cabbage. It had been delayed at sea by a storm. It was that close! "Thank you, St. Cecelia!" I murmured.

We gave the men the bonus we had promised them. John bought a Cadillac and disappeared into the solid south. Willie married a cute young "chick" and planned to start a family to "take keer uv him when he git old". Jeepers! Would he ever find out?!

And Bill did what every farmer does: he paid off notes.

"Couldn't happen to a better man," the bank president had beamed.

Bill then bought a new tractor, traded in our car, and bought a diamond-studded wristwatch for me. "What! No mop?" I queried. Bill just grinned.

Besides the beer party we threw for our crew on the last day, we invited them to a steak dinner. The Jamaicans we had hired from a nearby camp would soon be leaving for their homes and this would be a nice sendoff. Suddenly, however, every restaurant in town seemed to be booked to capacity for the week ahead. We finally had to go to a nearby town where a table was set up in the bar to accommodate us. When the steak was served, there was a dead silence. Bill looked from one face to another. Nobody stirred. What was wrong? Suddenly I got the message.

"Bill," I said softly, "aren't you going to say grace?"

Bill's face turned a mottled red as he bowed his head and said, "Lord, we thank Thee . . ."

The stars in their orbits were sure active, for a lot was happening in the house. While I was head-over-heels into the cabbage market, Katie's husband, Clarence, had bet on a long-shot and won. When we asked him how it happened, he said: "Well, the lead horse fell down, the next horse stopped to ask if he was hurt, and my horse walked in!"

He was able to borrow money and get his factory reopened, and Katie had her eye on a house on "Mortgage Parkway", where she could entertain their friends at intimate little soirees.

Dottie had gotten a cable from her husband that he would soon be home for good, and she was looking for a house so they could get going on their family.

Herta was firmly settled into her cobblestone with her antiques.

Bill and I were alone at last. "Seems kinda good," he remarked as he toasted his toes in front of the fireplace. "Just the two of us, for a change."

But, of course, that didn't last. A few days later, he drove up to the kitchen door with the pickup and a long, rangy, middle-aged man climbed out, followed by a short, squat woman, who had the build of a matronly American Native squaw.

"Picked 'em up at the bus station," Bill informed me. "Uncle Lewis says he knows about cows and he'd sure be a help to Willie at milking time. Aunt Bessie," Bill said, grinning, "allows as how she could show you how to bake corn pone. They've been traveling all night on the bus, and they've got no place to stay. Figure we could bed 'em down?" He looked at me.

"Of course," I said, cordially. "Come on in!"

This was my introduction to the Hill People.

CHAPTER 23

Aunt Bessie & Uncle Lewis

Aunt Bessie and Uncle Lewis sure made life easier for Bill and me. They were packrats, and their rooms were piled to the ceiling with all sorts of odds and ends. Whatever you were fresh out of, Aunt Bessie had it. I could stick my head in her door and yell: "Aunt Bessie, I ripped a hole in my jeans!" Aunt Bessie would have a patch. Or, "Oh gosh, Aunt Bessie, I forgot to get baking powder and Bill wants biscuits for dinner." And Aunt Bessie had an extra can. Even: "Hey! Aunt Bessie! How's about the loan of your extra television?" Uncle Lewis would then lug it over to our room. When I teased him about having two TVs in one room, he said solemnly: "Well, jes' supposin' one of them went dead during the Grand Ole Opry programmey? Well, jes' supposin'!"

Aunt Bessie and Bill clicked right off. She reminded him of his beloved Aunt Allie and, besides, she could make fried cakes (not to be confused with doughnuts). As my mother always said, "The way to a man's heart is through his stomach."

Aunt Bessie knew that Mom's death had left a big gap in my life, and she tried her best to "mother hen" me. She gave me the same stern advice that Mom used to give me, but when it came to a slight disagreement between Bill and me over items like new drapes for the living room, Aunt Bessie would always take my side; very nice. Aunt Bessie knew a lot about managing husbands. She had been sixteen years old when Uncle Lewis had wooed and won her. For a while, all was well. Uncle Lewis was in love with his "little woman" (Aunt Bessie weighed ninety pounds when they got married), and he was a good husband to her. But, like many of the mountain men, Uncle Lewis also loved his "moonshine" and, a drunk Lewis was a very different man.

Aunt Bessie stood it as long as she could, and then she took the bus back home to her Mamma in South Carolina. "Chile," her Mamma said flatly, "you are a woman growed and yur place iz with yur husband." She put Aunt Bessie back on the next bus, and told her: "When you git home, you empty out every bit uv water in the thuh bucket (they carted their water from a spring two miles away), an when Lewis craves a sip uv water, yuh hand him a mug uv moonshine." For three days Aunt Bessie plastered Uncle Lewis with moonshine, and when he sobered up, the smell of moonshine made him sick. Aunt Bessie put him on a "diet" of beer and an occasional jug of wine, but when he slipped off to town every once in a while, his cronies would be overly generous and Uncle Lewis would come home slightly bar worn.

"Have you tried talking to him?" I asked Aunt Bessie.

"Chile," she said solemnly, "I dun talked sweet to that man an' I dun talked sour."

"Why, so have I," I said, all agog at this meeting of the minds. "How did you make out?"

"Well," she started dolefully, "neither ways I din't git nowheres."

On the other hand, Aunt Bessie was the first to admit that she had her own little faults. She had been "spoilt rotten". When she was three years old, she had tried to walk into a bonfire, and by the time her father caught the screaming child and stripped off her clothes, Bessie had a hole burned in her back so big "so's you could see her lungs". She spent a year in the children's ward in Charleston, and she was such a cute little tike that the nurses had "baby-fied" her. At least she was spoiled until her baby sister arrived the next year. Bessie decided that she would fix that.

"What did you do?" I asked, mindful of my sibling rivalry with my own sister, Mary.

"I set fire to her crib," Aunt Bessie replied.

"Jeepers!" I gasped. "And what did they do to you?"

"Well," Aunt Bessie said with a grin, "I didn't iver try that no more!"

Bill put Uncle Lewis to work milking the cows. Willie thought this was an excellent idea. Willie wasn't too keen about milking, and Uncle Lewis had a way with the cows. He would slap "Carnation Pietje Dunloggin" on the rump and holler: "Git over here, Sairy Jane!" And Carnation Pietje Dunloggin would toss her head and git! After all, what's in a name?

Uncle Lewis' idea of milking was to grasp a teat in each fist and squeeze. Not too practical when there are forty cows waiting in their stalls. He learned to handle the milking machine, but he thought the sterilizing of the milk dishes was "dang foolishness", and washing the teat cups was "purely aggravatin'". A cow's teats, in case you haven't tossed the word around over the olive in your martini, are placed on her milk bag like the nipples of a woman's breast; and they serve the same purpose: they are faucets for milk. "Teats" and "tits" are the same thing, they're just spelled differently. The teat cups are hollow tubes of orange rubber wide enough at the top to fit completely around the teat and, with a very narrow extension at the bottom, fits over the air line. The air machine has a gentle squeeze-and-relax suction that persuades the cow to let her milk down. It works like a breast pump on a woman. The cow isn't completely satisfied with this arrangement. She prefers the soft warm feel of a hand on her teats, but then one can't have everything one wants, can one?

Bill could always persuade a cow to part with an extra quart or two of milk after the machine was taken off. Some farmers do this hand stripping because, if any milk is left in the bag, it is an incubator for the germs of mastitis; and mastitis is a word to make strong men flinch. A cow with mastitis gives milk that has lumps in it, and if any of this milk gets on the market, small children get sore throats and the Board of Health gets fits. It is possibly transmitted from cow to cow through dirty teat cups. To clean the cups properly requires a lot of elbow grease and a stable temperament. To make a dirty situation dirtier, our water is hard due to the lime in the ground, and, if even a trace of milk is left in the rubber, the hot washer hardens it into a scum called "milk stone" (a most appropriate name). Milk stone made our inspector break out in a rash, so there was a constant cold war between him and Uncle Lewis.

One day, Uncle Lewis stormed into the kitchen. "Git me un bran' new set of them there teat cups!" he ordered. "I'll fix that inspector!"

I wondered what the hell was going on, but I figured the less I knew, the better; so I delivered the teat cups as per Uncle Lewis's request.

The next week, the inspector stormed into the kitchen. "Pat," he said, "come out to the milk house. Want to show you something."

All innocence, I went out with him.

"See those cups?" he demanded, pointing to the cups on the wall in their draining rack.

"Why, yes," I said. "What's wrong? They're as clean as if they'd never been used."

"Exactly!" he said. "They have never been used! Look here."

He swept his flashlight across the tops. There was a fine spider web across each one. Poor Uncle Lewis! Finked by a spider!

"Now," said the inspector, "show me where he's hid the cups he's using! Jeez, Pat, I got to at least look at them!"

We found them in the refrigerator, next to the antibiotics. Luckily, they were reasonably clean. "And you tell Lewis," the inspector continued grimly, "I've been at this job a long time." Then he began to chuckle. "Son-of-a-gun damn near got away with it, at that!"

I passed on the message, complete with the last remark, and Uncle Lewis grinned. As Mom used to say: "Men are just little boys at heart!"

The months flew by, as usual. Except for Mom's death, it had been a good year. Our harvest was plentiful; the market was kind; our hay, oats, and corn were stored; our notes were paid off; our cows were contented; and one of our dogs had puppies.

Uncle Lewis cleaned out all of the fireplaces, and, on cold nights, it was heavenly to sprawl on the floor toasting our toes or poking at the logs to see the sparks fly. Often, I would put on my wooly pajamas and housecoat, and Bill and I would go in to visit Aunt Bessie and Uncle Lewis. One night, when we were standing around drinking tea, I backed up to the fireplace to warm my backside, and I backed one step too far. The hem of my robe caught on fire! The wooly material was flammable, and my hair was hanging loose to my waist. The men stood frozen with shock, but Aunt Bessie reached over and tore my pajamas off of me.

"It 'ppeared like you wuz better off nekked," she said calmly, "than to be burnt to a crisp!" I agreed with her wholeheartedly.

Soon it was Christmas; my first one without Mom. My sister, Mary, and I called each other every night, but it was a difficult time. Aunt Bessie tried her best to fill the gap, and she made dozens of nut cookies and kettles of fried cakes. When Bill grumbled that it was foolish to put up Christmas lights on our spruce trees outside, Aunt Bessie said firmly: "Now, Mistuh Bill, Miz Pat wants them lights so bad she can taste 'em. Iff'n I wuz you, I'd put 'em up." So, our lawns were a beacon for Santa Claus.

Bill did not give me a mop for Christmas. He bought me a string of pearls, instead. Another string of pearls? Oh well. It was the thought that counted. So, I went to sleep Christmas night and dreamed of sugar and spice and everything nice, but at the crack of dawn, I was shaken awake by Bill.

"Hey," I protested. "What's going on? I can think of a lot nicer things to do!" And I cuddled up to him.

"Not now, Dear," he said, gently. "I've been awake since midnight. You'll have to take me to the hospital in the city. I think I have appendicitis."

I scrambled out of bed and fumbled into my clothes. Aunt Bessie heard the commotion and came trotting in.

"You hev some hot coffee an' toast," she said. "You cain't drive all that ways on an empty stummick!"

"Not now," I told her, but she was firm.

Minutes later, we were on our way. Thank God the car started! Fog hid the road; not so completely that the Thruway was closed, but treacherously. Here a clear stretch and then WHAM! . . . a thick blanket. Add to the fog a not-too-good-woman-driver, tense with worry and pressed for time, and the total promised to be one hell of a trip.

When we were about halfway there, I turned to Bill. "How do you feel?" I asked anxiously.

"Watch out for the turnoff," he muttered, and slumped down in his seat.

I couldn't stop to check him. I had to keep going. By now the sun had come up full. Traffic was light and I pressed hard on the gas. Soon, thank goodness, the hospital loomed in the distance.

"Turn here," Bill said, rousing a little.

"I can't,' I said desperately, "we're in the wrong lane and there's a truck along side of us."

"Turn!" Bill said, and the truck driver swore as I shot across in front of him.

The hospital parking lot was filled, not one vacant slot. I jammed on the brakes, stopped in the "Fire Lane", and ran to the main desk.

"Patient of Dr. Jones," I sputtered (we had met him at a party). The receptionist picked up her phone, pressed a button, and reported languidly, "Gone for the weekend. Next?"

"But this is an emergency!" I insisted.

"Oh, Emergency. Second driveway to the right."

"Yes?" Bill mumbled, as I got back into the car.

"Soon," I promised.

The emergency room of the University of Rochester teaching hospital was crowded. Nurses were hurrying; loud speakers were blaring; sirens were wailing and coming to a crescendo; children were crying; stretchers were rolled in and stretchers were wheeled out; patients with blood-stained first-aid bandages were brought in; curtained cubicles were opened and curtained cubicles were closed; lights flashed; buzzers hummed; and, to me, the whole scene was bedlam. Bill was put in a wheelchair and whisked away, and I was shunted into the admissions office and fed into the computer. Ah! The computer!

Patient's name? Occupation? Symptoms? On and on until we got to the nitty gritty. Do you carry any insurance? Thank goodness we had insurance. There were no private rooms available, so Bill was placed into a curtained cubicle for the night.

"It was right interesting," he told me later. "Being as how it was Saturday night, they kept bringing in drunks off the streets. Heard sounds I never did hear on the farm."

By morning, Bill's tests had been read, the pain had subsided, and, except for a "slight cold", he was OK, and they discharged him. Thankfully, I took him home, but there was a nagging worry tucked into one corner of my mind. Bill had never before complained of pain.

"There must have been something wrong," I said to Aunt Bessie after we tucked Bill into bed.

Now, now, chile," she said, as she patted my hand. "Ain't no need fur you to fret. You done took him to thuh city and thuh doctors dun told you ain't nothin' wrong, an' they orter know."

Yes, of course, they ought to know, but still . . .

Bill's "cold" got worse, and I was glad that it was time for his checkup with the allergist that had been treating his asthma. This man had his office in another city sixty miles to the west of us.

"Now, you stop worrying," Aunt Bessie said, as we climbed into the car. "The Lord ain't gonna let nothin' bad happen to Mistuh Bill."

We waved to each other, and Bill and I set out. The day was cold, but the car was warm, and I was much more confident about my driving. The traffic was light ("Thank you, St. Cecelia!"), and I had high hopes that this doctor would help Bill. No sweat.

"Well?" I asked, as I went into the office after the doctor had examined Bill.

"Not well," the doctor reported. "He's got pneumonia. Don't see why they didn't keep him in the hospital. [I had told him of our visit to the emergency room.] We've got an epidemic of the flu and there isn't an empty bed in our hospital, or any of the other hospitals in the area. Get these prescriptions filled, and you'll have to take him home, I'm sorry."

I was stunned. I knew that pneumonia was no longer a killing disease, but when it is your child or your husband that has it, you really worry.

We set out for home. The day was still clear, and it was easy driving in the city, but the "snow belt" lived up to its name. As we drew into the country, the sky darkened and the fluffy white flakes started to fall; gently at first, then thicker and thicker. (Why had I ever thought that snow was beautiful?) Wind swept across the road, and sleet froze on the windshield. When the heavy swirls slacked for a second, I saw that I had been driving on the wrong side of the road!

"Warning!" the car radio blared, "visibility zero. No unnecessary travel. Repeat: No unnecessary travel!" Then the clutch started slipping, and there was a steep hill ahead. I stopped the car and started to bawl. "St. Cecelia," I sobbed, "I can't go on; I just can't. I can't cope!"

"Now, now," St. Cecelia staid sternly, "of course you can. You are a big girl now, and I'll help you."

Just then, Bill roused and said fretfully, "Honey, can't we go any faster? I'm getting cold."

An hour later (three hours for a sixty-mile trip), we pulled into our driveway. Aunt Bessie and Uncle Lewis came running and got Bill into the house and into bed. I stumbled in after them and collapsed on the sofa.

"There, there, lamb," Aunt Bessie said, comfortingly. "You're jes' plumb wore out. You git some sleep, and Lewis and I will sit up with Mistuh Bill." What would I have done without Aunt Bessie and Uncle Lewis?

Many of the Hill People had moved into our area, and our close-knit community had received them with folded arms and open hostility. "Damn freeloaders—want our welfare!" one of our friends had grumbled. They ignored the fact that the mines were shutting down and a lot of the men were here looking for work. They *wanted* to work. But we simply did not have that many jobs. Downtown in the bars, a yelp of "hillbilly" was enough to start a midnight rerun of the Civil War, and our cops started doing pushups. I even had my moments of consternation. One day, when Uncle Lewis and I were driving into town, I picked up one of Uncle Lewis's cousins (all of Clay County, West Virginia was related to each other) who was trudging along the road.

"Wanna lift?" I inquired. "Lewis, you get in back and Fernie and I will sit in front and get acquainted." Nobody said anything for a few miles, and then Fernie suddenly broke the silence.

"I kilt a man oncet," she said. "I slit my knife acrost his throat, jes' like this." She drew her finger across her throat in a sinister gesture. (Instinctively, I edged closer to the door and kept one hand on the latch. After all, what did I really know about the Hill People?)

"I kilt him. Me and three other girls (Fernie was crowding forty) wuz walkin' in the Gulch an' this man, he come up an' dragged me into the bushes and he . . . (she gave me one of those woman-to-woman looks) . . . so I kilt him."

The thought of Fernie, who was known to half of the men in town, killing someone to protect her honor, flipped me! However . . .

"So thuh Depitty come to my house and he says, 'Miz Fernie, I gotta take you to thuh Sherruff.' An' thuh Sheruff says, 'Now, Miz Fernie, we found this knife beside the dead man. Is this your knife?' An' I sez, 'No, sir; I ain't never seed that knife.' An thuh Sheruff sez, 'Miz Fernie, we know thet there's your knife.' An' I sez, 'No, sir. No, sir.' An' after a while I sez, 'Mistuh Sheruff, I got six chilluns' tuh home an' they's gittin' hungry 'long 'bout now.' An thuh Sheruff, he sighs an' sez, 'OK, Miz Fernie; that there man warn't no account no how, but don't you let me catch you killing any of my lawmen!'"

"Phew!" I said to Uncle Lewis after she got out of the car. "Do you suppose . . . ?"

Uncle Lewis chewed on his tobacco and said, "Wal', 'ppears like someone wud a tole me." And he spit out his cud.

Bill got over the pneumonia, but he stayed listless in spite of Aunt Bessie's herb tea and the sulfur and molasses that she dosed him with. "Ugh!" was his comment as it went down.

When I would say, "Dearest, I think Dunloggin is coming into heat—she's licking another cow," instead of checking for himself, he would say, "Call the inseminator if you think she's ready. You know as much about it as I do."

We changed doctors; perhaps a new man . . . ? But, when the new man said casually, "Let's see now, how old is Bill?" I knew it was hopeless. So, we went back to our family doctor who at least knew us. At last, not even Aunt Bessie's fried cakes tempted him, and, when he began throwing up, the doctor suggested a few days in the hospital and some tests.

"Just routine," he remarked, cheerfully. "I don't think there's anything much wrong."

Bill was admitted on Monday and all went smoothly. His roommate was Jake (an old friend), and the nurses assured me he was "such a good patient . . . no trouble."

Tuesday went by quietly, then on Wednesday, all hell broke loose on the farm. The cows spooked, machinery broke down, trucks failed to arrive on time, and some of the men were drinking. It was late by the time I got to the hospital. I knew at once something was dreadfully wrong. Bill's hands moved constantly, and he clutched at the bed sheet. I had to go to the head of the bed before he noticed me.

"Pat, is that you?" he asked fretfully. "Honey, get me a Coke. I'm thirsty."

I ran to the Coke machine in the hallway and poured a cup. He pawed at the air and I had to hold the cup to his lips.

"How long has he been like this?" I asked Jake.

"Since this morning, when he came back from X-ray. They could hardly rouse him to go down."

"When was his doctor in last?"

"No one has been in all day." Jake answered.

I ran to the nurses' station. "My husband is blind!" I said. "Get his doctor at once!"

"His doctor has gone on vacation," the nurse said, "and we haven't been able to reach his relief."

"You will have a doctor here in fifteen minutes!" I demanded slowly, "or I will call the Sheriff!"

A doctor arrived in ten minutes. Bill had had a stroke. He was given a shot. Twelve hours after Jake had noticed something was wrong! A cot was put up in the sun parlor, and I was urged to spend the night. "Bill is the one who should be getting the attention," I thought bitterly, "not me!"

By morning he was conscious and I had to go back to the farm. That night I was greeted by scandal! Bill had gotten up and wandered into another patient's room in his nightshirt, and the other patient was female! The nurse couldn't have been more shocked if Bill had tried to rape the woman.

"What happened?" I asked Bill when we were alone.

"Well," he said, "I went to the bathroom and, when I came out, I got kinda confused, and I went through the wrong door. You'd think," he added dryly, "some of those old hens had never seen a nightshirt before!"

When I told Aunt Bessie, she sniffed. "There, there, lamb," she comforted me. "Evrathin's gonna be all right."

"As long as I had Aunt Bessie to turn to," I thought, "it was."

But, then a phone call came for Aunt Bessie. It was from a neighbor in the hills. Mary Ann's husband (Aunt Bessie's own flesh-and-blood "datter" who was mentally retarded and whose husband was a bestial old man) had beaten Mary Ann up and she was pregnant and wanted her "Mama", and poor Bessie! She was so torn between the two of us that I had to make up her mind for her.

"You must go. At once!" I said. "I'll help you pack."

"I'll be thet worrit about you," Aunt Bessie said, as we went to the bus station.

"Now, now," I said, and Aunt Bessie smiled, "Evrathin's gonna be all right. You'll manage. Somehow . . ."

I was alone.

The Pillars barns (facing east)

The Pillars barns (facing south)

CHAPTER 24

No Woman Can Run A Farm!

That night, I called Willie to the house and told him that he would have to do the milking until I could find another man. Willie never grumbled a bit if it was to help Mr. Bill. Early the next morning I gulped some hot coffee ("You must eat!" Aunt Bessie warned me). I got the trimming crew started on pruning the apple trees (if they grow straight up in the air, the pickers demand more money because they have to use a ladder), so it was noon before I got to the hospital. I ate lunch with Bill, and that night I grabbed a sandwich at the cafeteria and we talked as he finished up his tray.

"Why do you visit your husband so often?" one of the staff doctors inquired. "The other wives don't."

I happened to know that this particular doctor was going through a sticky divorce. I replied, "Perhaps it is because I love him."

The next time I went in, Bill asked me to bring him a radio (there was no television in his room). I was delighted; this was the first time he had shown any interest in anything except staring at the ceiling; Step One. I rushed home, got the radio, plugged it in, and went down the hall to the restroom. A grim-faced nurse greeted me when I returned.

"Take that thing out of here!" she said icily, pointing at the radio. "Jake (Bill's roommate) is really sick and I can't have him disturbed."

After the nurse stalked out of the room, I stumbled over to the other bed. "Jake," I mumbled, "you have been so good to Bill. I would feel dreadful if we ever hurt you."

"Now, now," he said, reaching over and patting my hand. "Bill and I are old friends. We played football together and even tried to date the same girl for the Senior Prom! I am not all that sick. Sometimes I think those nurses get a bit uppity. Now, you be a good girl and stop worrying."

I put the radio under my arm and started down the hall. As I passed the nurses' station, I saw a cluster of nurses talking to each other. Lights were flashing over the patients' doors indicating that someone was calling for help, but the little cluster never moved. I overheard, ". . . so, he said to me . . ." as I went by. "And what did you say to him?" and there was a peal of girlish laughter.

Downstairs in the lobby a friend of mine stopped me. "How is Bill?" she inquired. "I'm waiting for my sister; she works here as a nurse. There she is now!" and she called to a woman in white who was striding past. "Hey, Jean! Wait up a minute. Where are you going? Emergency? My God, you look important!"

"As a matter of fact, I'm going to the cafeteria for coffee. I'm a nurse. Nurses are supposed to look important." And she clicked off down the hall.

"Par for the course," I thought, and that night I cried myself to sleep. "It's all part of growing up," St. Cecilia murmured.

Bill got spurts of energy, but they didn't last. When he got up in the morning, he would phone me. "Come and get me," he would say, but by the time I got there, he would be lying on his bed staring at the ceiling totally exhausted.

"Why don't you just put his clothes on him and take him home?" one of the nurses demanded. I thought of the times when he had been in the hospital for asthma. ("Such a good patient, no trouble.")

"When his doctor discharges him, I'll take him home. I'll be glad to." I replied.

Later in the week his doctor called me. "Perhaps . . . in familiar surroundings . . ." I got the message: Bill had been written off.

As we drove through town, I discovered that Bill could see physically but couldn't identify what he saw. "Something new?" he asked, pointing to the factory where he had delivered tomatoes for years.

The next day, the bank president and his manager came to the house. "How nice!" I exclaimed. "Come in. Bill is home."

They chitchatted for a few minutes while I made coffee. Then they got down to the nitty-gritty. "I hate to do this," the bank president said, "you are such nice people; but our board has decided that no woman can run a farm by herself, so we are giving you three months to liquidate. In the meantime, we cannot advance you any more money. Sorry."

I sat there with my mouth open while the roof caved in around me. This was the end of the road. When they went out the door, the manager, who had looked me over every time I went to the bank, lingered behind and said, "You know, I might be able to help you, if you would cooperate . . ."

"Not for sale!" I said flatly and slammed the door.

It was coming into spring; the time when all farmers, even the well-heeled ones, borrow money to get started and carry them until the crops are harvested. We had no income except from the dairy, and that brought up a serious problem. In the winter, our herd ran free in a loafing pen and the Board of Health required only that fresh straw be spread each day over the frozen manure. But, on their "cut-off" date, the barns had to be completely cleaned out so that the warm weather would not spread disease from the droppings. Otherwise, we could not ship fresh milk and would have to ship to the cheese factories at a starvation price. To clean out the barns would require additional labor, and more workers would mean a cash payroll. The bank had just cut us off without warning. Z-U-T! Just like that! We were hamstrung.

Two years before, when we had a good year, Bill had switched banks. Several banks had beamed on us (sure proof of solvency), and the bank that we had been dealing with assured us that the "light would be burning in the window." The bank Bill transferred to was, at that time, a small county bank, but it had merged with a state chain and the absentee landlords didn't know their local clients.

When I called the central office and pointed out that if we could not get a loan our milk market would be cut off, the officer said, "Bad planning somewhere," and hung up. When Bill had opened our account with the bank we were dealing with now, he had suggested that instead of going through the paperwork of a chattel mortgage each year, he would take out a real estate mortgage and, in return, the bank would finance him each year on notes. It had been a verbal agreement and the central office refused to honor it. With the real estate tied up, no other bank would touch us.

In desperation, I applied at the bank that had assured us the light would always be burning in the window. We could not afford to be proud. Anxiously we awaited the answer; it was our last hope. Each day I ran to the mailbox. One noon I was waiting there, as usual, and I was talking to a salesman (he didn't know we were broke). The mailman drew up and I saw the letterhead of the bank. "Excuse me," I said, and tore open the envelope.

"We regret to inform you . . ." That poor salesman! I started to scream.

"Go right ahead, lady," he said. "The bank did my mother the same way when my father died."

"Try the government agency," one of my friends advised. "They finance farmers who can't get loans through the banks."

But by now my courage was at low ebb. Maybe those men were right: No woman can run a farm. "Oh, come on!" St. Cecelia said scornfully.

I tilted my chin at a new angle and I went to work. I had learned that originally there had been just one man on the Board of Directors who had been hostile to me and he had swayed the others. So, Mom was right—as usual. One loud-mouthed bellwether could stampede any board. I went to each member of the government agency before the meeting. These men were farmers themselves, and they all knew me. They had watched me stand in a cold drizzle to watch a pruning demonstration. They had seen me plod through the mud to watch a demonstration of contour plowing (cutting the furrows across the slope so that, hopefully, in a hard downpour, the topsoil wouldn't wash down the hill). They had sat beside me during interminable seminars and egged me on to ask pertinent questions.

At one lecture, the professional egghead imported from the South talked on and on about "mah-jinal crops. "What's he talking about?" I asked Bill.

"Shhh," he whispered back. Apparently he didn't know either.

During the coffee break I asked every man in sight what he was talking about, and none of them knew. When we reconvened, I raised my hand. "Sorry," I said, "I didn't catch the word before 'crops'."

"Mah-jinal," the lecturer said impatiently, "M-A-R-G-I-N-A-L."

Everyone sighed with relief. Problem resolved.

Every farmer knew how much I had helped Bill, but would they risk money that I could make it on my own? If they turned me down, I would have very little money, a sick husband, and no home.

"I know what's going on," Bill told me on one of his good days. "Mr. X (an influential customer of the bank) wants our place, and the bank is trying to give it to him."

When I had spoken to every man on the board, I reported to St. Cecelia that there wasn't a male chauvinist in the bunch. St. Cecelia smiled.

A week later, we got a letter telling us that they would finance us! The next day, an old man who worked for us came to me and said, "Pat, there's a thousand dollars under the carpet in my living room. Ain't doing nobody any good there. It's yours for the asking."

So, I was in business. I soon found out that being an able first lieutenant was very different from being commander-in-chief. The decisions I had to make! And taking care of Bill ate into my day. He had progressive hardening of the arteries, and the best I could do was to attempt a delaying action. He hated to get up in the morning—it was so restful to lie in bed and stare at the ceiling—but the doctor had warned me that if I gave in to him, he would soon be bedridden.

One morning, when I was badly pressured, he lay there like a log and refused to budge. Cajoling, pleading . . . nothing worked. Finally I lost my temper. "GET UP!" I yelled, and slapped his legs. I did penance for days afterward for my tantrum.

The work on the farm went smoothly. Willie was my strong right arm, and he let the men know that I was the underdog and trying to hack it. Since they themselves were the underdogs forever and ever, they worked over and above their wages to help out. It was amazing how much more work a man will turn out when he is interested in it.

Aunt Bessie sent her love whenever she could get anyone to write for her (she could only sign her name); and I learned that her daughter was doing well with her pregnancy, so if Miz Pat needed her . . . . I know how much Aunt Bessie had longed for a grandbaby to cosset, so I wrote: "I miss you terribly, but you must stay to welcome that new baby. Bill is holding his own, and we are managing. Love . . ."

"Good girl!" St. Cecelia murmured.

"Yeah, but you know I was lying," I retorted.

St. Cecelia smiled.

Bill's illness was a heartbreaking game of cat and mouse. Many mornings he would try to pull his shirt over his legs or his pants over his head; but one day, when I took the truck downtown (I took him with me whenever I possibly could), I went to the bus station, and when I came out, some man said, "Lady, do you know your gas tank is leaking?"

I looked. There was a stream of gas pouring onto the street. I dashed inside and dialed the Fire Chief. "What do you expect me to do?" he roared. "Get it to a garage. Hurry!"

The truck had been parked on a hill on Main Street. When I ran back, I was just in time to see the truck pull away from the curb and weave through the noonday traffic with Bill at the wheel. Screaming, I ran after him on the sidewalk. Cars and pedestrians scattered before him, but there was a traffic light at the foot of the hill. If it was red . . .

"Please, St. Cecelia," I begged. "The light . . ." It was green. Bill turned the corner and stopped in front of a garage.

"Bill, darling," I sobbed. "Why did you do it?"

"Well, dear, somebody had to," he said, smiling. That night, he tried to pull his pajama pants over his head.

Once, I took him to visit my best friend. I had gotten him a new suit. On the farm, I wore Bill's old shirts and jackets; everything but his shoes. I could never fill Bill's shoes. Although he had gotten painfully thin, to my eyes he was still handsome. When we left, my friend whispered, "He's just a zombie, isn't he?"

But, he was not a zombie. He was NOT.

One night, we were in the living room listening to the news, and he said, "This must be so hard on you. Why don't you send me to a nursing home? Let them take care of me."

"Don't ever say that again!" I said fiercely. "I couldn't bear to be without you. I love you."

One noon, when I was at the kitchen table, hunched over the accounts book, he came up behind me and, bending over, kissed the back of my neck. This had been one of our most cherished love tokens, and I was overjoyed. That night, when we went to bed, he put his arm around me and I whispered, "Dearest, I want you so much. I need you so much. Couldn't you . . . perhaps . . ."

"It's too frustrating for me to touch you," he said, and moved away. So, the ache in my body was added to the ache in my heart.

The day-to-day pressure began to get to me and it climaxed one day later in the summer. I was especially proud of the tomatoes that we had grown. There were thousands of plants in the fields and I had helped to transplant each one. I had slogged down there at two a.m. to light the smudge pots so that the warm smoke would protect the vines against a freak frost. I had used the insecticide spray Cornell advised, and now the long vigilance was at an end. The tomatoes were ripe and that very day, the pickers had gone down the long rows and the baskets of luscious tomatoes were standing in the roadways ready to be picked up in the morning and shipped to the factory. Early that evening, the cows spooked. "They're headed down the lane to the tomato lot!" Willie yelled.

I raced to the truck; Bill got in with me, and we headed down the lane. As yet, the cows had done no damage. They had ambled the length of the field, but they walked on the roadways that the trucks used to get through. One of the men tried to get ahead of them and turn them, but suddenly, they heard the truck. Bill had thrown it into gear and he drove kitty-corner to the farthest end of the field. The plants had been spaced two feet apart and Bill cut through them so expertly, not a single plant was damaged! He turned at the headland and gently prodded the cows back toward the gate.

It was a feat only the most expert driver could have done. But, the gate was closed and, with the truck driving them from the rear, the lane blocked in front, they cows were boxed in, and they panicked. They tore through the field like maniacs. Tomato vines were squashed under their hooves and the filled baskets were trampled and smashed to bits. A hurricane couldn't have done half the damage. It was more than I could take.

"I hate you! I hate you! I hate you!" I screamed, and collapsed, sobbing.

"I know it's hard," St. Cecelia murmured, "but you are the one who must be strong."

It took the crew all the next morning to clean up the mess.

Later that week, Bill went on a hunger strike. He refused to touch food. When I said, "But you'll die if you don't eat," and tried to force a spoonful of oatmeal in his mouth, he spit it in my face and laughed. It was such an agonizing reversal of roles. Bill had always been the stable one, almost fatherly, and now . . . I called a friend of ours in New York City who was a doctor and cried, "They won't try . . . the doctors here—they won't even try."

"Now, now," he said gently. "You and I know that older people are slower to respond. I can't promise anything, but there is a new medication; I'll phone in an order."

Two days later, Bill walked to the refrigerator, opened the door, and called, "Honey! Any food in here? I'm hungry."

But, of course, the effect of the drug wore off. With hardening of the arteries, there is never complete hopelessness, but there is never a lasting gain.

By the end of summer, the men who had backed me were beaming. The care I had given to the crops paid off. The yield was excellent, and the price for a quality package was excellent. Oats, hay, straw, and wheat were stored in the barns to feed the cows during the winter, and we had started to trim out the cabbage that was in storage. We would be able to pay off our notes!

I was downtown buying a new watering cup for the dairy when the fire whistle blew: two long and one short. It was our signal! "Now, don't get excited," the clerk cautioned me. "It's at your place, but it's probably just a grass fire."

A grass fire? In November? I was out of the store before the clerk had finished speaking. A mile from the house, I could see heavy smoke mushrooming into the sky. We had the largest barns in the county, and the insurance agent had often told me, "Pat, if that barn blows, it will be the biggest fire we've ever had."

The barns were three stories high in places, and they were built onto the carriage house, with its ornate wrought-iron staircase that went to the bell tower. Our road was jammed with fire buffs (there is so little excitement in the country), and I had to park on the next road down.

"Bill is alright," one of the men called to me, "but he tried to go into the barns looking for you."

The fire had started in the south end of the barns where we had a wood-burning stove to keep the cabbage from freezing. We almost never have a south wind, but on that day, there was a wind of gale strength blowing straight from the southwest. Bill had gone to the milk house for some milk, and, before he got to the house, the fire had outstripped him. The barns were a hundred years old, and the dry wood burned like kindling.

The cows were loose in the loafing area and the men got them out, but the poor little calves were tied to the pens and were burned to a crisp. The volunteer fire company came steaming up, eager to show off their new pump, which they had bought after innumerable dinners and raffles. They laid their hoses to a neighbor's pond (the nearest fire hydrant was three miles away), and no one could get the motor started. I went to the window and stared at the ashes of my dreams; but Bill went to the desk and started looked for our insurance policies.

The fire burned far into the night, and the stored oats smoldered for days. We couldn't even clean up the mess until the insurance adjusters had come. Every time I looked out the window, I saw not the smoking ruins, but the barns as they had been.

Several days later, a friend of ours in the produce business in New York City called. "Got any cabbage?" he inquired.

"We had cabbage," I said, "but our barns burned."

"Tough luck," he said. "The price jumped fifty dollars a ton today. Florida cabbage froze last night."

Our cows had been spooked from the whole ordeal. All thoroughbreds have delicate nervous systems, and our best cows suffered the most. Their milk production went way down, and our income went way down with it. No one in our area had a barn big enough to hold our herd, so we had to rent two barns five miles apart. Poor Willie had to ferry between the two to do the milking, and since our car chose this particular time to conk out, I had to hire a taxi.

The whole schmeer was impossible, and I agreed that we would have to sell the herd. We decided on an auction and picked an auctioneer. He was a beaming, affable, slippery individual and Bill didn't trust him. Again, it was Bill who found out that the auction wasn't even advertised.

"I know what he's pulling," Bill told me. "He's sending notices to a list of his private customers. There will be no competition, and he can knock the cows down at low prices. We have got to advertise."

"Get on the ball!" St. Cecelia warned me; so we squeezed a last-minute ad in the local paper and got a rush order for posters. Then Willie and I plastered posters on every telephone pole for miles around.

The auctioneer showed up early on the day of the sale. "Make you a price on the whole herd," he offered. "Fair price. Better take it. Auctions are risky."

"He's bluffing," St. Cecelia said. "Call him on it!"

"Go for broke!" I told him, and the auction was on. We took in twice the amount that the auctioneer had offered us. The insurance was not adequate (is it ever?), but our creditors were kind. The barns were a total loss, but with no herd, it was not essential to replace them. AND, there was enough to pay off the mortgage.

After we had settled into our new routine with no cows to milk, Bill said to me one night, as I was planning what crops to put in for the spring planting, "Honey, I think we should put the farm in the Land Bank."

The Land Bank was a government agency that rented farms and paid the farmer NOT to raise crops. There had been an overproduction the previous year and the brain-trusters had thought up this gimmick in the hopes of stabilizing the agricultural economy. I was stunned. I had been proud of the way I had managed the farm.

"It isn't that I don't think you can run the farm," he assured me. "You've proven that you can. But, I think it is killing you."

I started to protest, but then I stopped. Technically, the farm was mine. He had given me the deed, but in my eyes it was, and always would be, *his* farm; forever and ever, amen. So, I put the farm in the Land Bank and, as soon as the papers were signed, Bill relapsed into a semi-stupor. When a new state trooper who had never known him as "Sir" called him "Pop", it was the end of the road.

As his illness progressed, Bill became more and more self-centered. I had hurt my back quite badly dragging a hundred-pound sack of cabbage from the fire, and driving the beat-up old pickup truck had become a chore. After a long day-trip, I was pooped. When we got home, Bill said suddenly: "Honey, I want a glass of milk!"

"Look in the refrig . . ." I started, then remembered we didn't have any. "Oh, dear, I'm so sorry. We used up the last we had this morning. I'll get some first thing tomorrow, OK?"

"I want it NOW!" Bill said in the factious voice of a spoiled child. "NOW!" he repeated.

"Please," I begged, "I'm too tired to drive to town to the store."

"Tired? You're just lazy!" he scoffed. "Why I've driven that truck a million miles and never got tired."

Broke as we were, I called a taxi. That quart of milk cost us $10.

Once more, I was concentrating on finding a doctor who might know the answer. I chose an older man with a reputation for being kind to his patients. I took Bill to his office once a week, not so much for treatment as to make him feel that he was still in the main stream, that he was being cared for. When Bill came out of that office, he nudged me and whispered, "Pay the bill."

"Oh, my no," I said, pretending to be shocked. "It's your bill—you pay it; you have money." (I always made sure he had money in his pocket.)

I knew what the hang-up was; he was afraid that he couldn't sort out the right amount. The doctor came into the waiting room, and he and I and the receptionist watched patiently. Bill fumbled in his wallet, and, when he pulled out the right change, the three of us praised him so lavishly that he beamed as though he'd won the Grand Prix.

This doctor still made house calls, and one night, when Bill complained of pain, I called him and he came at once. "Just a little touch of indigestion," he said reassuringly. "He'll be right as rain in a few days."

But, I had a premonition and I followed the doctor out onto the porch. "Is this the beginning of the end?" I asked.

"No, no," he said. "He'll be alright."

"But, what if he gets worse?" I persisted.

"Take him to the hospital and call me. I'll be home."

An hour later, Bill was rolling from side to side in agony and clutching the bed sheets. With the help of a neighbor, I got him to the hospital, and we called the doctor. No answer. Again and again the phone rang.

"I can't even put Bill into a bed until the doctor gets here," the nurse apologized.

Finally, I drove to the doctor's house. I looked through the window and saw him sitting beside the phone fast asleep.

Bill was admitted, and the wheels were set into motion. The next morning, when I went to the hospital, a strange doctor came into the waiting room. "Your husband's doctor has gone away for the weekend," he said, "and has turned this case over to me. We can't operate due to his weakened condition, and if we don't operate, he won't be here very long." Then *he* left for the weekend!

I was too numb to get the message. "Not very long . . ." Six months? A year? I started to go for a cigarette when some instinct alerted me. (Is it possible to hear the rustle of the Wings of Death?) I went back to Bill's room and resumed my vigil.

"Bill," I whispered, bending over him, "if you can hear me, shut your eyes." He blinked.

"I would be so lost without you. Please don't go away."

The wisp of a smile touched his lips, and then he was still. Frantically, I rang for the nurse. "I think he's dying," I said.

She pushed me out of the room and shut the door. "Don't go in," she said.

"He's dead, isn't he?" I asked flatly.

"Don't go in the room," she repeated and ran to a phone. "Emergency! At once!" I heard her say.

Five minutes passed; ten; the life of the hospital corridor swirled around me. I was an island. Alone. "I know he's dead," I told St. Cecelia. "Why don't they tell me?" But no one heard. Slowly, I began to beat against the wall with my fist. It was the only way I could vent my anger, my bewilderment, my anguish. "Why don't they tell me? WHY?" My voice rose, and people turned to look. The head nurse hurried over and gently forced me into a chair.

"I know what you are going through," she said, "I went home one day last summer and saw my husband sitting on the lawn in the sunlight. 'Harry,' I called, 'it's such a beautiful day, let's . . . 'and then I saw that he was dead. Dead! I am a trained nurse, and I hadn't realized that anything was wrong. His doctor hadn't realized it, either. He was just . . . dead."

"Just as Bill is dead," I said. "Please, tell me!"

"Yes, dear," she said slowly, aware that every word she spoke was a violation of her professional code. "Your husband is dead."

Forty-five minutes later, the doctor on call came bursting in from the golf course. "Where death is so sudden, we would like to do an autopsy."

I agreed at once. What did it matter? What did anything matter now that Bill was gone? The autopsy showed that death had been due to gangrene that had set in the spot where Bill had had the agonizing pain two years before; the time when there was "nothing wrong".

CHAPTER 25

Bunny, Dear

"What in hell now?" I grumbled sleepily as I reached for the phone by my bedside. If the illuminated dial on my wristwatch was correct, it was four a.m. Of course, there was a perfectly good chance that the thing wasn't working; nothing else around this place did! Why, oh why, had I ever thought I could run a farm? When you came right down to it, I could; but in this crass and materialistic world that is all enamored with inflation, could I run it for money?

All this time the phone was buzzing. The heck with it. I turned over, resolving with great will-power not to answer. But sleep was not for me. Duchess began to bark; Cricket flopped all forty pounds right on top of me. Suddenly I sniffed the air. In the country at four a.m. Good Heavens! There had been a rash of barns burning lately . . .

"Central!" I yelped into the receiver. "Hello, hello? Get off the line! I have a perfect right to use the party line in an emergency! What? Oh, Bunny; Bunny Dear." Who else?

Bunny was my next-door neighbor, about a mile away. At eighty, she gets so much joy and zest out of just living that innocent bystanders are often bereft of both. She was my friend and comrade-in-arms; my gadfly pain-in-the neck! Our friendship was solid as long as I remembered one thing: Bunny was the Boss! Born to the purple, she was now reduced to a violet magenta pink, but the transition bothers her not a bit. Although, mind you, she still clings to certain heirlooms: a magnificent jet-fringed shawl, that was Mama's, for instance; or an amethyst brooch or a gold-headed cane that was Papa's; a John Frederick's hat purchased at an auction for 25 cents (I wouldn't call that extravagant, would you?); a pair of size four Russian boots with fur, the whole topped off with stockings that barely held together, and a perfectly horrible pair of men's work gloves ("A lady always wears gloves!"); to say nothing of a petticoat that droops. But she will sail into an exclusive restaurant (me quaking behind her, expecting to be bounced) and the maitre d' will bow to her! Any dame that eccentric has got to be rich!

So, here she was, yipping into my phone at her usual chirping speed. "Whoa!" I said; "Wait till I get Cricket off my chest. Now, huh? What do you mean, I'm not up yet? At four o'clock in the morning! Darling, you've gone around the bend. Last night I said . . . OK, OK, I'll be right over."

It was Bunny's Midas Touch again; we did have a beautiful crop of tomatoes, but the factories (Big Business) wouldn't pay the little guy (me) enough to cover the payroll. So, the chairman of the board (Bunny) had devised a plan to outwit them. We would load Jezebel, the friendly pickup truck, with baskets of the best tomatoes and go to the public market, which opened at five a.m. There we would sell them at outrageous prices to other little guys (suckers) and come home with gobs of money.

A minor earthquake hastened my dressing. My mother had always insisted that I be dressed for emergencies. But, all that rumbling wasn't an earthquake; it was Willie tinkering with Jezebel. On first seeing Jezebel, no one is every able to refrain from asking: "How in hell did you ever get that thing to pass inspection?"

I used to wonder myself. I guess it just goes to prove that friendship transcends all. Her headlights were temperamental; her doors were loose; her battery was chronically anemic; and her rear fender was permanently squashed. But, she carried a sticker and she was loyal. So was Willie.

When Bill died, the sensible thing for me to have done was to shed the farm pronto and head back to where I came from, which was Forty-Second Street and Broadway. But, here was Willie on the one hand, trained by my husband to plough and cultivate and spray; and Bunny on the other hand pointing like a coon dog all aquiver at the fun it would be to run me whilst *I* ran the farm. I was outnumbered and outflanked.

So here I was at four a.m. of a chilly morning sniffing at the air. The stars were still out and the moon was full. Maybe there was something to this country bit! I stood in the floodlight that the troopers had firmly insisted I install after they had answered a few of my unfounded alarms and watched Willie count the baskets of tomatoes that he had loaded on the back of Jezebel the night before.

"Willie," I said, "don't you just love to be out so early in the morning?"

"Nope," he replied, "I'd rather be in bed." He went back to counting baskets.

"That's a waste of time," I said, just to pay him back. "You counted them last night. There's a hundred and fifty."

"That was last night," said Willie, always the realist, "that truck done stood here all night. Las' time the truck stood out all night, we lost a tire iron an' the wrench an' the flashlight and my las' can of snuff!"

"I reported it," I said defensively. (Willie seems to think that everything is my fault.) "But it's hard for the troopers to trace a can of snuff!"

Willie treated this remark with the silent contempt it deserved.

"When the needle shows half-full, the darn tank is empty, you know," I said.

"I oughta'," he replied, "I done hauled you home behind the tractor often enough."

He had, too. Little things like remembering to check the gas and oil were pushed right out of my mind by bigger problems; such as how could I meet the payroll and would that last check bounce and why, or what would Bunny do next?

Bunny was a blithe spirit; she turned worrying over to me to chew on. When I had exhausted my capacity, I became a blithe spirit, too, and turned the worrying over to Willie. Willie accepted this fate. He and Jezebel and my dogs carried on a running feud. I once caught him surreptitiously kicking Duchess on one side while Cricket was nipping him on the other. I felt almost maternal about Jezebel.

"Spark plugs goin', two quarts of oil a day, headlights don't work, starter goin' bad; when is you goin' to get a new truck?"

"Willie!" I answered, shocked, "Jezebel is our friend! Besides, she's paid for. Tell you what, if Bunny and I get to the market really early and sell out at a good price, and if the crop holds up and the price holds up and I can meet payroll and we can get the help, maybe I'll get a brand new used second-hand truck. I'll let you pick it out," I promised. "Oh, and Willie, look after the dogs while I'm gone, won't you?"

"Nope," answered my trusty servant, "if those dogs git lost, they's stayin' lost."

I turned into the road a little gingerly. One-hundred-and-fifty baskets of tomatoes on a half-ton pickup truck is as touchy as a load of TNT; and of the lovely squashy catsup-y mess they would make if they overturn! The street runs with gore and troopers.

I upset the big truck once, right in the factory yard and I was so completely crushed that the yard boss, after pulling me out, mopped off my face and said, "Never mind, the boys'll get the truck right again. The inspector isn't here today. We'll scoop the tomatoes up in tote boxes and use them for juice."

I coasted down the hill cautiously and slammed on the brakes as Bunny darted out in front of me waving half a sheet. "Bunny!" I yelled, as Jezebel swayed, "what do you think you're doing?"

"Well, I thought maybe you wouldn't see the house in the dark. Are you dressed?" she answered.

"I certainly hope so," I replied, "and in my right mind. At least I was until you shook me up. What on Earth are all of those packages?" I asked, pointing to a mound of boxes.

"Just a few things we'll need for our trip."

"But we're only going to the market. Where do you think we'll put all that junk in the front seat of a pickup?"

"The truck is amply spacious, Dear, if you'd just manage. My mama always taught me how to manage. Now, this little package will fit right here, between these two little pedals . . ."

"Bunny, Dear," I said, "that's the brake and the clutch. You're not leaving room enough for my feet."

"Well, I could get my feet in there. But, of course, mine are only size four." At my offended snort (mine are size . . . well, never mind), she hurried on, "Dreadful circles under your eyes, Pat. Especially for a woman the age you say you are! Don't squash that paper bag—our lunch, you know."

I groaned. I knew Bunny's lunches: stale cream doughnuts, last week's bread, apples that had fallen off some truck onto the road. She once told an income tax inspector that she lived on $600 a year and went to Florida for the winter. He just patted her shoulder and told her not to worry, she reminded him of his mother, and at eighty years old, she didn't have to file.

"How come you're wearing your boots?" I asked, "on a hot day like this?"

"That just shows that you don't plan for anything," she replied, busily stowing packages. "I'm saving space. The hard-boiled eggs for lunch are in the tops of my boots. Besides, I always wear them with my John Fredericks hat."

I squawked loudly about the family Bible she put on the dashboard, but she refused to budge without it. "What if the house burns down while I'm gone?"

Her papa's gold-headed cane was perched perilously on top of the seat. "I've always envied you that cane," I said, as we sped along at 30 miles an hour.

"Papa got it in Buffalo. Roll your window up, it's a trifle chilly." She pulled her jet-fringed shawl tighter around her. "This reminds me of the night of the big freeze. The forecast was for a frost and Papa had a load of pumpkins on the barn floor and he said 'Oh, my pumpkins!' and he went and got Mama's Oriental rug and spread it over the pumpkins. That night, one of Papa's Percherons got loose!"

"Bunny, Dear, I know I'm dumb," I said, "but what are Percherons?"

"Purebred Flemish horses that weigh a ton. One got loose and walked all over the pumpkins and put a hoof right through Mama's Oriental rug, and Mama cried like everything, because of the Ladies Aide meeting there . . ."

"In the barn?" I asked, scandalized.

"In the parlor! And Papa had to drive into Buffalo and get Mama a new dress before she'd stop crying. My, but Mama was . . . Didn't you see that bump? Mama was beautiful and the next week Papa was in the barn and Mama went out to call him and some hired man that Papa had fired was out there, all full of revenge, and Papa yelled to Mama to get his pistol and Mama was so scared that she ran . . . Pat! You almost hit that adorable little kitty!"

Since the "adorable little kitty" was a skunk out for an early morning stroll, I decided I couldn't drive and listen to Bunny at the same time, so I parked the truck.

". . . into the house," continued Bunny, "and locked the door because she didn't want to get killed, and when Papa finally knocked out the hired man and climbed in through the window, he was so mad, he made Mama take the dress back! Papa and Mama loved each other dearly. What are we stopped for?"

"Nothing," I answered. "Bunny, Dear, where did you ever get that cliff-hanger of a story? Did you make it up?"

"Certainly not!" she sniffed, "I had a very interesting childhood."

"I had an interesting childhood, too," I said, "my Pop used to wallop me when I told whoppers, though."

Fog hid the road; not completely so that the wary traveler stayed indoors, but treacherously: now an open space, now a blind stretch; not too good for a woman driver. Familiar landmarks disappeared into nothingness. Add to the woman driver a beat-up old truck loaded with one-hundred-and-fifty baskets of tomatoes, and the chances for trouble increase. Add headlights that don't work and a horn that blatted like a lost calf and the luminous gray of four-thirty a.m. and you were asking for it!

We rode on in silence. Our mission: To get to the Public Market. Our goal: Cash money for the tomatoes. I had recently received a notice from the bank that the bank note payment was past due. When I showed it to Bunny, she said, "Well, thank Heavens the tomatoes are ripe!" So, we picked tomatoes, we polished tomatoes, we packed tomatoes, and we tied up the tailgate on Jezebel at midnight last night. Now, our mission was under way.

Bunny stared grimly into the darkness ahead. Having driven her papa's team of Percherons, she was the pilot and I merely the co-pilot. Although the title was honorary, Bunny's instructions carried weight. "Gracious, child, don't back up now! There's a car right behind us!"

Both the truck and I aged considerably, but Bunny was awful good with the cops. "Let me see," she would muse, gazing at the stalwart form while I fumbled for my license and registration, "you're a Nichols, aren't you? I knew your grandfather; handsome man. You look just like him!" And the cop would wave us on.

The pilot was also the Senior Business Consultant. Bunny had lived through the Great Depression, and "All we have to fear is fear itself!" The huge house and their farm had been foreclosed and had gone to strangers who converted it to a fox farm. A breeding station, no less! Outraged (and curious), Bunny had prowled the ancestral grounds at night until the new owners protested to the Law. She was disturbing the love life of the foxes. "It was interesting!" Bunny told the judge.

There was no self-help housing for the newly poor. If Bunny wanted a roof over her head, she would have to put it there herself. So, she did. With no blue prints or cellar or well, and almost no cash; just the knowledge that she needed a place to live, she set to work. Nail by nail, with scrap lumber, the one-woman project forged ahead. Completed, it had a sort of romantic air, a sort of "Babes in the Woods" gingerbread look. But, it was hers.

With all this wealth of experience under her belt, the Senior Business Consultant was inclined to sniff at my moans about the bank notes and working myself to death on the farm. "You make such mountains out of molehills!" she reproved me. "We've got the tomatoes, don't we?" She glanced back to the truck bed to make sure. "And, we'll get scads of cash at the market, won't we?"

To all other woes besides monetary, Bunny listened with all of her heart. "Yes, Dear," she would murmur, "I know." And the moaner would immediately rejoin the human race. According to legend, there was very little Bunny didn't know.

Past a certain point, Bunny will not stand for sass from her juniors. There were times when Bunny got herself all mixed up with her Mama, who had been a regal beauty; and her aunt, to whom she referred as "The Queen" behind her back. Bunny had inherited her mother's classic features, but not her height; she was only five foot one inch tall, and only weighed a hundred pounds, counting both wedding rings. Her hair was truly magnificent: a pure white that reached down past her waist. But the thing I loved most about Bunny was the fact that a side tooth was missing, so that when she grinned, she looked like a mischievous child that had succeeded in getting away with something. She had gotten away with plenty!

One of the first stories I ever heard about her when I came here was that way back, when Bunny was in her teens, she had evaded Mama, and, with an excess of youth and imported vodka, had danced on top of the bar in one of the saloons in the village, to the edification of her friends. Apparently nobody had had the heart to tell her mother. If some of the stories that Bunny told me were true, nobody had had the heart to tell her mother a lot of things!

But, dear oh dear, Bunny could be dignified; especially when I didn't follow her advice and she disapproved. To hear her tell it, I could be wearing mink if I would just listen to her. Once in a while, she came up with a very practical suggestion, though. When I was sputtering about the money I had spent sending for garage men to rescue me when Jezebel conked out in the hinterlands, as I watched them squeeze one little wire against another one and charged me $6, Bunny replied loftily: "If you'd remember to put some lipstick on and look as dumb as you are, men would gladly do little jobs for you!" Dear Bunny! At eighty, males were still gladly doing little jobs for her. Right now she was probably planning something!

Years later, I asked a solid-type middle-aged citizen if he had known Bunny in her youth. "No," he replied, regretfully, "I was a little too young. I have always felt that I missed something, though," he added, thoughtfully.

"Pat! Slow down! You're going ninety miles per hour—that little hand says so!" Bunny yelled.

"Bunny," I replied, "you know perfectly well that 'little hand' is broken! We busted it down in the back lot when that bull was chasing us."

"And when the trooper stopped us the next day, you said 'Yes, sir, I'm on my way to the garage right now,' and that was last year."

"Well, I was on my way to the garage, but it was to get a tire fixed."

Good Heavens! The headlights went out again! Just like that. We have to get to the market early to sell the tomatoes, or they'll be pigs' feed! I got out and looked at the wires, did some tinkering, and Jezebel blossomed in full glow again.

A sign post up ahead pointed to the market. The Public Market covered a square mile of land. A million dollars of state funds had gone into its construction and it was a miniature village laid out in broad streets with long one-storey sheds divided into outdoor stalls with an imposing Administration Building and produce terminals for the wholesalers. The mob was hell-bent to grab a stall, unload produce, load produce, or set up a stand in time to catch the early trade. The keynote was speed, which seemed like chaos topped by bedlam! Bunny and I turned into one of the broad lanes. A huge tractor trailer truck sped toward us and swerved at the last possible moment. An eight-wheeler in back of him barely missed us, and another and another. A cop flapped his arms frantically. As fast as I swerved and avoided one truck, another would zoom down on us. A sign loomed in front of me: "EXIT ONLY" it said, with an arrow pointing in our direction. We were on a one-way street going the wrong way! I tried to back up, but as fast as the traffic parted in front of me, it swung around me and closed in again. "Bunny," I cried in a panic, "what shall I do?"

"Pray!" replied Bunny, "Our Father . . ."

I waded upstream to the nearest crossing. A boy with a pushcart skimmed across in front of me so close that I didn't even try to put on the brakes. There was an empty stall ahead, but before I could reach it, someone else backed in. The noise couldn't have been worse in a bombing raid. All I could do was to go with the tide.

"Oh, St. Cecelia," I beseeched, "please don't let Jezebel stall!"

Way down at the end of the line, in the most undesirable part of the market, there was an empty stall. I backed in and stood there shaking. Bunny alighted briskly. "My," she said, "wasn't that interesting? Now all we have to do is unload the tomatoes and set things out attractively I do wish I had a broom so we could tidy up a little. If I just had something to stand on, I'd unload the truck."

Gone were my hopes of selling out at big prices. In this maelstrom of people pushing, people grabbing, and people shouting, there wasn't a chance for two women. Bunny's little coquetries wouldn't even be noticed, and I couldn't yell loudly enough to be heard. The country mice were in way over their heads. It had been a nice dream, while it lasted.

"Go get a cup of coffee," said Bunny. "Papa always got a cup of coffee when he went to the market. And don't worry about a thing. I'll have the tomatoes sold by the time you get back."

"The hell you will," I thought to myself, but said: "Remember, Bunny, Dear, the tomatoes are a dollar a basket."

"A dollar and twenty-five cents—didn't I promise you that you'd get a dollar and twenty-five cents? And Mama always said a lady should keep her promises."

Dragging my heels, I went in search of a cup of coffee. The coffee bar was filled with six-foot-tall prosperous-looking farmers clad in dungarees. The bank wouldn't have intimidated them!

"Tomatoes went good early today—two dollars a basket!" they told me. "Then a couple of big trucks pulled in, and . . ." They shrugged their shoulders and advised that I take what I can get and consider myself lucky to be rid of them.

When I got back to the truck, it was empty. One-hundred-and-fifty baskets of tomatoes were unloaded and gone! Bunny was counting bills, "one-hundred-twenty, one-hundred-forty . . . don't mix me up, Dear, one-hundred-sixty . . ." she continued, then crammed the wad of greenbacks into the money bag. "Isn't that what I promised? One-hundred-eighty-seven dollars and fifty cents . . . did I get enough?"

A nice man had stopped and bought all of our tomatoes for his restaurant. He had been raised on a farm himself and was quite neighborly. He said he hoped Jezebel would get us back home again.

I dropped Bunny off at her house, and she was still clutching the money bag. I might lose it, in her opinion. The next day, she called me up and asked me to come over.

"Something wrong?" I asked.

"No, not really, but it is kind of a dull day, and I don't have anything better to do," she answered.

"Try getting your furnace fire going," I advised her. "That might liven things up a bit!"

Bunny had one standard procedure for starting her fire: Open the furnace door, stand directly in front of it, and heave a bucketful of raw kerosene on the glowing coals!

Sometimes I get bored, too, and chastising Bunny was like spanking a butterfly—nothing you could get your hands on! Last week, I got a letter from my Congressman about a committee to investigate ways of bringing interest into the lives of our Senior Citizens. How Bunny would have snorted! In her later years, Bunny returned to the teachings of her youth. On her eighty-first birthday, her swain appeared to offer his congratulations. An unexpected blizzard blew up and the poor guy couldn't get his car started. Bunny thrust him firmly into the night. "I will NOT," she told him, "have the neighbors saying that you spent the night with me!" Since the swain was in his Golden Years as well, the resultant pneumonia almost finished him off, but he was awfully flattered.

No memoriam for Bunny would be complete without a moment of silence for her bicycle. That bike! It was an antique which she rode with her long skirts decorously concealing her legs, long white tresses unbound to the breeze, as she wove in and out of traffic, waving gaily to all. These friendly salutations gave fits to tailgating motorists who mistook them for hand signals. Once in town, she parked her bike, did her shopping, and got a cup of tea. She parked it in the most incredible places, and then she confided winningly to utter strangers: "I've lost my bike. Would you please help me find it?"

Into the drowsy languor of a small town's Main Street on a lazy summer's day, when most of us are curled around a Coke at the corner Sweet Shop or watching fishermen idly casting their lines from the bridge over the Canal, the news would burst. "Miss Bunny's lost her bike, again!" the small boys would yell.

Since Bunny combined the innocence of a child with the assurance of a beauty queen, and the downright gall of a panhandler, people who didn't know her, overcome by the pity of it all, would drive Bunny all over town looking for her bike! The meter maid hadn't seen it; the garages were bare; people would even check in the most unlikely of places, like the cemetery ("By Mama's grave," Bunny would plead). No bike. Enthusiasm would mount; tension spread; shopkeepers would call the police chief. With her innocent blue eyes getting more innocently blue by the minute, Bunny would plead, "What will I do?"

Rumor has it that even our local police chief would go mighty easy on some of our chronic offenders if the bicycle should disappear. But, the chief had tangled with Bunny before, so he let it be known that if that damnable bike ended up at the bottom of the Canal, there would be no questions asked. He didn't mean it, though; not really. With the nearest movie theater fifteen miles away, our town needed Bunny and her bike! Of course, some of us noted, it was a mite peculiar that the bike seemed to turn up missing on those days when Bunny got to thinking how nice it would be to get a ride home. Dear Bunny!

Toward the end, Bunny grew a little wimpish. For the first time in her life, she didn't know what she wanted. Her mail lay unopened and her bills went unpaid. A wispy voice would call me at daybreak and announce plaintively, "My fire has gone out."

Her friends formed a tight little coalition to protect her; but we were the ones who needed protection! With ludicrous ease, she bypassed our well-intentioned plans. We located a distant relative who needed a good home, but Bunny threw her out. No house was big enough for two ladies. As for nursing homes, her doctor refused to commit her (he told us we worried too much), and Welfare couldn't touch her (she had means of her own). Her lawyer wouldn't help, either. So, the coalition called each other daily and decided firmly that something had to be done.

Winter brought ice; ice brought falls; and, in Bunny's case, a fall brought the ambulance. From the hospital, she went to a nursing home where the staff agreed that she was one to keep them on their toes. The last time I saw her, I said to the nurse, "Want to bet she tells me I'm to take her home?" Sure enough, that's what she did. She was still The Boss.

Bunny, Dear, never really did anything with her life. It never occurred to her that she should. While the rest of us were concerned with making a living and paying our taxes, she just lived; lived and loved. She took exquisite self-sacrificing care of her invalid mother; there had been a husband in her distant past, as well as a miscarriage; she was reared in luxury, but tossed poverty over her shoulder, surmounted untold obstacles (Bunny could tackle anything), yet still had a ball with the whole lot! What more is there to life?

P.S. Bunny, Dear—I finally paid off the notes!

APPENDIX A

Memories of Pat Carr

Ruth Eileen Carr Miller:

The Carrs were readers; they just devoured books! Perhaps Pat wrote her book in an effort to tell her side of the story. Yes, the step kids rejected her, and she rejected them. They were all strong-willed and had strong personalities. You may notice that Pat doesn't call the three oldest by their names (except where we interjected), just their order of birth. She seemed to want to rid the house of Myrtie, Bill's first wife, who had died just eleven months before Pat and Bill were married. How do you deal with a ghost? Myrtie's things were destroyed and disposed of behind the barns! Myrtie kept the house and the gardens, and she never ventured into the barn or the fields. Pat wanted nothing to do with cooking, cleaning, or keeping the gardens. She preferred to work with her new husband side-by-side. Pat wanted Bill all to herself, so the youngest of her stepsons, Charles, was driven from the house and lived with neighbors, relatives, and friends until he went into the Merchant Marines, then into the Army. Charles had intended to farm with his father and had taken care of the place so his dad could go to New York City. When Charles (Chuck) left the house, Pat disposed of all of his personal belongings! There! She had Bill to herself!

My mother, Dorothy, Chuck's first wife, would walk to The Pillars from town (about five miles) when she was in high school and Chuck was off in the Service. She would bring out homemade cookies and would sometimes fix a meal. She remembers cleaning up the dining room one time and setting flowers in a vase on the table. When Pat came in, she screamed at Dorothy and scared her away! There! She had Bill all to herself!

As a child, I remember visiting The Pillars. I loved all of the animals, but did think it strange when Grandpa would let the dog eat off his fork at the dinner table! (Grandpa said that the dog just pulled the food off with his teeth, and that was OK.) I loved following him out to the barn and would play around the cows. I remember pulling up a chair in the kitchen and washing dishes—a lot of dishes! Dad would say "Aunt Pat" (that's what we called her) told Grandpa that she didn't cook nor did she clean, and she didn't! We never stayed very long.

Grandpa died in 1960 and the major portion of Pat's book is about their 16 years of married bliss. Bill had shown his Last Will & Testament to the family and left the Porter farm to our father, Charles. Mysteriously, though, the will was "lost". There! Pat now had The Pillars to herself!

Pat continued to farm until the 1970s. Fred, a neighbor, remembers when one of Pat's workers rinsed out a chemical jug for water for the crew. Pat filled the water jug and off went Megal to the fields. However, Megal took some water from the jug before giving it to the crew and keeled over dead! Fred also remembers when he came to the house one time and Pat had a live lamb in her oven! What else do you use an oven for, but to warm newborn lambs? Pat teamed up with Pete Dragon, who took over much of the farm in the 1970s. He grew lots of questionable crops, which sold for a small fortune!

Pat never got along with her sister, Mary, who was a school teacher and ballroom dancer out in California. Mary was her only family besides Bill's family, whom she didn't like much either. Pat established her own "family" in the tenants at The Pillars. Rent was cheap. Pat remembered her early days, when she needed a leg-up, so to speak. Pat worked with Community Action, which helped establish a clinic for migrant works, and is still going strong today. She also helped establish the Council on the Arts and brought "culture" to Orleans County. The "Go Art" today encourages local artists, as well as brings art into the county. She also worked hard to establish a place for battered women and victims of rape. Her biggest love, however, was her house. When the waterline was put in on County House Road, plans were to take down the big trees in front of the house. Pat fought long and hard to keep those trees. Mind you, she was 90 and fought the law like a trouper! The trees are still standing. She loved and cared for her tenants and expected them to take care of her, too. Some did; some didn't; and some ended up robbing her. Her hope for the future included continuing The Pillars as an affordable home for folks who needed a place to live. She entrusted this hope to her friend, Annette.

As an adult, I visited Pat from time to time. She loved chocolate, and I would take her brownies. Pat loved the idea that I had been to college and then married a farmer. We could talk farming. She would come to the house to see her "grandchildren", and fell in love with the "grandson", Richard. As the years passed, Pat connected with my oldest daughter, Julie, and they became friends. Pat was delighted when Julie gave birth to her first son, Jonathan. Pat called him her "great-grandson". Pat would have her driver, Vinnie, bring her to our house just to see all of the kids and animals. We would meet in a store in Albion from time to time. Even in the heat of summer, she would be dressed in her fur coat and always had a little dog in her car. Trips to The Pillars were always a mystery to me as she never let me come past the door. She was also a mystery to me as she rarely shared her life with me. Now that I have read her book, I begin to understand. She was one of a kind!

The Reverend Gary Saunders of the First Presbyterian Church of Albion shared this story: He first met Pat in 1998, when she called him one day wanting to ride the church's bus on Sunday morning. Gary invited her to dinners and would personally pick her up. Pat became friends with the Ladies of the Church. One day, he asked her to come to the classes for joining the church, and she did. Upon completion of the course, and after many, many interesting discussions, he asked her to join the church. Pat declined. As Gary went through his records later on, he found out why. Pat had joined the church back in 1946 with her husband, William! Gary remembers her as being witty and intelligent, even though she did trick him!

Gary is the person who took Pat to Strong Memorial Hospital, where she was found to be "mentally incompetent" and not allowed to live on her own. I think that she knew she needed help and trusted the good reverend to do the right thing. Before this, her Pillars residents were pilfering her things. She would hand them her checkbook, and they would write their own checks for whatever they did for her! She was held captive by Vinnie for a time against her will—but I never really believed her! I think that calling for the bus rides was Pat's escape from Vinnie, and I guess she was telling the truth, after all.

Fred would come to The Pillars whenever she called him to do minor repairs, break up a fight, or whatever. When Pat needed someone to act as her Power of Attorney and Guardian, she contacted Fred and it was made legal. He and his wife did a wonderful job of managing her affairs and caring for her.

There were some folks, though, who worried about their own pocketbooks; Pat would pay them for whatever they did with a signed blank check. So, if a hot dog cost $100, who cares? The old lady wouldn't know! But, I think Pat knew. She was just helping them out. She also knew that things were getting out of hand, so to speak. These "low-life" people wanted to remove Pat from the assisted-living facility, Orchard Manor, where she received excellent care. They made her life hell in the name of selfishness and greed.

Fred fought just as hard to make sure that Mrs. Carr (as he called her) received the best care possible. Pat said that she wanted to live to be 100; she did live to celebrate her 99th birthday, and passed away peacefully three days later, on Thanksgiving Day, 2003. She and Bill would have been married 59 years on her 99th birthday!

When the time came to probate Pat's Last Will and Testament, the original could not be found. Luckily, she had given a copy to me for safe-keeping. After reading parts of Pat's book and, with our family's encouragement, the judge ruled to honor the copy that I had. Many of her possessions had already been stolen. Fortunately, before she died, she had donated the old piano, a Square Grand Piano, built in the 1860s by the New England Piano Company, to the Cobblestone Museum in Murray, Orleans County, New York.

The "treasure" that was passed on to the Carr family were boxes and boxes of Pat's writings. The project was a huge puzzle in that Pat had written the chapters of the book, and then rewritten again and again, all on her old manual typewriter! My sister, Nicki, spent four years putting together Pat's tales contained in "The Long-Legged View". At last, the puzzle is completed!

Nicki Ann Carr Tiffany:

My first memory of Pat is from when I was very young—four or five years old. Our maternal grandmother lived in the village of Albion, on Main Street. Sometimes, while we were visiting her, "Aunt Pat" (as we called Pat Carr) would be in town on errands. She always wore lots of jewelry and a fur coat! She always had a big smile on her face when she saw my sister, Ruth, and me. She would stop and talk with us in her poshest accent, and she always listened with rapt attention to anything we might say.

I also remember visiting our grandfather, Bill Carr, at The Pillars. He was ill and bedridden, but sitting up, and we would climb up on his bed with the three or four dogs already there, and he would put an arm around each of us. As youngsters, we never thought it was odd that Grandpa's bed was in the parlor!

For holidays or birthdays, Aunt Pat always gave us the strangest gifts. The ones I remember the most were a soft plastic rendition of mounted safari animal heads; I think I got a lion and Ruth got a tiger! I wonder whatever happened to those . . .

I always regretted not visiting Pat more often and getting to know her better, but I think it was mostly out of respect for our father, Chuck, who despised her. He was the nicest, friendliest man on Earth, except when it came to Pat Carr. She hurt him deeply when she deposed his position on the farm, and she is the one person in his entire lifetime that, while he may have been able to forgive her, he was never able to forget what had happened. Because of this, I kept my distance when I was older, but I would always speak to her if she attended any family gatherings.

When Ruth and Julie shared Pat's book with me, I was blown away by her stories and writing style. My first thought was to share these tales with the world because she told them so well. It's a bit of a history lesson, the statement of a strong-willed woman, and a collection of anecdotes unknown to most of us in the family. She has captured the essence of our Grandfather very well, and, although told from her own perspective, the stories ring true and bring them both back to life for us to enjoy, if only for a little while.

Julie Carr Miller Trembley:

My name is Julie Carr Miller. I belong to the "Carr Club" of children in my family, all first-born, who carry the surname "Carr" as our middle names. I'm seven to thirteen years older than my siblings, so the references that my mom makes to their experiences with Pat are quite different from my own memories.

I first understood who Pat Carr (aka Helena Carty, anglicized from the French Cartier) was when my husband Tim and I were planning our wedding. While addressing invitations, my mother Ruth suggested I invite my "step" great-grandmother. "I have a step-great grandmother?" I asked. "Yes," was her simple, short reply.

I knew that my Grandma Millie would tell me more. The details of the history of my great-grandparents, family tensions, properties, marriages, and more unfolded over several days during a visit to the Carr vacation spot in Myrtle Beach, South Carolina, in 1990. While my grandfather searched for shark teeth and other treasures on the beach, I learned, from his wife, the story of why Pat Carr was the only person he would never get along with. She warned me not to ever mention her name in front of him. (Grandma Dorothy, Chuck's first wife, later filled in the few remaining holes in my understanding of the story and reiterated the warning, "Don't let him find out you've seen her.")

Even my Aunt Helen Carr, whose name carried Pat's legal first name and married name, would speak of "HER" with only the pronoun. She would, from time to time, receive Pat's mail by mistake (all of which Helen forwarded until one day, an entire suitcase came to her by mistake in the mail and she was "forced" to deliver it in person). Aunt Helen has been my grandfather's confidant and caregiver after he left home as a minor, shortly after Pat's marriage to his father.

I was always highly respectful of my Grandpa Chuck (Charles Carr). A certain stern look from him or a finger pointed my way could straighten every hair on my body. I therefore, avoided the topic in his presence as had been recommended. However, I was responsible, only a year or two before he died, for inviting both Pat and Grandpa Chuck to a family gathering, and I was quite nervous about the potential encounter. When he saw HER there, he asked me, "Who's that?" I nervously spoke her name. He replied, "I really don't care." And he meant it. I had two riveting, concurrent reactions at that moment. I wished then that I'd dared before to ask him all of the questions I'd bottled up about his past. Mostly, I was astounded at his capacity for forgiveness. He'd forgiven the woman who had stolen his father and his birthright. He had let go of the years that he'd been forbidden to pass through the doors of his childhood home. He modeled Christian forgiveness forty times and then forty more.

My wedding day, amidst other "blurry moments," was my first memorable glimpse of Pat, dressed in a black and white polka-dot dress, high heels, and her signature fur coat, leaving the church with someone I assumed to be her driver. She was petite with sharp features and long hair. She carried a midsized handbag at the elbow.

I don't remember exactly why I was determined to befriend Pat. I wasn't interested in the house (moreover, I was terrified of the The Pillars, often overwhelmed by its smell and the reputation of its inhabitants). I remember thinking that someone in the family SHOULD see after her, since she was family, after all.

Sometimes, I sat in her kitchen while she drank coffee, usually instant, always black. It was sometime difficult to concentrate on her words because my ears would pick up the sounds of music, movement and words from the adjoining apartments and the creaking of the old radiators. I was distracted by the panting and rushing around of her little dog "Bobo."

Her apartment was messy and very, very dirty. (The dining room, in particular, was always "proper" and buried in a very thick layer of dust.) I always imagined, as I sat, that it hadn't changed much over forty or even fifty years.

Pat loved to go out. We drove around to see Christmas lights. We ate at "The Basket Factory" restaurant, The Apollo and the town of Elba's only diner. We went to the circus and took drives to the lake. My dear husband lifted Pat in and out of his big truck, always waiting with a smile to be her chauffeur as she shuffled down the ramp from her apartment with her walker.

Oh, the circus! She couldn't wait to see the lady riding the white horse (there's always one of those in any circus, she stated). She was as giddy as a toddler about theater. She was as mad as a dog about social injustice or the unnecessary removal of old growth forest trees. She loved drama, literature, politics, and art. She read many newspapers and in her 90's, exercised daily on a stationary bike. I understand that she also pursued Reiki treatments until the provider became wary of adjusting her frail, elderly body.

I appreciated her wisdom. She said that if parents provided a roof and basic nutrition, "the rest is gravy" (referring to parenting skills, in general). She claimed that she was unable to bear children of her own because she'd been the recipient of experimental radiation treatments as a young adult. She was contributing to a trust fund for one child among her tenants, who, in particular, showed promise of breaking the cycle of poverty. She seemed, somehow, to sense my fatigue as a working mom. She would talk and I would sometimes simply listen, settling in to a deep chair around the dining room table set with mismatched china under very dim lighting.

Our relationship waxed and waned over the years. I sometimes found it very difficult to manage my jobs, school, and my own growing family and her care. At times, I lacked the energy to even return her calls. I sometimes resented what at times seemed to be a one-sided relationship. Couldn't she write to me as I'd written her? Couldn't she, once and for all, learn to trust me? When Grandpa Chuck became ill, I felt I should concentrate on him.

I tried, however, to enlist myself as her agent with the Office for the Aging or the hospital's social work department, with little success. She was ever suspicious and forever independent. I reported the abuse that I witnessed. My calendar was full of notes that I would make about the payments she was making to people posing as contractors or aids. Looking back, I realize that I did not fully understand the intricacies and the demands of elder care.

Before her good neighbor, Fred, was "contracted" as her power-of-attorney and Rev. Saunders began to visit regularly, Pat became panic-stricken about the whereabouts of her walker, her purse, and her dog. She feared for her own safety. I am, forever, grateful to them for caring for her where I could not. I am also grateful to the nursing home staff and the volunteer advocate from the Office of the Aging for their excellent care.

There are many memories of Pat or the interesting stories she told over the years for which there is insufficient space here (maybe another book?). Even her funeral was not unlike an episode of a television drama.

Pat was funny, witty, and often her words carried double meaning. She was calculating, brilliant, and sometimes naïve. In a way, the house was her most loyal friend and her longest-living companion. It sheltered her, and it became the stage she forever longed to return to.

Some of my strongest memories are random. Mom and I sang hymns at her bedside before she died. I'll never forget discussing lipstick and nail polish colors with Rev. Saunders and Pat in the nursing home (Pat did know color!).

When I called ahead to announce that our cousin, George Hirsch, was coming to meet her (how she flirted with him!), she readied herself with enormous costume-jewelry rings on all ten fingers and a feather boa. He was rightfully awe-stricken when she showed him her professionally taken stage photo from the 1940's, a black and white touched with color on the lips, cheeks, and hair.

Whenever we ate out with my children, Pat would introduce herself to the waitress as their GREAT great-great-grandmother, with emphasis on the first great as to mean outstanding." The waitresses would always put on the "what a sweet (crazy) old lady look" while they took her habitual double order (one order for now, one to go, for the little dog waiting in the car). But Pat was never crazy or senile, even to the age of 99. Imaginative? Absolutely. Creative? Definitely. The time I spent with her, whether it was a short visit or a trip to the city, was always like attending a theatrical performance. The visits were full of highs and lows and unexpected turns. What a great, great, GREAT act she was.

James Powell Ganley:

I only met Pat twice; the first time was probably in the summer of 1945, when Mother, myself, and perhaps my brother, Bill, visited Albion for two very short holidays. My memories of (Grandfather) Bill and Pat are very vague, due to the passage of time and the short period of the stay. My most vivid memory of both visits was the older car that they owned in that post-war era. The back floor of the automobile had rusted through in several spots and exhaust fumes flowed freely into the rear section of the car, almost asphyxiating me with carbon monoxide poisoning! I was probably only about eight years old during these visits to my mother's family home.

Ruth Rebecca Ganley Hirsch:

I only met Pat twice. Once with Mom and Alice, about a year before Aunt Mim [the eldest of Bill's children, Mariam] died. I don't remember her at all from that visit, but I must have met her since Mom walked us through the downstairs of the house. The second time I met her, I think, was at our family visit up there for the reunion we had in 2002. I believe that I only was in the kitchen portion at that time, where she was sitting. She was rather elderly at that point and I'm not sure that she was mentally healthy. She had already started having one of her boarders take care of the finances for her. I just thought of her as quite the character—sort of like Shirley McLaine.

APPENDIX B

Photographs of the Carr Family

"Drawing of The Pillar Farm Barns (facing north) for Pat and
Bill's 1959 Christmas card".

"Myrtie Powell Carr circa 1900",

"William Mortimer Carr, Jr., circa 1910"

"The Three Eldest Carr Children (from left—youngest at the time to right—eldest): William Franklin Carr, Ruth Alice Carr Ganley, and Mariam Ida Carr Hollingsworth, with their father, William Mortimer Carr, Jr. circa 1920"

"The youngest Carr sibling, Charles Arthur Carr circa 1944"

Edwards Brothers,Inc!
Thorofare, NJ 08086
13 April, 2011
BA2011103